Max G[...]

Max Gordon

Life, Loss and Baseball's Greatest Comeback

JACOB KORNHAUSER *and*
DYLAN KORNHAUSER

Afterword by Pat Casey

McFarland & Company, Inc., Publishers
Jefferson, North Carolina

ISBN (print) 978-1-4766-8483-3
ISBN (ebook) 978-1-4766-4255-0

LIBRARY OF CONGRESS AND BRITISH LIBRARY
CATALOGUING DATA ARE AVAILABLE

Library of Congress Control Number 2021035135

Front cover image: A ritual he did in every at bat for the rest
of his career, Max looks up to the sky to remind himself
who he's playing for (Gordon family)

Printed in the United States of America

*McFarland & Company, Inc., Publishers
Box 611, Jefferson, North Carolina 28640
www.mcfarlandpub.com*

To the memory of Nick Gordon:
In hopes that those whom you never met
and those who knew you best
can share in knowing the legacy you left.

And to the coaches:
Dave Kitchell, Grampy Norman, Pat Casey, Charlie Hall,
Rob Willson, Terry Baumgartner, Pat Bailey and others

And to Max Gordon
and all the kids you've kept in the game.

Table of Contents

Acknowledgments

I have to start by thanking Stan and Michelle Gordon for their openness on this project. A large portion of the book is about a time in their life they'd rather not look back on too often. But they welcomed me into their home to discuss some very difficult topics because it was important to them that Max's and their family's story be told in the right way. I can only hope they're confident we've done exactly that. Secondly, I'd like to thank my beautiful fiancée, Khaki, who is always my sounding board for any and all ideas on projects like this. I'm not sure I could have ever reached the clarity I needed to tell this story without her guidance, love, and support.

Another huge shoutout goes to Gary Mitchem and the McFarland team for taking a chance on this book. Getting a book published these days is as hard as ever, and we couldn't be more thankful that Gary believed in us enough to help bring Max's story to life. To my countless friends and colleagues, including Nick Yahl and Jake Garcia, who gave me notes on draft after draft, you have my deepest gratitude.

For fostering my love and propensity for writing, I thank my mom and dad, Angela and Ari, as well as influential teachers and mentors like Lori Ratliff, John Anderson, and Tim Kurkjian. Most of all on this project, I'd like to thank my brother Dylan. For taking this project on and helping Max's story jump off the page, I'm deeply appreciative. Ever since we were little, we've wanted to work on a writing project together, and on these pages, for the first time, we got to do just that. Here's to the first of many...

— **Jacob Kornhauser**

Firstly I must acknowledge my most vital support system: my family. My mom and dad, Angela and Ari, my little brother Devin, and especially my older brother and co-author, Jacob, for bringing me this project. Without the home we come from, we lose the ability to feel at home anywhere. To Max, for seeing his story through that we might one day tell it. And to all of the mothers, fathers, sisters and brothers who have received the call or heard the knock at the door that would rend their lives irreversibly. Healing is possible. If this story has taught me one thing, it's that.

— **Dylan Kornhauser**

Introduction

Baseball reflects life. That's why it's such a useful tool for the 99.9 percent of young children who never end up playing the sport professionally. It teaches them life lessons in a way nothing else can. Hustle, play fair, always try your best. Those are the obvious lessons, but there are some subtle ones too. Play for the team instead of yourself because the name on the front of the jersey is more important than the name on the back. Virtually everybody who has played baseball has learned these lessons. But every now and then, it works the other way around. Tough lessons you learn in life become the basis for how you play the game of baseball. In those cases, baseball *becomes* your life. That's the situation Max Gordon found himself in.

Max's story is important for a couple of reasons. First, the personal success he was able to find in the face of unthinkable tragedy is inspiring. Anybody who has ever been through something close to what Max experienced—losing his three most beloved mentors in a two-month span and staring death straight in the face himself—can be sure they are capable of achieving whatever they set out to do. In this book, Max effectively lays out the blueprint for how to do it. But his story is also important, because it doesn't focus on a baseball player whose career ended in the major leagues. We know most of those stories. For some of the most fortunate players in the country, the highest level of competition they will face in their careers is in NCAA's Division 1. Their stories are just as deserving of inclusion in the public conversation as those of big-league ballplayers.

Through interviews with Max, close friends and family, former teammates and coaches, his story has been brought to life. Firsthand accounts and records shared by his former high school and colleges helped provide the framework for the unique narrative that is Max's life. From his time growing up in the Scott Valley of Northern California to his move to Ashland to his ascent while playing baseball in Corvallis, Max's life story is shared. It is a biographical account that is not just the biography of a man, but the biography of a family. This family, bonded by blood, strengthened through loss, and defined by resilience is the family that took life lessons

1

and applied them to baseball. Their story of healing and Max's story of athletic excellence are one and the same.

Some may find they have something in common with Max on the field or off it. His life lessons can become yours. His lessons learned through baseball can become yours too. And let the story you're about to read, as a whole, serve to teach one more lesson: no matter the score, in baseball as in life, as long as you have one more at-bat, you're still alive.

CHAPTER 1

Etna

Here we go boys, he said to himself, looking his bat up and down as he turned his attention skyward; he was a long way from home. Max Gordon stepped into the left-handed batter's box and dug into his stake in the dirt. He wasn't just competing for himself, his teammates, or his parents in the stands. He was playing for those who couldn't make it with him to Omaha.

Before his ascent to one of sports' most iconic stages, Max's signature toughness was forged in the dirt of a forgotten town in the Scott Valley; Etna, California, is a speck on a dot on the map. Population: roughly 700. The town was originally settled as "Rough and Ready" in the 1870s,[1] a nod to the style of ballplayer it didn't yet know would call its city limits home.

What was once merely an open field surrounded by mountains, the Gold Rush turned Etna into a bustling mining town by the turn of the century. The area was also replete with beavers, which invited the likes of Hudson Bay Company trappers to the region. The 1930s brought changes to town, including a shortening of the town's name from "Etna Mills," a nod to the town's former staple flour mill, back to simply "Etna." By the early 2000s, the town still hadn't grown much.[2] Etna is a working town, one where the field-handy folks tend the fields, and the linemen stay up on the lines. Outside of that? Well, there's not much to do in Etna…

That's why Max Gordon, his older brother, Nick, and the other neighborhood kids, Jared, Trevor, Clint, Glenn, Adam, and others had to put the "creation" into "recreation." Most families on the block where the Gordon boys grew up seemed to have sons in pairs, each one right around either Max or Nick's age. When the whole group hung out, Max was usually the youngest. He was always the smallest.

As such, Max became the group's test dummy and, more often, their crash dummy. Need to try out a new shoddy bike ramp? Have Max go off it first to see if it's safe. It often wasn't.

"I was always the guinea pig," Max remembers. "They'd build some horse shit jump and I'd have to test it out and then I'd hurt myself and start crying. I learned pretty quickly that would get the older kids in trouble and I wouldn't be able to play with them anymore if I cried."

He kept his mouth shut, gritted his teeth, and as a reward, he got to fit in. Football games would often end with the pigskin sitting in the middle of someone's yard and the entire neighborhood fighting in a playful brawl. Of course, when it came to Nick and his little brother, who was three years younger, it wasn't always 100 percent playful.

Take the time Nick and his good friend, Jared, were jumping on the Gordon family trampoline along with Max as Michelle, Nick and Max's mom, watched through the window from inside the house. Max was still very young and was enjoying being bounced high by two older kids.

"Okay, now let's do a really high one," Nick suggested to Max.

He was all for it. Jared jumped onto the trampoline and launched Max into flight. Standing off to the side, Nick timed his own jump and spartan-kicked Max all the way off the trampoline. He was sent flying, his small limbs twirling through the air. As he hit his apex and descended toward the ground, he ventured dangerously close to a horseshoe pit post installed for a party celebrating Max's Grammy's and Grampy's 50th wedding anniversary. Surrounding the pit was a circular bed of rocks, which Max's body crashed into as the force of gravity could hold him up no longer. Stan and the boys' mom, Michelle, looked on in horror from inside the house.

"Dad, dad, dad!" Max screamed as he raced toward the door. The chase was on. Nick hopped off and darted after him, hoping to pound him into silence. Max reached the door and tried to open it, but Nick had caught up. Just as he reared to strike, their father swung open the door.

"Whoa, hey, what's going on?" Stan asked his two sons. With a knowing glare of agreement between them, the brothers decided to leave the issue at that. For now, there would be no major clash between the boys. This was a style of crisis aversion with which Stan had grown quite familiar over the years.

From this moment and countless like it, a rivalry was born between the two Gordon boys. The family had a beautiful 72 × 40-foot backyard, perfect for playing sports. It was on this ground where the rivalry grew. On one occasion, the pair played "Three Flies Out," where the objective was for the batter to hit as many home runs as possible before the other brother caught their fly ball three times. As always, Stan was the one pitching the Wiffle balls.

Nick stepped up to the plate and took a huge hack, lining it down the left-field line. Max sprinted with impressive closing speed, sprawled, and made a diving catch for out number one. Nick was already pissed off. Next pitch, he lined it down the right-field line. Once again, Max gave chase and snagged it on a full-extension dive for the second out. The third pitch, Nick finally hit it where Max couldn't get to it. He smacked the Wiffle ball to straightaway center, ticketed for the home run barrier they had constructed. At the last second, Max found his way right onto the barrier and robbed his brother of a home run. Three outs. Nick threw his bat down in frustration and went back inside. For a little brother, it doesn't get much better than that.

Max (left) looks in wonderment at his first-ever pair of batting gloves as his brother Nick looks on. Max would have to wait to use the gloves, as he had a broken arm at the time.

Stan wasn't the only one who inspired the boys' passion for sports, specifically on the diamond. Michelle was Max's tee-ball coach for several years. At first, she didn't even have her kids, or the countless neighborhood kids who would join them, hitting off a tee. She coached a group of tee-ball all-stars against Weed, California, and the group won, 23–22, in an 11-inning thriller. By this point, Michelle recognized tee work was important for her son to improve. Max was just eight years old when he started devoting himself to taking 100 swings off the tee outside his house the instant he got home from school.

Before she and Stan decided to have children, Michelle worked at a high-powered job in bearings. She was good at what she did, but the couple agreed that if they were going to have kids, they could live on Stan's

A young Max Gordon gets his tee work in. He was taught from an early age that tee work is of paramount importance.

paycheck from the power company, where he worked as a lineman. Michelle walked away from her job and undertook the more difficult task of raising two young boys. Above all else, she wanted her boys to know the value of determination, dedication, and perseverance. Too many times, she had seen other parents place limits, spoken or not, on their children, and she was not going to fall into that same trap. "If you ever give up, you never have a chance to succeed," she would say.

She put 30,000 miles on the family van when the boys were young. Driving to and from baseball and golf was time-consuming. That made it all the more rewarding for her to watch the rare times when her boys got to play on the same team.

Max was always the batboy for Nick's Little League baseball team, and when the team didn't have enough kids, Stan would let Max play. When the boys transitioned from tee-ball to Little League, Stan took on the role of coach. Early in his young baseball career, three years younger than the boys he was facing, Max stepped into the box to face the almighty Anthony. Max was downright puny compared to every other kid on the field, but none loomed so ominously over him as Anthony did. Max would have to get used to being the smallest kid on a lot of fields and learning how to compete; he didn't have any way to know this yet, but he wasn't exactly going to grow up to be the biggest, strongest kid in Etna. This at-bat was a baptism into the type of competitor Max might one day become: would he meet this beast head-on, or would he be stomped into the dirt?

Every town has an Anthony. He's the kid who can throw 70 miles an hour before most kids know how to properly hold a bat. He's the towering, weakly mustachioed pre-teen with the thunderous steps and powerful thighs all too big for his Little League pants. He's the kid who causes smaller, weaker kids to cower in fear. As Max dug into the lefty box and stared at the beast, he felt no fear. As it turned out, he should maybe have been a little more afraid. Of course, Anthony's first fastball drilled Max in the ribs, and he went down like a ton of bricks. "He's going to be scared of the ball forever," Stan worried at that early stage of his son's playing career.

Max was fine as he ran out of the box and was incredibly happy to be on first base. "Any way on base," that's what his father (and coach) had always taught him. Nick wasn't a great hitter, and he certainly didn't have the same passion for baseball that Max did. The two saved most of their competition for less formal events than organized ball games.

There was an ebb and flow to Max and Nick's rivalry. Although they constantly craned their necks to peak above the other in any competition they could find, they also implicitly recognized that in their own little existence, they really only had each other. They had a love forged by the mutual respect that only two true competitors can have for one another, but they also had a love forged by the sheer strength of their family bond. This reality was not always apparent right on the surface, however; that was never more evident than when Stan Gordon heard a loud thud and cries coming from the living room one afternoon in the family's Etna home.

"Son of a bitch. Nick get in here!" Stan yelled, assuming he had hurt Max yet again. Instead, it was Nick who came running into the room.

"Max hit me!" he screeched, holding his hands to his eye.

At the ripe old age of six, Max punched his brother in the face for the first time in his life. Stan put Max in his room and gave him the old "words over violence" spiel, but he admitted years later that he wasn't entirely upset with how Max handled himself.

"While taking a trip down Memory Lane, my dad told me, 'I couldn't really tell you this at the time, but that was one of the proudest moments of my life when you finally socked him,'" Max recalls.

"I watched him torment you and beat the shit out of you your whole life and you finally got him," Stan told Max years after the fact. To his face, he told Max, "Hey now, don't hit your brother," but under his breath, he was saying, "Never let anyone push you around."

Stan and Michelle did not shelter their kids. The only way for them to learn, they said, was by making mistakes. They were allowed to attempt dangerous stunts (within reason and oftentimes with a helmet) because frankly, what else was there to do in the Scott Valley?

Nick wasn't a bully. He was simply doing what any older brother does:

show little brother who's boss. While their rivalry never dwindled, the boys' relationship grew closer as they worked together around the house. Stan would have them haul away limbs from trees that he had cut down. The boys would have to drag the trees to a burn pile, which is no easy work. At first, the pair whined and complained. However, once they realized that the more quickly they were done with house work, the more time they'd have to go swimming or ride bikes or do literally anything else, they became a well-oiled machine.

"We started working really well together," Max says, "We started getting things done and weren't bitching and moaning anymore. We were out there doing what we needed to do. . .We didn't really talk about how close we were, but we were always next to each other."

A common spectator to the boys' antics was their grandfather, Norman McPhail, who took every opportunity to visit from his home in Oregon. He couldn't help but smile as he watched their rivalry turn into something more supportive and mutual. To Norman, family had always come first.

Norman's dad had passed away when he was just eight years old, leaving his mother to care for four boys all by herself. How did she provide for four hungry, growing boys? She ran moonshine through the house for Al Capone during Prohibition. Although it was a good way to keep food on the table, it also made for a less-than-ideal home environment for children. She would hide booze in the floorboards and wheel wells of a big Studebaker to conceal the illicit libations. When they were feeling bold, the kids would sneak upstairs and watch people hanging out in the Speakeasy. Who knows the stories and jokes they heard, setting their young imaginations alight and also probably frightening them back to their rooms before long.

Soon finding this roaring underground socialite lifestyle to be unsustainable, Norman's mother took off; the boys, now technically orphaned, were sent to a dirt floor shack along the Missouri River in Missouri Flats, Montana. Norman's oldest brother Alan, just 13 when the boys moved, went homesteading. Norman went to school. By age 12, he was breaking horses, and he just hated that. It slowly tortured him to always have the scent of manure in his nostrils and caked dirt under his fingernails; he was clearly not one for the cowpoke lifestyle. In his own visions of himself, Norman wore a suit and tie. He wanted to be distinguished, to make something of himself.

So he set out to find his mother and go to school. Industriously and however gradually, Norman began to save up cash. When he had saved ten dollars, he sewed the bill into the cuff of his jacket, so that it wouldn't get stolen. He took a buddy along with him on a train. They were just a couple of runaway kids looking for their place in the world. Of course, some runaways have more resolve than others; his friend got homesick around Seattle and headed back, leaving Norman on his own.

"Well," Norman said after his friend's departure, "I'm traveling on."

He forged his way down to Klamath Falls, Oregon, and though he still had the $10, he had to work for food. If he bought food with his money, the bums on the train would see he had cash and take it from him. In Klamath Falls, he knocked on a woman's door and offered to do chores in exchange for lunch. She obliged, so he worked for his keep. He lost some pride over it, but his eyes were opened by what it felt like to work just for the simple pleasure of a meal. At any rate, he left with his belly full.

The lunch made him drowsy, sending him adrift into a long nap. When he woke up, he realized he had missed his stop. He had to get back on another train in Red Bluff, California, going the other way to make sure he got to Redding, which was his final destination. Norman found his mom and lived at the Joss House, a well-known, beautifully decorated Taoist temple of worship, the oldest Chinese temple still being used in the State of California.[3] It struck a rather ironic chord that it was from this house of peaceful worship that Norman went to Weaverville, where his toughness in high school athletics earned him his nickname: "Killer Mac."

There were 25-year-olds playing high school football in Happy Camp, one of the teams Weaverville played against. He wasn't scared so much of the players, but he was scared that if he hurt one of his opponents, their wife or girlfriend would come after him. Due to that fear, he stuck to student-coaching basketball. Norman excelled in school and was accepted to San Jose State to study journalism. Before he could make any progress on his degree, however, Japan attacked Pearl Harbor.

Immediately, Norman and his brother, Jack, signed up to defend their country. Overseas, "Killer Mac" became the guide for the driver scopes, which dropped bombs. He would sit in the back of the plane using Norden Bombsight, a state-of-the-art technology, which calculated speed, wind, and much more. Norman displayed an inherent knack for it, and those in his command took notice quickly. He was the only one who could hit the "x" on the bomb practice runway with a sack of flour.

"Holy smokes, you have to become an instructor now," the powers that be relayed to the young bomb scoper.

That's where Norman spent the rest of his time during the war. His brother Jack drove one of the boats which dropped soldiers off on the beaches of Normandy on D-Day, when thousands of soldiers laid down their lives in the name of country and the shores were lined with the bodies of a generation of young men. Jack saw thousands of American troops gunned down. Miraculously, that day, his life was spared. The brothers returned to civilian life, Norman now wanting to settle down and start a family.

Of course, that would require finding a girl. That's where Dorothy came in. Dorothy's mother wanted her son to bring someone home for his sister. He obliged by bringing home a recently discharged World War II veteran with dead aim named Norman McPhail. Once in Philadelphia, Norman quickly fell head over heels for Dorothy. She fell just as fast. However, he needed her to move to "God's Country": California.

Moving away from an abusive father, Dorothy used the situation to move on up in the world while helping four of her five siblings move away as well. Norman and Dorothy set up a life together and soon adopted three children, including Michelle, Max's mother. Norman wasted no time instilling the value of family in his children. "Dad would always say, 'When you die, it doesn't matter how much money you have. All you have left is your family,'" Michelle Gordon still remembers.

The message was received loud and clear: you have to take care of your own before you can take care of anyone else. As Michelle went on to have a family of her own, with Nick being born in 1987 and Max following soon after in 1990, Norman would still call Michelle twice a day from Southern Oregon. While Norman legally adopted Michelle, her brother, and sister, he also informally adopted Stan, the father of two of his grandchildren.

Grampy Norman, Grammy Dorothy, and Michelle (back row, left to right) smile with Max (middle) and Nick (right) sitting in front of them in 1991.

"Michelle's mom and dad were closer to me as far as parents go than anyone who raised me," Stan recalls.

Stan was taken in at age four by Ken Gordon, whom his mother married after splitting with his father. Ken was 18 years older than Stan's mother, who looked like Jackie Kennedy and was the apple of many an eye. Ken taught Stan the virtue of hard work; he also whipped him constantly. Stan despised Ken, because of the beatings and the fact that he and his mom would jet off to Mexico for six months at a time, leaving him to fend for himself on the couches of friends. Stan vowed when he turned 18, he would leave for good.

"I'll never come back," Stan told himself at the time, "I'll live in a box under a bridge before I come back." He wasn't kidding. The day he became an adult, he got on his motorcycle and rode away, taking nothing with him from the past except for his abusive stepfather's last name, a name to which he would spend a lifetime trying to give his own meaning and values.

It was from these roots that Stan and Michelle helped ensure that Nick and Max had the most stable home life of any generation either family had seen. They got the love and support they needed without being coddled. The two boys entered their teenage years still rivals, Max still looking in awe sometimes at his brother and his array of skills.

One afternoon during these times, Nick, who had just gotten his driver's license, had driven Max and himself out to the bridge at Kelsey Creek in the Scott Valley. There was a 40-foot drop off to the water below, and Nick stepped up and pulled off a "gainer," where you jump forward and do a backflip. Max was beside himself.

"I thought it was the coolest thing ever," Max remembers.

Inspired by his brother's bravery, Max decided to do a front flip off the bridge. What Max didn't know was that his older brother had been practicing that trick for two years. Max was in the air for what felt like two minutes. He over-rotated on his flip and smacked his face against the water. Woozy and sore, Max swam to the river's edge, gasping for air. His competitiveness had driven him near insanity, but his blatant disregard for the safety of his body showed no signs of slowing down.

Being three years older, Nick was the first to play high school sports, starring for the basketball team. The rivalry continued, but Nick's elevated status as a high school athlete made him an even bigger idol to Max. When Nick started sneaking out of the house and getting into trouble, Max would cover for him. Nick frequently sneaked out to drink, something Max vowed not to do until age 21, thanks to a $5,000 deal with his mom. Though Nick was Max's biggest rival, Max would never rat on his brother.

He saw the pain Nick's behavior was putting his parents through and he thought, at the very least, he could spare them a little more if he kept his

Nick (left) and Max smile at the top of Etna Summit on Christmas Day after being gifted new snowboards for the holiday.

mouth shut and vouched for his older brother. It all, again, came back to there being nothing to do in the Scott Valley. For generations, kids would go up onto a mountain, start a bonfire, and drink. After one such outing, Nick was a passenger in a car with a driver who was drunk. When the police called the Gordons, there was nothing Max could do to save his brother from trouble and his parents from anguish. "I was really upset with him," Stan says, "Not that the cops called, but the fact he was driving with somebody who was drinking. I didn't want him getting into an accident."

Stan was a line crew foreman for the power company and had seen how deadly drunk driving crashes could turn. He worked on power poles regularly which had been crashed into by drunk drivers. Working for the power company was good, honest work, but it left him exhausted by day's end. With Max heading into high school and Nick entering his senior year, the family felt that a change of scenery might do something to shift the momentum their lives seemed to be picking up.

Stan and Michelle had considered moving a couple of hours north to Ashland, Oregon, for a while, but hadn't yet pulled the trigger. It was just a short 20-minute drive to Grampy Norman and Grammy Dorothy in Medford, which was an important factor in the family's consideration. The tip of the iceberg came after a long couple of days of yard work.

All weekend long, the three Gordon boys logged their property. Stan cut down trees, while Nick and Max methodically piled up the rounds and cut them into firewood like they had so many times before. Finally, they were done and nobody was in any shape to fix a meal. "I'm too tired to cook anything," Stan said, "Let's go out. We just worked hard all weekend. Let's go have some dinner."

The family loaded into the car and checked out every one of the few restaurants Etna had to offer. All of them were closed. It wasn't even seven o'clock. Etna's small-town charm was noticeably beginning to lose its luster. Stan sometimes felt as though he was losing his mind. Ultimately, he and Michelle left the decision up to Nick, who would be entering his senior year of high school. Unsure of the motives driving his choice and nervous that they'd have to stay in Etna all their lives, they awaited their son's decision. In the end, the parents got the answer they were hoping for.

"Grammy and Grampy need us," Nick said, suggesting the family should move closer to Norman and Dorothy in order to see them more often. It surely delighted Norman, the old orphan bomber, "Killer Mac," that this was his grandson's reasoning for making such a momentous decision.

With that, the family relocated to Ashland, Oregon, population roughly 20,000. Though some might pass through Ashland without giving it much attention, to a kid from Etna it felt like New York City. It was also the next step on the way to the battle of a lifetime.

CHAPTER 2

Ashland

Before he had time to react, Josh Scarminach's dad, Michael, was summoning him to his truck.

"Hey, hop in. We're going to help another lineman move in," the elder Scarminach said.

Michael had caught word that a lineman from the Scott Valley was being transferred to Medford, Oregon, where he worked. Power linemen are a breed that stick tightly together by nature. Michael figured he'd bring his son along and see if he couldn't make friends with the new guy's kid.

The Scarminaches arrived and began helping the Gordons move into their new home in Ashland, away from everything they knew in Etna. The first thing Josh and Max did together was move a coffee table inside. The way they conducted themselves in this exchange served as a sort of precursor to the tone of the friendship to come; the two managed to snag the table onto the corner of one of the door sidings, ripping a piece clear off the doorway. As if thinking with minds alike, Max and Josh each quickly looked in each direction. Exchanging a knowing glance and judging that nobody had witnessed their mistake, the pair kept on with their work and didn't mention it to anyone. Naturally, from that point on, the two friends would always be flirting with trouble together.

Josh was a major welcoming presence for Max as he assimilated into his new environment; it quickly became apparent that the boys were kindred spirits. Stan's youngest son was not excited to move to Ashland to start high school, and he was even more perturbed when he saw groups of kids who sagged their pants and wore styles with which Max was entirely unfamiliar. Ashland's size, whilst still considered a small town by city-folk, overwhelmed Max at first. Compared to Scott Valley, his new setting offered perhaps too much all at once for him to handle. He didn't know where to begin, and he felt almost paralyzed by the branching possibilities with which Ashland, Oregon, presented him.

On that first night in Ashland, upon finishing the preliminary unpacking, Max had one destination in mind for his first meal in his new state;

every kid coming from a speck on the map dreams of its iconic golden arches… Max wanted to go to dinner at McDonald's. While living in Etna, the closest fast-food establishment to the Gordons was 35 minutes away in Yreka. Now, he had one right in town.

So Max, now 14 years old, decided he was going to take big brother Nick's nice bike down to McDonald's to grab something to eat. His dad gave his blessing, so he raced his way down the street toward the land of Big Macs, chicken nuggets, and crispy, golden french fries. He quickly arrived, parked Nick's bike outside, and went in to order and eat his dinner. After less than half an hour inside, he came back out to grab the bike and ride home. The only problem was, the bike was nowhere in sight.

Nick's bike had been stolen in the short time Max was inside. The natural trust in one's neighbor that comes with growing up in a very small town had been immediately violated, and Max would come to learn that a half-hour was no longer a short time to leave his belongings unattended. The family decided to file a police report, although Max and his family knew it was likely to no avail. They were never seeing that bike again. The whole episode was a wake-up call. "We're not in Etna anymore…." Stan chided his youngest son. The privilege of naiveté was no longer something he or his family could afford.

Max did not make the same mistake twice. Yet as the summer wore on, freshman football practice was in full swing, and the youngest Gordon boy once again ran into some bad luck on his bike. While riding to practice (on his own bike this time), Max had a major wipeout and gashed his hand wide open. Blood rushing out of the wound, he hurried over to the Minute Market in town. "Hey, do you guys have a Band-Aid or tape or something?" Max asked as he walked inside, clearly rattling the woman at the front desk who examined his hand.

In her state of panic, all she could offer him was a meager attempt at wrapping his hand up with some toilet paper and tape. Having bought himself a little time, Max thanked her and hopped right back on his bike, racing toward the fields. His heart was beating out of his chest with nerves and excitement at the prospect of getting out on the freshly cut grass and into the action. As his body pumped adrenaline, his heart pumped blood to the site of his wound, so that by the time Max hit the brakes in front of the baseball field off campus where the freshmen practiced, blood had seeped through the toilet paper wrap and had dripped down his arm. As he approached his coach, blood was streaming steadily off his elbow.

It looked like Max's hand was about to fall into two distinct pieces. It was gruesome. He was quickly shuttled from the coach to the team's trainer, who examined the injury and determined the wound too deep to treat by himself. This would require a trip to the hospital. His mother was called and quickly, Michelle found herself driving her son to the hospital.

Many would panic due to the nature of the injury, but soon after arrival, Max wasn't sweating it. The nurses had already administered him some painkillers, so he was as cool as a cucumber. As a result of their very nature, he and Nick were no strangers to hospitals. Eventually the doctors got him all stitched up, sending him back home with nothing more than a killer scar by which to remember the incident. Ashland had left its mark on him for the first time.

Nick (back left) and Max came right off the practice field and joined Grampy Norman and Grammy Dorothy in the fall of 2004. It was one of the last times the two shared an athletic field together; Max was a freshman and Nick was a senior, and both played on the JV squad.

Max was back on the football field in no time. Nothing was going to keep him off the gridiron. For one, he couldn't afford to miss much time as he was battling for a starting spot; but there was also the fact that the football field was one of the very few places that felt welcoming to Max during that first summer in Ashland. In his first week of practice, "Coach K," varsity assistant coach Dave Kitchell, stopped by freshman practice to get a look at his new crop of future varsity hopefuls. "You guys are still a part of our program," Coach K said, "You're all the young crowd and you're not going to be playing varsity this season, but we're still watching you and paying attention."

Coach K, by this time, was a fixture in Ashland. He had been coaching in the Ashland Schools since 1984, when he was just 28 years old.[1] He was a quiet but fiery man and a coach whose demeanor demanded one's respect. He could have been the head coach at Ashland High School or elsewhere by this point in his career, but he fancied being an assistant. This way, he didn't have to deal with the "junk" around which head coaches are generally required to operate.

Kitchell was raised in a rough and tumble neighborhood near Chicago in Hammond, Indiana, which forced him to carry himself a certain way to thrive. The color of his background put a sort of mystique around him. As a result, the students whom he coached generally paid attention to what he had to say. His fight with cancer was just one more thing that led his players to hang on his every word.

Coach K had been diagnosed with colon cancer five years earlier and had never gone into remission. He would go in and out of good times and bad, sometimes facing very aggressive forms of treatment that left his body utterly depleted. As a runner, Kitchell tried to sweat it out, to put the disease behind him or at least enter a temporary escape. Just the fact that he was fighting was enough to inspire a group of young kids.

Max was as yet unaware of Coach K's story; all he knew was that something about his coach scared him. He was seemingly omniscient, and it served his players well to know where he was at all times. "He had a presence, some sort of voice," Max recalls of that time, "His talks would get you excited or they would scare the life out of you, but it taught you not only how to attack the game of football, but how to attack life."

Kitchell's legacy had grown even larger thanks to the Pacific Rim Bowl, an idea he began in 1988.[2] Every two years, the Ashland football team played a team of Japanese all-stars in what was meant first and foremost to be an important cultural exchange. It always culminated in a football game. Home games were alternated, so every four years the game would be played in the United States, and every four years it would be played in Japan.

In Max's sophomore season of 2006, the team was set to travel across the Pacific to play at Oji Stadium, in Kobe. Upon the team's arrival, the extreme language barrier immediately became apparent. Japanese host families knew more English than the players knew Japanese, but neither knew enough of the other to communicate very effectively. Max, for instance, knew how to count to five and say the pre- and post-meal prayer in Japanese, but that was it.

The cultural differences put him into some less-than-ideal situations.

For example, he was always taught to clean his plate as a sign that he liked the food his host had prepared. He did this in Japan to be polite, even though he wasn't a huge fan of the predominantly fish dishes being served. Unfortunately, in Japan, clearing your plate is a sign you want more food, so for days, he would get seconds and thirds until Coach K told him what he was doing wrong.

Ashland lost the ninth-ever Pacific Rim Bowl, 28–6, which proved an ominous warning of things to come for the sophomore team. The group had already gone winless as freshman, and the loss to the Japanese All-Stars sounded alarms that potential disaster lay ahead for Max's class when they reached the varsity level. Most of the good players from that team were plucked and placed onto the varsity anyway.

Head coach Charlie Hall and Coach K had coached together off and on for nearly a decade and had a great admiration for one another. When Coach Hall got the nod for the head coaching job in 2005, it was Coach K who alerted him to the opening. Together, they developed pre-game and pre-practice rituals players would never forget.

At the center of the ceremonies were the positive affirmations the team would make before each game. Everybody would drop to a knee in the locker room and hold the hands of the boys on either side. The entire room would be locked together, and Coach K would run through simple affir-mations, slowly making them more and more serious. He would start with something like: "I will do my job."

"I will do my job. I will do my job. I will do my job," the team would recite back, saying each affirmation three times.

"We will all fly to the ball."

"We will all fly to the ball. We will all fly to the ball. We will all fly to the ball."

The first few affirmations were subject to be changed on a game-to-game basis. If the team needed to be reminded of a specific area of strategic emphasis, or maybe if a single player was going through some-thing and needed extra support, for instance. The team's final affirmation before taking the field, however, always stayed the same:

"We love and care for each other."

"We love and care for each other. We love and care for each other. We love and care for each other."

All previous activity in the locker room effectively built toward that moment. Coach K could scheme and game plan with the best of them, but at the end of the day, he wanted the kids to know that really, football doesn't matter. What matters is building relationships, loving each other, going to war, fighting for each other, and knowing when the final whistle blows that you've given the competition and your teammates every bit of effort that you could muster. It was the main message he wanted to deliver to every kid who took the field under his command.

Of course, he was also a football coach, so he used his fair share of tough love. As a sophomore, Max was placed in a hitting drill with junior running back Justin Mesa, who had at least 40 pounds on him. It was Max's job to hit Mesa and stop him at the line. On his first attempt, things didn't go as planned. Mesa blasted through Max, nearly taking his head off with him.

"Max, what the hell was that?" Coach K asked his sophomore defensive back.

"Sorry, Coach, I'm trying," Max responded, stunned as he picked himself up off the hard earth. It was the worst retort he could have made.

"You're trying?" Coach K asked, grabbing Max's facemask, "Stop trying and fucking do it." He delivered the message a little less eloquently than Yoda had, but the sentiments were the same.

Something about how Coach K delivered that message to Max stuck with him. He hopped back into the drill, lining up once more across from the imposing figure of Justin Mesa. Mesa was just another "Anthony," the massive boy who had drilled Max's ribs with a fastball years ago in Etna. He was another Goliath.

Six or seven more times these two collided, and neither backed down. There was a full-on collision each time, registering a resounding POP! as the two helmets and pads came crashing together. On the final rep of the drill, Max again jumped forward to stop Mesa, but this time, Mesa stepped to the side like a matador sidestepping a bull, causing Max to stumble. He looked back in confusion at his much larger, older counterpart, not understanding why he had avoided the final contact.

He didn't have to wonder for very long. Mesa came up to Max after practice and admitted, "I think you gave me a concussion, man. I couldn't do that anymore. That was starting to hurt."

Although Max walked away from the confrontation far from unscathed, he realized with excitement that he had used enough will-power to outlast a bigger, stronger opponent. He had risen to his coach's challenge and been tougher than his adversary out of sheer resolve. This proved to be a powerful realization for Max going forward.

His toughness continued on the baseball diamond, where he played the sport about which he was most passionate. He was a utility player, a lefty hitter, capable of playing middle infield and outfield, even a little catcher on occasion. As had been the case with football, Max's all-out style of play and limitless resolve won him popularity among his teammates. During the summer after his sophomore season, he and his team watched the College Baseball World Series as Oregon State made its miraculous championship run. *Wow*, Max thought, *The College World Series is a bigger deal than I thought.*

The Beavers lost their first game in the College World Series, 11–1 to Miami, pushing them to the brink of elimination. They proceeded to dispatch No. 7 Georgia (5–3) and then got revenge on the same Miami team (8–1), pitting them against No. 2 Rice in the semifinals.[3] Coming out of the losers' bracket, the Beavers had to win two games in a row to land in the championship series. Rice didn't score a run in either game, and Oregon State was suddenly two wins away from a national championship.

Once again, the team was pushed toward elimination after losing the opening game of its best-of-three series against North Carolina, 4–3, in a game that included a 77-minute rain delay. An 11–7 slugfest victory in Game 2 assured a winner-take-all title game the following day. Tied 2–2 in the bottom of the eighth inning, the Beavers scratched across a run, and closer Kevin Gunderson shut the door in the ninth. The Ashland High School players, including one of Max's best friends, Sam Gaviglio, couldn't believe it. A team from the Pacific Northwest had won a major collegiate sports championship.

Collegiate sports were always on Max's radar. Decisions he made about how much time and energy to spend on each sport started to be shaped by what he saw as his best chance to play sports at the next level. He knew Power 5 college baseball might not be in the cards due to his size, but he was convinced that it was this sport on the diamond, not the gridiron, that was calling his name. He decided against playing football his junior year in order to focus on baseball and play in a fall League. The pressure he placed on himself mounted. Junior year is the big one, the year when serious prospective collegiate athletes expect to receive scholarship offers.

He went to Ashland High for the first football game of the season, and after seeing how much fun his friends were having without him on the field, he decided to play again. He tracked down Charlie Hall the following week and told him he'd like to rejoin the team. That was fine, but since he had missed summer workouts, it would be at least six weeks until he could actually suit up for a game, based on Oregon safety regulations. Max realized it was too late. He was angry with himself. Just because he'd thought for a minute that he didn't feel like playing football, now he would have to miss out on his entire junior year football season. He would have to put all of his energy into baseball. That didn't prove to be as productive as it may have sounded. "I put a lot of pressure on myself junior year," Max remembers, "I was going to conquer the world. I was going to hit 1.000 with 100 home runs."

The pressure got to him. Things went horribly wrong at the plate. Max became neurotic in the box, trying dozens of different batting stances as well as numerous different types, weights, and sizes of bats. No such simple solution was found. Pressure evolved into panic as the clock began to tick seriously on his hopes of receiving a college offer. Ultimately, the clock ran out. He didn't get a single Division-1 college offer. It was the first and only time in his life that he had been playing a sport more for himself than for his team. Without a college career to focus on, Max vowed he would be a team-first guy in his final high school season.

Just months after his disastrous junior baseball season ended, his senior football season began. As they had every four years, Coach K and the Grizzlies welcomed the Japanese all-stars to Southern Oregon ahead of the 2007 season. In a hard-fought game at Phillips Field, Japan came away with a thrilling 28–21 win. It indicated to Ashland how far they'd come in just a couple seasons. Japan was always tough, and to fall only by a late touchdown was a sign that this could be one of the best seasons in years for the Ashland football team.

Max, now a senior and a major weapon on the Ashland defense, hoped to leave his mark on the area with his final football season and make a name for himself in athletics. He only wished that he had the support he'd always counted on from his older brother to help him make that goal a reality.

Nick was no longer living at home, and Max was worried and annoyed. His older brother was studying to be a firefighter, but his punk-rock attitude made it clear that he would clash with the traditional trappings of establishment. Now he was sharing an apartment on the other side of town with a girlfriend and another friend he let stay with him for a while. His girlfriend had a kid from another relationship, and his lovable friend did little else but chill on the couch and smoke weed.

Feeling the burden of compassion that almost always guided his actions, Nick worked at a grocery store, Shop 'N Kart, in Ashland full-time and bussed tables at a Mexican restaurant at night in an effort to take care of everyone in his life. He worked close to 12 hours a day, and while Max didn't like the direction his brother's life was headed, he saw exactly why he was behaving the way he was: "Nick doesn't want to see anybody suffer, so he takes his friends in," Max says, "He's looking out for his girl. He's buying diapers for this baby that doesn't belong to him and all this stuff. He's putting on the cape and being the hero."

Since Nick seemed to look out for everyone except for himself, Max decided to be the one to look out for his big brother. He went over to his apartment one evening during the football season and put it to him straight: he told his brother that it was time to start looking out for himself and to get an education. Otherwise, he insisted, Nick would wake up one day and realize that his whole life had been lived for nothing. Max was the first one in a long time who got through to Nick and forced him to look inward.

All the while, the football team was in the middle of one of its best seasons. The Grizzlies were 8–0 following their final home game of the regular season and were closing in on a conference title. Normally, following a big win, Max and the "Man Clan" went hot-tubbing. The Man Clan was a group of Ashland's defensive starters who assembled every Wednesday night to watch "Flavor of Love," starring Flava Flave.

On nights after a win, however, the Man Clan just couldn't be satisfied by reality TV. They would go to the richest part of Ashland and try to get away with hopping in the nice hot tubs of the town's most affluent residents. On this night, the final regular season home game of his high school career, Max would not be joining his best friend, Josh Scarminach, and others in their usual escapades. Nick gave him a call after his game and asked if he would come over.

Max, of course, obliged and went back to Nick's place that night. His older brother walked him outside onto the porch and shut the door behind them. Shortly after the conversation started, Nick's girlfriend opened the door and asked what the brothers were talking about.

"Hey, I'm talking to my brother," Nick shot back. "Please stay inside."

Nick had always referred to Max as his "little brother," but not this time. Max took notice. Nick turned his attention back toward Max, who had just helped the Grizzlies to their eighth straight win to start the season.

Nick began to reflect on the conversation the two of them had previously had: "Man, I'm really proud of you and I'm really glad you told me that," Nick told his little brother, "You're right."

Max had never talked to Nick the way he did in their prior conversation. Nick had always been the alpha in the relationship, but that status was beginning to fade and become unimportant between the two boys.

"I can't treat you like a kid anymore," Nick continued. "You're smart, you're grown up, you're not an idiot."

"We're equals."

Max had been waiting to have this very conversation with Nick for 16 years, and here it was, finally. All the years of getting picked on and of being "little brother" were gone. The two brothers were on level footing. It was an arrangement that would have to be lived to be confirmed, but the words still meant a great deal to the youngest Gordon child.

From there, Nick and Max hatched a plan that night that they would attend junior college together. Nick wanted to go back to school, and Max had decided to attend Sierra College in the Sacramento area after visiting two different schools: Sierra and Feather River College.

He met Feather River College head coach Terry Baumgartner during an indoor practice (not exactly the best sell for a California school), and Baumgartner could tell he was a good kid. "He was exactly what we thought would work for our program," Baumgartner recalls of Max, "He was undersized, a great kid, great family. He was going to do anything he could to get on the field."

Max liked Baumgartner and Feather River, but his visit to Sierra College put it on slightly higher ground. His parents both came from the Sacramento area, and he still had family there. Sierra was also well on their way to a California state championship that season. Max attended a game in which Sierra beat a solid junior college team soundly, 11–1. Facing a pitcher who would later be drafted in the 10th round, Sierra teed off moonshot after moonshot.

Never wanting to over-recruit, head coach Rob Willson wanted an honest opinion after the game.

"Do you think you could play here?" Willson asked Max as his dad stood by.

"Oh, 100 percent," Stan shot back before his son was able to answer.

Willson himself wasn't entirely convinced. *This little guy? Really? We've got a guy who hits cleanup who's 6'3", 220 pounds*, he thought, but the certainty with which the boy's father spoke resonated with the old coach. "Okay, if you think he can play here, I'd love to have him come to Sierra College," Willson told Stan and his youngest son.

Max's mind was quickly made up. Sierra had the better baseball pedigree, and his mom was convinced of their academic prowess as well. Sacramento would be the next stop in his baseball journey once he graduated from Ashland.

On the night of their momentous talk, Nick made plans to join Max there. The pair would get an apartment together, and Nick would go back to school, applying himself once again to become a firefighter. Max came home from Nick's that night, and his mom could tell he was emotional. Michelle asked about his day.

"I just had the best conversation with Nick," Max told his mom.

"Oh really? What just happened?" Michelle wondered out loud.

"Well, he asked me to come over after the game and I did," Max responded.

"I'm glad you did," Michelle said.

Michelle knew her youngest son was frustrated by her oldest son's direction in life. When Max told her that Nick had tagged them as equals, she couldn't wipe the smile from her face. She knew better than anyone that this marked a major shift in the way both of her boys would approach the rest of their lives.

The following week, the Grizzlies wrapped up their Southern Sky Conference title with a win over Eagle Point, pushing them to 9–0 on the season with one non-conference game left before the playoffs. Every year, Coach

K would dance a jig in the locker room after a late-season win in order to get the team ready for its playoff run. In Eagle Point's locker room, Coach K stormed in and started dancing to the Motown song, *Tighten Up*. As he danced around on the floor, the team followed his lead. Players were dancing all around him. It was a great time to be an Ashland Grizzly.

In his 24th season as a coach for Ashland Schools, Coach K was having as much fun as ever. He was also using the dancing, and coaching as if nothing was wrong, to cover up the fact that he hadn't been feeling too well as of late. The following day, just a handful of hours after he danced on the floor of the Eagle Point locker room, he rang up Coach Hall.

"I need to go to the hospital," Coach K told Hall.

"Oh, are you all right?" Hall asked his good friend and assistant coach.

"I'm not feeling too good," Coach K responded. "I talked to the doctor."

Hall was taken by surprise. Based on Coach K's demeanor over the last several weeks, he seemed fine, but then again, he had always kept his cards close to the vest. Because of the toughness Kitchell had shown in the past, his head coach knew deep down that for him to miss such an important game meant something really was wrong.

"I've been struggling this whole week," Coach K continued. "I'm not sure what's going on, so I'm just going to go in."

The team traveled up to play Crook County without Coach K as the players speculated about his condition. After yet another win, helping them end their regular season a perfect 10–0, Coach Hall received word that Kitchell didn't have long to live. Doctors had discovered more cancer and said he was up against a time limit. This seemingly sudden turn of events left Coach K in hospice care in his own home, where he would be more comfortable.

Following a bye week they'd earned with their perfect regular-season record, the Grizzlies learned they would take on Corvallis at home in their first playoff game. That week, Max and several other players visited their beloved coach at his home as his wife, Trish, took care of him. His guard was down when the players walked in, and they could tell the toll the cancer was taking on his body.

His skin was beginning to yellow and his body seemed frail. It frightened his players. The same man who simultaneously represented to his players vitality, power, and an undying winning spirit was withering quickly before their very eyes. The moment he saw them walk through the door, he straightened up and asked Trish if she could give them a couple minutes. She nodded, gave her husband a kiss, and left him with his players, the young men whom he cherished most.

"What's up, boys?" Coach K asked the group.

"How are you doing, Coach?" they asked.

Coach K said he was doing fine, but his players could tell that he was simply protecting them from having to hear the reality of the situation. The group talked about football and game plans as they always had as if nothing was different, but the air around them had an entirely different feel to it. It was unavoidable. Max kept trying to move the conversation back to how Coach K was doing, what the doctors were saying, how he was going to beat this. His coach kept deflecting the attention from himself as he had for decades.

"Oh, don't worry about me," Kitchell said in a response true to his entire coaching ideology, "You have to focus on your job. Focus on what you guys have to accomplish this week."

His response provided inspiration for the team's upcoming playoff game against Corvallis, but it also gave them a pit in their stomach knowing there must be a reason he kept dodging the questions about the status of his health. No matter, they just enjoyed being able to spend some time with Coach.

Everyone turned to leave after a while of chatting. Most had gotten to the door when Coach K shouted to the group.

"Hey!" he yelled.

Max and the others turned around, the faint voice of a once-powerful man still commanding the attention of the room. His eyes and Max's met.

"Hey man, I love you," he told the young man, allowing the facade of authority between player and coach to dissolve momentarily. He was cementing a genuine connection he felt with one of the men whose lives he had touched in such a fundamental way.

"I love you too, Coach."

With the playoff game looming in a couple of days, Max took a few seconds to fully appreciate what was going on. He lingered slightly, getting one last look at his coach, one of the most significant figures to that point in his life. He turned the corner and walked away after the rest of his teammates. He left his coach's home that day with a mental snapshot etched in his mind of what he assumed was his final encounter with Coach K. He would carry this moment with him and resolve to live a life that might honor one of his heroes, a man who was—to many budding athletes in Ashland, Oregon—larger than life.

CHAPTER 3

"We love and care for each other"

On the eve of the big game, one could see a rather peculiar sight at the Ashland High athletic complex: a long wire snaking all the way from the football field to the field house gym. The wire connected two antennae, one on the field and one on the gym. It would take some ingenuity to rig this sort of technology, but assistant football coach Steve Mitzel was determined to get it done. He would find a way for fellow assistant coach Dave Kitchell to see his boys face off at home against Corvallis in the playoffs. Since the illness rendered Coach K too weak to attend the game himself, there was little hope that he would get to see them play in person.

Mitzel sought the help of his brother-in-law, Jim Teece, the head of Ashland-based Internet and tech firm, Project A. Mitzel himself was the IT Director for the Ashland School District. At this time in Ashland, if there were any pair of men who could make this happen, it was these two. Sure enough, through the complex system of wires and antennas, as well as playback at Coach K's house, live streaming was made possible.

Kitchell had been made aware of their plan in the days leading up to kickoff. As days of arduous planning and hours of painstaking work came to fruition, the playing field at Ashland High School buzzed into clear view on the coach's TV screen in his own living room. The year was 2007, and Dave Kitchell had a premium live-stream of the Ashland-Corvallis playoff game thanks to two devoted colleagues.

Back at the stadium, Coach Hall felt rudderless as he looked out at the young men preparing to do battle. Coach K's gusto in the locker room had become the lifeblood of many a young squad over the years he and Coach Hall had worked together. Although Hall was a seasoned leader on the gridiron, making stops in the NCAA coaching for the likes of Northern Arizona and North Texas, his soft-spoken nature was not always tailored to these intense, high-octane moments. Nevertheless, he knew his team needed something from him to light the fire inside before they took the field for this crucial matchup.

The solution was simple: have Coach K call in. Ashland players, preparing for the biggest game they had ever played, gathered around Coach Hall and the room went silent. Coach K was on the other end of his cell phone, and the entire team—players and staff—was hanging on his words. With the same forceful resolve he always displayed, he began to recite the team's affirmations. They went through each one by one, like always, and like always, they knew what the last decree would be:

"We love and care for each other," Coach K said through the phone as he had so many times before.

"We love and care for each other. We love and care for each other. We love and care for each other," the young men resounded their reply.

As he looked around, held up his phone, and listened to the words of his dear friend, repeating them back with the team, Coach Hall let the tears stream down his face.

"I knew that was probably going to be the last time," Hall said.

Emotions running high, their beloved coach ailing in his living room just a few miles away, the Grizzlies stormed out onto the field. Corvallis met them with a similar flourish, and the first half of the contest was a deadlock; it was a chess match of defensive strategy, and each side stifled the other's efforts at every turn. By the time the scoreboard indicated halftime, it had still not been lit up by either side. The teams would enter the second half no closer to victory than they had been at the time of the opening kickoff. Players covered in mud filed in one by one as they prepared to hear what their respective coaches had to say about the first half of the game. As he pondered personnel changes and game-plan adjustments, Coach Hall's phone started ringing.

"Hey, Coach," the voice on the other line said.

"Hey Kitch, how are you doing? Are you all right?" Charlie asked Coach K, who had surprised him with a halftime phone call.

"Yeah, I'm okay," Kitchell said. He wasn't interested in talking about his health: "Damn it, you guys need to onside kick. The tackle is bailing out on that side. Just give it a shot."

Coach Hall, by now, had his phone on speaker once again so the entire locker room could hear Coach K speak. He continued, saying that a surprise onside would work and after it worked, the Grizzly offense was going to shove it down Corvallis' throat. Kitchell was always a big visualizer. As they listened to his vision, players' minds returned to how he would often end practice by having every player lie on their backs and visualize exactly what he was saying.

"You guys are going to wake up, you're going to brush your teeth and get ready for school. You are going to have all your homework done. You're going to say 'hi' to Father Sean when he comes in and gives us the prayer before the game," and he would move onto more football-related visualization, "Sam is going to make a 25-yard catch for a first down on a long third down. It's going to be a big play."

It seemed impossible, but nearly every time he mentioned something specific, it would happen. These visualization exercises began to turn into self-fulfilling prophecies. He would say it, and so it was. There are people who believe that if one can hone the power of visualization enough, they can actually begin to manifest the things in their visions. It's uncertain whether Kitchell, Coach Hall, or any of the Ashland players believed such a thing. But one thing is certain: when Ashland lined up and opened the second half with a kickoff, it was an onside kick. Just as Coach K had envisioned, the tackle on the far side left his post early to go to his blocking assignment. This left the gunner on the Ashland squad with an open path to the ball. He sprinted down that path until he could feel himself falling down on top of the ball. The kicking team had recovered, and one more of the old coach's visions had been realized on the gridiron. To manifest the rest, the offense marched down the field and found the end zone to nab the first points of the day, giving the Grizzlies a 7–0 lead. They shoved it down their throat, just like Kitchell said they would.

They nursed that lead for most of the second half. After Corvallis scored and missed the extra point, the Grizzlies hung onto the lead for dear life, up 7–6. With less than two minutes to play, the Grizzlies were forced to punt from their own 30-yard line. Sam Gaviglio was the school's punter in addition to the baseball team's ace pitcher. As long as he got a decent punt away, the defense should have no problem holding Corvallis off.

The snap went over Gaviglio's head. To salvage the play and keep the Corvallis defense from scoring, Sam dove on the ball on the Ashland two-yard line. The Spartans had first-and-goal from the two with a minute to play. A touchdown would all but guarantee a victory for Corvallis and a stunning, last-minute defeat for the Grizzlies.

Earlier in the season, Ashland players had watched the movie *300*, and now Max took the film's message to heart. He channeled an us-against-the-world mentality to fire the team up with its season hanging in the balance. Coach K watched on his TV screen as his defensive players, the ones he had groomed so carefully over the past three or four years, had the fate of the game resting on their shoulders.

"This is where we hold them!" Max screamed. "This is where they die!"

He was like Leonidas, drawing a line in the sand. On the first play, Corvallis handed it off up the middle, and Josh Scarminach blew the guy up at the line. On second down, the Spartans threw a fade to the corner of the end zone which got knocked down. On third down, they pitched the ball to the outside; Max tracked his man with ferocity and dove to make the tackle just short of the goal line.

It all came down to this one play. Fourth and goal, season on the line. This was high school football after all, and the weather was crumby. A field goal attempt simply was not an option. Coach K's defense was given the chance to win a playoff game with a memorable goal line stand. Ultimately, the final stop did not take a heroic effort. Just as the play began, it was over. Corvallis fumbled the snap on fourth and goal and their season came to an end. As in *300*, the Spartans ultimately fell. But in this iteration, the heroes lived on the other side of the line of scrimmage.

"It's Coach K's defense out there and it's time to show up," Max says. "Me and all my friends just shut these guys down. We just manhandled them, didn't let them have an inch."

Jubilation painted the scene as the young Grizzlies began to celebrate their epic victory; players jumped around, arm in arm, chasing and tackling each other with glee as they rejoiced in the fact that there would be more football for them to play this season. Coach Dave Kitchell watched with pride from home, knowing he had helped these young men manifest one more dream out on that field. Coach Hall and the players would hope

Ashland head football coach Dave Kitchell (left, middle) draws up a play as Max (right, middle) and others look on during the Grizzlies' 2007 season.

after the fact that this moment of vindication had brought the old coach's soul some peace. As Coach K reveled in one more sweet victory, he slipped off into a deep, contented sleep. As Hall and the team would learn the next morning, Dave Kitchell passed away peacefully mere hours after the final whistle rang out in Ashland's favor. He was only 51 years old.

Dave Kitchell and the Ashland football team show intensity during a muddy Friday night game.

Word circulated early in the day. It was Sunday. That meant no one was in school, and many had been out celebrating the big playoff win the night before. Coach Hall was among the first to get the news, and he started spreading it to current and former players as well as parents and high school staff. Max got a text from a friend early that morning: "Did you hear about Coach K?" He knew this question could only mean one thing, but he responded anyway. He needed to see the words.

Once he got the reply he'd been expecting, Max sat down. He simply fell to the floor of his room and sat there, stunned. He doesn't know how long he stayed there. It felt like an hour, but it could have been five minutes or an entire afternoon. He was in a daze. At some point, he finally pulled himself up off the floor and hopped in his car. He drove to the one place that made sense: the Ashland High School football field. Within hours of the news circulating the town, more players pulled up and poured onto the field. Most simply shared a wordless embrace with their fellow mourning comrades. Few actual words were spoken, but they all carried the sentiment of love and care for one another which Coach K had spent his entire adult life trying to impart. He lived in them, through their words and actions, their mannerisms and their priorities. He not only molded young competitors, he molded young men who learned how to be compassionate and generous and caring.

"We were coming off our first playoff victory in a long time," Max recalls. "Typically, you wake up and you've got that king-of-the-world feeling after winning a football game, but that was pretty devastating to get the news the next morning."

Beyond losing an inspiring football coach, kids had lost their rock, their leader, their mentor. They wouldn't be able to ask him questions about life anymore, and the passing of one of their foremost spiritual guides presented even more vexing questions about the nature of their existence. Players held onto the knowledge, wisdom, and class Coach K had shared with them, because it suddenly dawned on them that the only way he and his message could live on was through them.

"In terms of mentality, this guy was built of stone," Max remembers. "Nothing is going to put this guy into the ground. When that happened, it was a rude awakening . . .It doesn't matter who you are, what your goals are, or how mentally and physically tough you are. Death is inevitable. It's coming for everybody. And you never know when it could strike."

A sizable crowd gathered at Ashland's football stadium that night. Candles were lit in vigil and placed in the shape of a "K" at midfield. Today, you can find a "K" in the middle of many Ashland Grizzly paw logos associated with the football team. Coach Hall felt he had to say a few words to the crowd that had gathered. "I had to put on a face and stay strong," Hall says, "I needed to share his legacy with people I thought it was very important to know, who didn't know him."

Compared to others in the community, Hall and Kitchell didn't go back very far. Some knew him for two decades, while Hall had coached with him for just a handful of years. In that time, Coach K made a lasting impact on the way Hall looked at his role as a high school football coach and as an educator. He spoke at the vigil that night and later at the memorial service, which was also held at the field.

> Speaking for all the coaches who have worked with Dave Kitchell ... we have been blessed and fortunate. For all the players here today and all those who have ever played for Coach K, you too have been blessed and even more fortunate.
>
> As a fellow coach and colleague, Kitch personified dedication, work ethic, knowledge, the desire to improve, the ability to teach, and the ability to coordinate. He had great insight on how things should be done. His positive attitude

and sense of humor made any job at hand worthy and fun. No job was ever too big for Dave Kitchell and no job was too small. No team was too good that he couldn't put together a game plan and get our kids to play hard.

As Coach Hall spoke, Max's mind raced back to the lessons Coach K had taught him. He thought back to when some players on the team had bullied a kid named Edwin. He was in Max's close group of friends, and one day before practice, a teammate said, "Hey Edwin, cool Bronco," before kicking the door of his Ford Bronco, leaving a huge dent in it.

Some players denounced him while others laughed. The coaching staff quickly found out. Coach Hall and Coach K had clearly had a long discussion during practice before calling the team to gather around them.

"What are the four key words for Ashland High football?" Coach Hall asked.

Players looked blankly around at each other, no one able to name the four pillars on which the program is built. Coach Hall started ripping into the group for bullying Edwin.

"We're going to run until you guys learn our four key words," Coach Hall said. Players continued to run, receiving scolding messages intermittently.

"How could you do that to one of your brothers?" he asked, some players now starting to huff and puff.

"This is someone who fights with you and you disrespected him like that. We're going to run until you guys figure out what those four words are," Coach Hall said, not giving a single hint.

Finally, the running stopped. Coach Hall called his players into a big circle at the end of practice, normally a sign that everyone was going to stretch and that practice was over. Once every varsity player gathered in the circle, Coach Hall just left. He walked off the field, stopped at his office, got into his truck, and drove away. Ashland players looked around in disbelief. Coach K was still in the center of the field with the team. The look on his face told them that practice was not quite over.

"Coach Hall is a good man," he said, "Now you have to deal with me."

The kids had to do up-downs for 15 more minutes, leaving them exhausted. Then they were placed back on the line, only to run more. At every sprint, Coach K would say one of the program's core values and the team would have to shout them back.

"Class!" Everyone sprinted, imprinting the first pillar into their brain.

"Effort!" Tiring, the team shouted at the top of their lungs.

"Tradition!" The team yelled in between deep breaths.

"Family!" Bursting off the line, the team's collective voice grew to a fever pitch.

This continued until it got too dark to run any more. Nobody on the

"Family," "Tradition," "Effort" and "Class," the four pillars of the Ashland football program. The Class of 2008 sign still stands at Ashland High School to this day and can be seen here in December 2019 before Max gave it an updated paint job.

field that day would ever forget the program's core values again. In case future classes face a similar predicament, Max made a big sign for his senior project. It hangs on the back of the football stadium, the side facing the practice fields. It reads: "Class. Effort. Tradition. Family."

The center of the grizzly paw has some more text on it. On a closer look, it reads: "Forever Coach K."

"Football is a violent game, a game full of aggression, a game that requires both mental and physical toughness," Coach Hall continued, his speech building to an emotional close.

> Football is also a game of emotion, and the *one emotion* that Dave Kitchell used to get Ashland Grizzly players to play to the best of their ability was *love*. He was able to get kids to love the game and love each other. What a great gift you've received from a great man.
>
> Even though he's not here with us, he continues to coach and guide us. His spirit lives strong in all of us who were affiliated with him. I know we will ask ourselves from time to time, "What would Coach Kitchell do?" Thank you, Coach K. We love you.

There was nobody better prepared to handle a team and community in mourning than Charlie Hall. His speech at Coach K's memorial service

And the sign from afar after Max removed a decade's worth of wear and tear with a new coat of paint.

"Forever Coach K" painted inside the Grizzly paw on the sign Max's senior class put up next to the football fields as their Senior Project.

struck all the right notes. Max saw more people at the stadium for the memorial than he had ever seen for a football game. There wasn't an empty seat in the stands or a dry eye in the house. It was so crowded, in fact, that many had to stand on the sidelines just to make room. Max looked around at teammates who had tears rolling down their faces.

"Coach Hall was so tough throughout the whole thing," Max remembers. "He gave everyone on the football team and staff a backbone. He was close with Coach K and went up there, delivered his message in such a strong, passionate way and he didn't waver. He didn't show signs of weakness, which I think Coach K would've been really happy with."

As hard as Coach Hall tried to keep morale high and channel his players' grief into useful energy going into their showdown with Glencoe in the next round of the playoffs, the team had simply endured too much. They lacked the fortitude without their spirited North Star, Coach K, to give them the affirmations they needed. Ultimately, the Grizzlies fell to Glencoe, ending their season. They returned home to Ashland without a state championship.

"The energy just wasn't the same," Max recalls. "We were missing him on the sidelines."

Even though the team had missed Coach K on the sideline for a couple games before his death, he still had at least been watching them and had a hand in the game plan the team would roll out. Now he was gone, and the team lost its sense of direction. But Coach K's life and his death had prepared his older players for how to deal with hardship and tragedy. "It brought my friends and me much closer together," Max recollects. "Going through that together made us all really understand the bigger picture and how it all works."

Unfortunately for Max, this was simply the first in a series of lessons it would take a lifetime of tragedy to learn, and his next brush with death would come much sooner than he anticipated.

CHAPTER 4

Family First

It had been a couple of weeks, but the town of Ashland was still in a state of mourning. The football season was over, and winter was ready to rear its ugly head and send baseball players indoors for a couple months. Max turned his attention toward the senior baseball season. He felt that he would mainly be out there playing for Coach K this season, even though Kitchell had never so much as helped him adjust his batting stance. He had been somewhat of a spiritual guide for many of Ashland's athletes over the years. Thus, it was no surprise that Max thrust his late coach into the role of actual spirit guide as he began training for the biggest baseball season of his life.

There was an unspoken consensus among the players, coaches and fans going into Ashland's 2008 campaign: This is the year. In 2008, the Grizzlies returned most of their key performers from the previous season. Max was among the team's leaders despite a down year in the spring of 2007. He had a lot to prove, but that was not at the top of his mind as the season drew near. He heard echoes of Dave Kitchell's affirmations replacing his most selfish, arrogant thoughts. He knew he had to help his team succeed. He wanted to win at all costs, and he knew that a few core guys like him and his pal Sam Gaviglio were the ones who could actually go out and make it happen. He had already set his mind on Sierra College, so his sole competitive focus was on doing whatever he could to help the Grizzlies bring a state title home to the City of Ashland. Anyone familiar with Ashland baseball knew that for that to happen, they needed Sam Gaviglio to shine.

Sam was one of Max's quiet, soft-spoken friends. He wasn't one to gloat or showboat despite being the best athlete in school. He was the Grizzlies' ace, and their season rested squarely on his ability to take his game to yet another level. Without his steady contributions, the Ashland squad would likely be outmatched by most of the competition throughout the state playoffs. Sam was among the neighborhood kids with whom Max made quick friends when he moved to Ashland, along with the Scarminachs and Rasmussens. Just as in the Scott Valley, each household had two boys separated in age by roughly the same amount of time as Nick and Max.

Although he wasn't always the most outgoing, growing up with a brother meant that Sam knew how to be friends with the other boys. He knew how to be daring, and he didn't back down from anything if it was going to be a thrill. He and Max, always pre-game catch partners, had a ritual where they would get close together after long toss and throw the ball at each other's chest, hard. This is how the duo would get themselves pumped up before a game. Sam would rear back and hit Max squarely. Then, Max would pick the ball up off the ground and return the favor. By this time in their baseball careers, both of these guys could throw the ball *hard*. This ritual may have seemed juvenile or maniacal to some onlookers, but it got their blood pumping, and to the young ballplayers, it just made sense. Max had an Energizer bunny mentality; he and Sam both just wanted to keep going and going and going. "My first impression of [Max] was that he was small and full of energy," Sam recalls. "He was fearless."

Sam's parents had a very similar background to Max's: a blue-collar family with small-community values. His dad was a handyman carpenter, and his mom worked in the Southern Oregon University main office. Max's dad, too, worked with his hands up on the power lines, and his mom was likewise an office worker, working in the main office at the high school. Naturally, the two families found themselves compatible from the start.

Those families' youngest sons had just done battle together on the gridiron, and now they were ready to do so again on the diamond. Both had won considerable personal glory from accolades during the football season, and that helped their status among the baseball crowd. "It gave us confidence," Sam says. "Once we were winning in football, it gave us more confidence when we took the field to play baseball."

Every student in town, not just the baseball players, was counting down the days until winter break in Ashland. It was just around the corner. While working in the counseling office at the high school, Max's mom, Michelle, got a phone call from her father, Norman. This was not enough to alarm her, because they spoke regularly on the phone twice a day. The calls, however, did not usually come while she was at work.

"I'm not feeling very well," she heard Norman say on the other end of the line.

"Why don't you call your doctor?" Michelle replied. "I'll tell him I'm leaving work and I'll come by and get you."

Michelle arrived at his house soon after. Norman had called his local physician, but unfortunately their CAT scan machine was out of order. This meant that they would have to go all the way to Asante Rogue Regional Medical Center. Asante was the very same facility where Norman had once frantically sought medical attention for his grandson's wounded hand. Finally, the father-daughter pair arrived at the hospital and waited to be seen by a doctor. Norman went in for his CAT scan. Michelle could tell something was unusual in that he wasn't feeling well. Norman was a healthy guy who lived with vitality. He never complained, and he was always feasting on the delicious Italian food his wife, Dorothy, made for him from scratch.

He wasn't one to eat fast food and remained in pretty good shape. What could be making him feel so sick? She wouldn't have to wonder long. When the very first CAT scan results came back, they already had their answer. The doctors found cancer. Unfortunately, they caught it extremely late. They told a shell-shocked Michelle and a crestfallen Norman, who silently sat and weighed their next steps. Hospice care would soon be required, a hospital worker told them. Christmas was just three days away, but it seemed apparent to Michelle that they would need to set up hospice care for her dad before the holiday.

When he heard the news, Max had been reasonably upset. But then he heard that word. Hospice. He knew what that meant. Coach K had just been in hospice a month earlier. He was heartbroken.

That means time is running out real fast.

Michelle quickly called her brother, Bub, and sister, Patty, and relayed how dire the situation was. Everyone, including Max and Nick's cousins, came down from Portland, a five-hour drive from Ashland. They all celebrated Christmas together on that Monday. The following day, less than a week after his diagnosis, Stan and Michelle could tell that Norman was nearing the end.

Nick, Max, and their cousins hung back at the Gordons' house while Michelle, Stan, Bub, and Patty stayed at Norman's bedside with Dorothy. The mood back at the Gordon house was somber, knowing only bad news awaited them. It was simply a matter of how long they would have to wait to hear it. They sat around in relative silence for a long time, reflecting. Then the phone rang out through the tension in the air, relieving the suspense but also signaling a dark recognition in all the kids.

"Your grampy passed away about 30 minutes ago," Stan said over the phone. He had to be the one to call. Norman's children were all still in there, saying their last goodbyes to their father.

The Gordon boys and their cousins exchanged hugs, and cried some, after hearing the news. Quickly, they loaded into the car and drove out to Medford to be with the rest of their family. Just one month after Max had lost one major male role model, he'd lost another. This time, though, he noticed something more: at the loss of his grandfather, he had truly lost one of the few meaningful ancestral bonds which he would ever know. This was a privation he felt mostly beneath the surface at the time. It would take many years, and far more tragedy, to put this event into context. "It takes me a while for things to sink in," Max says. "If I get news someone died, it usually takes a few weeks for me to understand the whole magnitude of the thing. But when grampy passed away, I went into 'How can I help?' mode."

Max knew he had to provide the support both his parents needed. Norman was the father Stan never had and was the best man Michelle had ever known. Before Norman's passing, Stan already had a sense that Max would be the rock that this family might need, even though the teenager was the youngest among them. There had always been something about Max.

"Stuff isn't going so well for the family, so when grampy goes or whenever anyone asks you to do anything, you just need to do it," Stan instructed his son. "Don't ask questions, just do it. Be there to help. I don't care what it is, big or small, just make it happen."

And so, Max did. When Stan and Michelle finally came home from Norman's and Dorothy's place, they came back to a clean house. The family would go back over to see Dorothy in the coming days, and Max would wash dishes to take at least a small burden off the family.

Of course, all the kids just wanted to help. It was hard on them; they had lost their rock in their grandfather. Max was still numb. He wanted more than anything to feel the full weight of the loss he had experienced. He knew what his response should be, which made it all the more frustrating when his emotions did not follow suit. He would sit, head in his hands, and try to cry. He wanted to cry for his grandpa and for his coach. He heard crying could be therapeutic in times of mourning. He just couldn't do it. He wondered if something was wrong with him.

During this time, his mind raced back to when he was eight years old, trying to do his first back flip on the trampoline. His grampy was the only one there to make sure he didn't break his neck trying.

"You can do it," Norman repeated enthusiastically.

Five, six, seven failed attempts went by. Max would land awkwardly after each one, undeterred.

"Come on, you've got it," Norman said, still cheering his grandson on.

More than a dozen attempts later and after an hour had gone by, still Norman was locked in, trying to will his young grandson to land it.

Finally, Max took a strong bounce off the surface of the trampoline, getting more air underneath him than he had in all his previous jumps. As he soared skyward, he tucked his body gracefully into its own center of gravity and did a form-perfect back flip, landing on two pointed feet and taking a couple final bounces to dispense the rest of his momentum. He looked immediately to his grandpa, whose face was lit as brightly as a Christmas tree. He was over the moon for his young grandson. The pair screamed out in jubilation as they celebrated this athletic feat. Max had completed his first back flip, and Grampy Norman was the only one around to see it.

Norman's death hit the adults harder. They had, of course, lost their dad. Bub, Patty, and Michelle were all adopted, all taken in by Norman and Dorothy and loved as their own. And so they were. Michelle's mind lazed back into a simpler time, when her parents took care of her. "My parents were Ozzie and Harriet, I swear," Michelle recalls. "I lived across the street from a baseball park and I learned how to walk along the fence chasing balls."

She was allowed to sleep on her dad's shoulder during Sunday Mass, which the family attended every week, until she received her First Communion. Dorothy once even met Pope John Paul XXIII and had a private audience with him. Norman worked in bearings and was home by five o'clock each evening, which was a nice perk about the job. Dinner was on the table by 5:30.

On Saturday mornings, the girls would do housework, and nobody was allowed to go anywhere until it was done. Bub, the only boy, got off easy. His morning paper route took up most of his free time. On Saturday nights, after dinner dishes were cleaned, each of the McPhails was given a nickel to buy a candy bar at the Little League park snack shack.

Every Sunday after Church, the entire family would come over for a barbecue. Norman would have a couple of drinks, pop inch-and-a-half steaks on the grill, and be the life of the party. He dressed up in his hat and apron and served BBQ almost too good for words. Those were the memories dancing around Michelle's mind as she mourned her father's death. No matter how close she got to smelling the smoke of the grill or tasting the sweet vinegar of his BBQ sauce, she could never reach out and touch these memories. The comfort her father's shoulder provided her as she dozed off in church would elude her for the rest of her days.

Of course, her mind kept returning to the importance of family as well, which was something Norman pounded home his entire life. It's something he didn't have growing up, but he made sure his kids would always be able to cling to it.

"When you die, it doesn't matter how much money you have," Norman would always say. "All you have left is your family."

In that regard, Norman left the world as a very rich man. As she thought on this sentiment, Michelle knew a way to help her most immediate family, her sons, Nick and Max. The brothers had always been avid snowboarders, so Michelle got them lift tickets and the Brother's Room at McMenamin's in Bend, Oregon. They would get to snowboard at Mount Bachelor, one of the best slopes in the country, a popular training spot for winter Olympians.

This will help get their minds off things and bond, Michelle thought.

Nick sports his sunglasses and takes a load off while out for a meal.

Max had lost an iconic coach and dear grandfather in the matter of a month. The conversation which had taken place between Max and Nick kept occurring to her as well:

"We're equals."

She was so happy the two of them had come this far in their relationship, and she just knew the snowboarding trip would help them set their minds at ease and build on the progress they had made in their brotherhood over the past month or so. Nick had been working so much and Max had been so wrapped up in high school sports that the pair didn't see each other often, especially considering they still lived in the same town. This, Michelle hoped, was the start of a new chapter.

"My parents thought, 'This is great. They get to hang out, do a little bonding, get out of town, relax, and mourn for grampy while having fun snowboarding,'" Max remembers. "I agreed with them. It was the perfect gift."

On New Year's Day, the brothers were ready to take off. Max had a GMC Jimmy, a car that could easily get through the snow. Michelle suggested they take Max's car.

"Max should drive, let Max drive," Michelle said, her motherly instincts kicking in.

Nick had just gotten a new Subaru, though, and there was no convincing him they wouldn't be taking his new ride up to the mountain.

Okay, well whatever, Michelle thought, just happy her two boys would get some quality time together.

The three-hour trip north to Bend began, Nick chugging along in his hot new Subaru, Max in the passenger seat. In a lot of ways, this time of their lives existed in a world apart from the rest of the times they'd known together. Their grandfather was gone, a reminder to both boys that the security of family was not guaranteed and that they would soon have to go out and find families of their own like Norman had. It was a new year, and both had resolved to leave a lot of the bullshit behind in the old one. Max had his senior baseball season to look forward to; his performance had the potential to unlock an entirely new world for him as he moved on to collegiate ball. He wanted to make his coach and his grandfather proud. For Nick, the new year was about getting his priorities back in order and making something of himself. For both of the boys, this trip was supposed to signal the ushering in of a new era in their lives. They were men, going out into the world together and submitting to whatever comes next, knowing they had the resolve to see it through. These new truths thought, but left unspoken, Max and his big brother cruised toward the mountains, feeling invincible.

Max, Nick, and Michelle Gordon have fun at the photo booth for Nick's senior pictures in 2005.

CHAPTER 5

Big Brother

While the trip of a lifetime kicked off for the boys in January 2008, the situation back home in Ashland was still bleak. Michelle Gordon sat in her living room with her mother, Dorothy. Both had lost their guiding light, and they looked to each other for what to do next. Although Michelle herself was still freshly mourning the death of her father, she recognized the responsibility she had in this moment: it was her turn to take care of her mother.

"What do you want to do, mom?" Michelle asked.

"I want to go and I want to go now," Dorothy responded frantically.

"What do you mean, 'now'?" Michelle asked, confused.

"Now, right now," Dorothy basically repeated herself, like that, for a while until she could make it more clear what she really wanted to do.

What she really wanted to do was to go immediately into assisted living after Norman's passing. Michelle could tell by the unwavering position her mother took that this was clearly the right choice for her remaining healthy days. With the boys out of the house, she had time to help her mom look for a place to stay. Their preliminary searches returned nothing that fit Dorothy's preferences, so the pair quickly realized they were assuming a heavy undertaking in finding Dorothy a place to call home during her twilight years.

Meanwhile, Nick and Max arrived near Mount Bachelor in record time. Their mother had booked them a night at McMenamins, an upscale hotel near the slopes. They planned to get a jump on the morning and spend the whole following day shredding the region's epic slaloms. They would need a lot of energy for a snowboarding day like that, so they fueled up the way only a couple of brothers on their own in a hotel know how: room service. They had a few pizzas sent to their rooms and settled in for the evening.

They chowed down on the pies while decompressing about the drive, and then their conversations started turning toward more salient topics: they talked about their grandpa, about the football season and Max's hopes

44

for his senior season on the baseball team. They talked about college plans. In both of their minds, the plan to continue together to Sierra College that fall was still full steam ahead. They tuckered themselves out with chatter until they ultimately turned out the lights and got some rest to prepare for the adventure the next day had in store for them.

After mere moments at Mount Bachelor, both boys knew it was the nicest place they had ever gone snowboarding. They learned to board on Mount Shasta, a course that offered little excitement to the seasoned winter sport athlete. They also tried out Mount Ashland back home, but to Max, both were dwarfed in comparison—literally and figuratively—to Bachelor. The brothers eagerly took to the slopes, and it was magnificent. The hills were stacked with fresh, powdery snow, allowing for perfect runs the entire day. On one trip down, Nick checked over his shoulder to see where Max was, snagged his board on an edge, and face-planted hard. His goggles went flying and he was thrown head-first into a heap. Max couldn't help but laugh at the sight in front of him.

Nick suffered no injuries except maybe a dent to his pride, and the two happily broke for lunch around noon. After they ate, they headed back out to the hills for a few more runs before they had to start the trek back home. They picked out a run they both particularly enjoyed throughout the day; it had a significant stretch that was covered in tricky moguls, making for a more turbulent and exciting ride down the mountain. They took several more runs down this course after lunch, and once they had their fill, they called it a day.

Both Max and Nick were exhausted from the snowboard-filled morning and afternoon as they packed up the Subaru with their clothes and gear. Once Max plopped into the passenger seat, he realized how sleepy he really was. Nick wouldn't expect him to do any driving, so he allowed himself to fall into a pretty peaceful sleep, despite the aggressive volume of Nick's music. They drew nearer and nearer to Ashland, and Max awoke for a pit stop in the town of Shady Cove, just 45 minutes from home. They parked in front of a Subway and stopped inside for a drink and a bathroom break.

Gatorade bottle in Max's hand, water bottle in Nick's, the brothers made their way out of the building and headed back toward the car. Nick had driven the entire way to Mount Bachelor and thus far had driven the entire way back as well. Max felt like he ought to at least offer to drive the final leg of the trip, although he knew Nick would probably want to stay behind the wheel of his beloved new ride.

"Hey, want me to drive the rest of the way?" Max asked. "You've driven the whole way."

"No, I've got it," Nick responded, perhaps protective of his new Subaru. Max quickly capitulated, pulled open the passenger-side door, sat inside, and waited for the short remainder of the drive to be over. Back home, his mom was just finishing setting his grandmother up in her freshly-picked-out community.

Finally, the two had decided on a place. After a tumultuous search, Michelle was still able to get her mom settled into a new home within two days of when their search began. She and Dorothy had agreed on a complex of six-person adult foster care apartment facilities. Once she knew she'd done all she could to make her mom feel comfortable starting life in her new environment, Michelle turned for home. She drove anxiously toward Ashland, eager to put this air of tragedy behind her and return to some sense of normalcy. At the Gordon house, Stan patiently awaited the return of both his wife and his boys. Max and Nick would be arriving shortly, and it seemed the worst days would be behind them all when the family soon reunited.

Max and Nick continued on, passing by field after field on wide-open Oregon Route 62. *Misty Mountain Hop* by Led Zeppelin was playing over the car's stereo system as it steamrolled south. The pair was passing through Eagle Point, still about half an hour from home, as they started going up a road with a gradual but persistent grade. The car directly in front of them was puttering along slowly in the snow, frustrating Nick. Feeling impatient, he decided to pass the car. It was an aggressive move for sure, but legal. There were dashed lines to his left, indicating that it was a safe passing zone.

With Nick's foot on the accelerator, the Subaru soon drew even with the vehicle which he was trying to pass. He was about to execute the next part of the maneuver when he saw headlights dead ahead. It took him multiple seconds to process his mistake. In the low visibility, and without accounting for the steady grade of the hill, Nick had failed to notice a vehicle approaching in the distance. He would not have time to pass the car completely and return to his own lane before being forced to confront the oncoming 2005 Toyota Highlander.

The Highlander was driven by Erik Larsen, 77, and his wife, Susan, sat in the passenger seat.[1] He also could not see what was about to happen until it was too late. In a last-ditch effort, Nick abruptly slammed on the brakes and attempted to turn sharply back into the right lane, but the lack of traction on the road caused by the snow sent the Subaru fishtailing out of control. It was sent spinning sideways and back into the oncoming lane of traffic. Max could feel and see what was about to happen. With his seatbelt tucked below his armpit, Max locked up his whole body and flexed every muscle, bracing for impact.

There was a loud screech, then a louder metal crunch. The Route 62 speed limit is 55 miles an hour, and the forces of both moving cars packed an intense jolt as the two vehicles slammed into one another. The Subaru was a free projectile, slingshotted right into the path of the Larsens' Highlander. The Highlander slammed full speed directly into the Subaru's driver-side door, T-bone style. Max was hurled forward by the massive shift in momentum, and his head slammed hard into the car's center console. The car slammed to a halt. The blow to his head registered immediately, and Max went into a haze.

"Nick…" was all he could process as he realized he needed to check and see if his brother was safe. The effects of shock were clearly already setting in, but he needed to get to his big brother and make sure he was okay. Still dazed, Max clutched the passenger-side door to escape the smashed vehicle, and suddenly his whole world went black.

CHAPTER 6

Up in the Air

As Michelle Gordon pulled onto Lupine Drive, she felt relieved; she had managed to make it back to the house just in time to meet the boys. She was greeted in the front entryway by Stan, who was already home; then she plopped onto the couch in the back of the living room. A few minutes later, there was a knock on the door. The couple looked at one another, and Stan gave a slight nod that told his wife he would get it. He opened the door and was surprised to see two uniformed officers on the front step. They were from the Oregon State Highway Patrol.

"Are you Mr. Gordon?" one of them asked.

"Yes, I am," Stan responded, puzzled. He looked down and saw that the officer had two driver's licenses in his hand. He glanced at each as he read, sensing by now that something wasn't right.

"Are your sons Nicholas Gordon and Maxwell Gordon?" the officer asked.

"Yes, they are," Stan answered with a gulp.

"There's no other way to tell you this, but your boys have been in a car accident." the officer said, maintaining a stoic expression as he watched Stan's entire demeanor change, "Nicholas is deceased at the scene."

Stan stared straight ahead. It was as if he was hearing the words through the head of a pin, miles long. His chest felt hollow and he said nothing, felt nothing for what felt like a long time. He heard the officer speak again.

"Are you okay, sir? Do you need a ride?"

Dazed, Stan turned his back on the officers and traced his way back through the entryway toward the living room, thinking in that moment only of Michelle. She was his best friend, and they had built a life together. How was he going to tell her that that life would never be the same again? Michelle did not know what to make of her husband when he came to face her in the living room. She never saw him looking so serious, and she prepared herself for one of his deadpan practical jokes or misdirections. She wanted to know what was up. Then, over his shoulder, she saw the two

48

officers shuffle into the room behind him. The curious smile drained from her face. As Stan began to speak, Michelle was already putting the pieces together. Why hadn't they heard from Nick or Max?

"The boys have been in an accident." She heard her husband speak, but she was falling before he even finished what he was trying to say. She felt her legs go out beneath her and she fell into a heap against the back window, pressing her face to the glass as she wept. She looked out over the backyard, a space here and in Etna where her boys had played sports and let their imaginations run wild. Michelle began immediately to feel the great weight of loss. After a while of her wailing uncontrollably, Stan managed to subdue his wife long enough to give her the rest of the information, which the officers had delivered to him moments earlier.

"Honey," Stan said, with a somber but reassuring tone, "We lost Nick."

Michelle looked at her husband with shock and confusion. By the tone and tenor of the initial reaction, she had assumed that they had lost both of the boys. She had been so inconsolable that they hadn't yet been able to tell her that Max had survived the initial accident. Suddenly, the world she thought had shattered completely was left with one glimmer of hope.

"Max is alive, he's being life flighted to Rogue Valley," Stan continued, and by the time he was finished speaking, Michelle was on her feet, frantically preparing to leave the house.

"Well, let's get the hell out of here and go!" she shouted, shoes already on. They raced out the door and jumped into the car to be by their son's side.

It felt like they spent a small eternity on the highway, but finally the couple got to the emergency room and hustled inside to find where Max was. They approached the front counter.

"Are you the Gordons?" the worker at the front desk asked.

"Yes, we are," Stan replied.

"Go in this room right over here," he responded, pointing them toward an emergency room off to the side intended for traumatic and critical injuries. Still having no details, but having sheer faith that Max would be all right, the Gordons entered the room, sat, and waited to speak to a doctor.

Coach Charlie Hall lay in bed late that night. He had had the past couple months to bounce back from the difficult loss of his colleague, Dave Kitchell. He had done a lot of reflecting and was just happy that he got to continue the legacy which Coach K had started at Ashland. He loved the group of young men he got to coach, and he felt an enormous amount of responsibility for them. He was about ready to fall asleep when the phone rang; a man coming fresh off a major tragedy knows a bad time for a phone call, and this was not a good time for one. An uneasy feeling grew in the pit of his stomach as he tried to imagine who could be on the other line.

His mother was advanced in age, living on her own in Arizona. He felt queasy as he put his mouth up to the receiver and said, "Hello?" Of course, his intuition had been correct. His mom was okay, but that was where the good news ended. He patiently listened to the voice coming over the other end of the line.

"Honey, I need to go to the hospital. Now." With little more than that, he got dressed, got into his car, and drove to the hospital, heartbroken.

About the time Charlie Hall received that phone call, word was rapidly spreading to Max's friends. Sam was in disbelief; he had seen Max just a couple of days prior, on his way to pick up his brother for their snowboarding trip. As soon as he got the news, he didn't even think before getting into his car and making a beeline for the hospital. When he walked into the lobby, he saw his teammate, Josh Scarminach, arrive as well. Josh's parents, of course, were friends with Stan and Michelle, and as soon as they told him what had happened, he came right away. He couldn't help but think of his little brother, Jake. He couldn't imagine if he were going through this right now. But he wasn't, Max was, and Josh realized in the moment how much Max meant to him, his teammates, and the entire Ashland High School community. When Coach K passed, the whole school felt like its collective pulse had slowed, its spirit diminished. There was an eerie sense that if Max couldn't pull through this, the school's heartbeat might stop completely.

Baseball and football players filled the lobby of Rogue Valley Asante Hospital, anxiously quiet. There was an unspoken tension in the room. Little was said, half out of the difficulty of the situation and half out of the fear that saying the wrong thing might speak it into existence. All awaited some type of update on Max's condition. Charlie tried asking parents for word on his status, but nobody seemed to know what was going on. All they knew was that Max was being treated by the critical care unit. Every player, parent, and member of the high school community stayed in the lobby and prayed.

Father Sean Weeks received a phone call slightly before others had been informed. He was the chaplain for the Ashland Police Department and was also the unofficial chaplain for Ashland High School athletics. January 2, 2008, was his first day on the job for Ashland PD. His job was to provide what he calls "trauma first aid" by accompanying officers on next-of-kin notifications and giving families emotional and spiritual support after officers give them life-altering news. On this night, he was summoned to the hospital where the Gordons sat, looking for hope from wherever it might come.

He stood by as officers debriefed the family once again. As he gathered his thoughts and began preparing to go about his duty to the family, Michelle noticed him out of the corner of her eye and trained her attention on him as she addressed the religious leader.

"You know my son," she said assuredly. Father Sean was confused. Rarely did he know the families or individuals whom he served in this capacity. The desperation in her face worried him. He feared that she might be looking for something from him which he could not give her.

"Max was on the Ashland football team," she explained further.

That was all she needed to tell him. Father Sean led pre-game prayers for the football team. He didn't have the names and faces of most of the players down, so he hadn't realized until this moment that he had actually already shared prayers with the boy who lay motionless in the next room over.

"Oh, okay. I do know your son," Father Sean assured her, recognizing in her face that it was extremely important to Michelle that Max had someone familiar helping him through this. She just didn't want him to be alone.

"Would you mind if I prayed over Max, so that he can get through the procedure well?" Father Sean asked Stan and Michelle.

"Please, will you please?" They urged him with enthusiasm. The Gordons were not a religious family, but in trying times they had faith that there was a higher plan at play, something that would make some sense of all of this suffering. Doctors led Stan, along with Father Sean, through the door to the CCU. Max had suffered severe head trauma during the crash, and as a result, pressure was mounting rapidly on his brain. In an effort to ease that pressure, the doctors were preparing Max to be placed into a medically induced coma. They explained that unless they could do something to alleviate the swelling around the brain, Max's odds of survival were very thin.

"I felt that God put me there," Father Sean recalls, looking back. "I became very aware that I was going to be an important part of this family's tragedy."

When the trio looked over Max, all Father Sean saw were two small slits where Max's eyes were supposed to be. Father Sean began to pray over Max, administering the Catholic rite, Anointing of the Sick. The local priest didn't realize that he was praying for one of Ashland Football's fiercest defenders. He didn't see "Max," lying there so quiet, still, and weak. Max's fighting spirit could not be seen below the surface. The three were moved to a private room in the emergency department to wait. That was when Michelle realized Father Sean didn't know that it was Max for whom he was praying. He was shocked, and it became personal. Max was a young man that he knew.

He made the Sign of the Cross over Max's body and asked that he respond to God's healing will and that the Holy Spirit would guide the doctors and nurses caring for him to make sure he recovered from his injuries. He delivered his message and finished administering the ceremony by blessing Max in the name of the Holy Trinity, then turned him back over to the doctors' care. Time was of the essence, and Max's soul had no intentions of leaving his body any time soon.

The team of doctors succeeded in inducing the coma, and Max was stable but far from in the clear. This process created a frustrating complex for all those awaiting news on his condition. Although the first step was a success, it was the first step in a long process of making sure that Max's body could stay alive long enough to be treated for his extensive injuries. They had to preserve his body temperature to keep from frying the circuitry of his brain, so they set the thermostats as low as they would go. This was going to be a long, delicate, arduous process.

To the still-growing number of supporters pouring into the hospital's waiting room, there would be no concrete news for some time. They all sat on pins and needles awaiting a prognosis, whether it be good or bad. The reality, however, was that no such concrete insight would be available for days. Ashland High athletes, teachers, parents, and even Stan's fellow county power-linemen waited with bated breath for news that was not going to come.

Eventually, the hospital staff realized the nature of the problem that was developing in their lobby. Max had so many concerned community members there for him that there was no longer enough room in which actual patients could wait.

Stan had a word with Coach Hall, who relied on his skill as a leader to offer what he could to the Gordon family in their moment of need. He got up in front of the tired, uneasy crowd and delivered the update that Max was in a coma and that no more updates would be coming in the near future. He suggested that everyone head home, seeing that it was late and the hospital staff needed the space. Most of the group were reluctant to leave Max's side until they had more definitive news, good or bad. But with no such news on the way, they all had their own lives to get back to and continue living. As Max's supporters filed out of the Rogue Valley lobby, however, they left knowing one thing: Max had a fighting chance.

As soon as word got out to family, Stan's brother Ron and his wife, Helena, hurried to Max's side from Colorado. Michelle's brother, Norman, quickly made his way down from Portland with his two daughters. Regina Scarminach and Jodie Haag arranged to have meals sent to the family every day they were in the CCU. Max's support system was growing by the minute.

When morning broke, Max's grandmother, Dorothy, awoke to the first day of the rest of her life. This would be her first full day in her new adult foster care community. As she sat down to her breakfast, an orderly handed her the paper, and she settled into what she assumed would become her new morning routine. She ate as she leafed absent-mindedly through the day's stories, reading the headlines to herself and moving on casually. Suddenly, one headline caught her eye and she homed in on it, beginning to read. What she read she could hardly make any sense of, but she was suddenly frantic. Nobody had contacted her, and yet here were her two grandsons in the paper, in an article about an auto accident.

"These are my grandsons," she cried out in confusion.

The staff was rather dismissive of her at first. The community was full of seniors who constantly told tall tales about their distant relatives who never seemed to visit. They had heard it all at this point and didn't jump up every time someone said their grandson made the morning paper. However, Dorothy was becoming so distraught that a few workers were forced to take a closer look at the story which had sent her into such a commotion.

It appeared that in the chaos of the previous day, nobody had reached out to the home to notify Dorothy of the accident. After the foster care staff confirmed that the article was indeed about her grandsons, they wondered what steps to take next. Word of the accident had spread, and no one knew how to best handle this woman who had just lost a grandson and had another whose life was hanging in the balance.

Back in Ashland, support for Max was growing with the help of the Internet. Stan had a buddy named Roscoe, and Roscoe's wife had a knack for making websites. So every time a noteworthy update came out of the Critical Care Unit, Stan would relay it to Roscoe, and his wife, Tracy, would post it to the new site. She developed the site specifically to help the community stay plugged into Max's fight. They even supplemented the posts with photos and were flooded with testimonials from supporters about Max's impact on the community. Tracy also set up a fund to help take care of the family's remaining medical expenses from what everyone knew would be a lengthy stay in the hospital.

The pair of grieving parents fell into an operative rhythm, with Stan handling communications and Michelle handling the doctors. It gave them both a role in a situation in which they felt truly powerless. They knew that neither of them would ultimately have any say in whether Max walked away from this but establishing themselves as a presence throughout his battle was the way that they showed themselves and one another that they would never, ever quit on their son.

Night after night, it was Michelle who sat at Max's bedside. She would gaze at him, breathing peacefully with a pressure monitor affixed to his head and breathing tubes snaking down his throat into his lungs. She held his hand in the dim light, hours after visitation was officially over. She prayed for the inflammation to subside. She wanted relief for her son, but more than that, she wanted a life for him. There had never been any quit in this boy, and the last thing she wanted for him now was to give in to the pressure. The doctors could do nothing until the pressure subsided, but it persisted night after night, and Michele settled into her new role. The first few nights, she sat rigid in the chair beside him without blankets or a pillow and shivered in the pale light of the machines responsible for keeping her son alive until the morning light touched her face again through the window. The hospital staff soon realized what Michelle had known since she first sat beside Max's still body. She gazed at him; he didn't look as though he was under pressure. He looked calm. And she hoped that inside, wherever his mind was at that moment—that he was as calm under pressure as he had always been so far in life. She wouldn't be leaving until something changed. They gave her some blankets and another chair, and she made herself more comfortable at her post.

It was a constant battle to keep Max's body at a safe temperature. When his pressure monitor indicated that he was overheating, the doctors would lower the temperature in the room until he was stable once more. Quickly, however, he might become too cold, sending his muscles into violent spasms. His rampant shivers sent horrible chills down Michelle's own spine as she watched, day after day, as the doctors fought to keep him viable. After days of constant surveillance and adjustments, the doctors in charge of Max's care decided it was time to try temporarily bringing him out of his coma by slowing his medicine down.

When Max awoke, the first thing the doctors did was ask if he could move his fingers or wiggle his toes. He showed them that he could. He saw his dad, and his mind was flooded with thoughts. He made a steering wheel motion, while locking onto Stan's eyes. He could not yet form a sentence, but his father knew what he was asking him.

"Yes, you were in a car accident," Stan told him. "You just do what they tell you and you're going to be fine."

The only intent in bringing Max out the first time was to check his reflexes and motor skills; satisfied by his demonstration of the dexterity of his fingers and toes, they induced him back into the coma once more. While they were now faced with the imminent situation of having to explain the accident's aftermath to their son, Stan and Michelle had just seen his first tangible sign of progress. The life was back in his eyes ever so slightly, and it was clear his resolve was bubbling to the surface once again. Immediately, Stan updated Tracy on Max's progress, and she got the update posted to the website, so supporters could read the good news.

Max's wordless inquiry to his dad did, however, make it apparent to Stan and Michelle that they needed a plan for how to explain to Max exactly what had happened in the accident. They turned to the nurse who had been supervising his care for advice. They asked her when the right time was to break it to Max that his brother hadn't made it, or when to explain the great hardship he was now facing. "You'll know when it's time," she told them. It wasn't the answer they were looking for, but something told them both that it was what they needed to hear.

Over several days in the care of the Rogue Valley staff, Max had already lost nearly 25 pounds. All those years of athletic training and competition had toned him into a lean, forceful young man. There was no evidence now that this had ever been the case. He was skin and bone, only around 130 pounds at the end of the day. He was a shell of his former self.

The second time they pulled him out of the coma, the doctors wanted to see if Max could stay out of it for good. He had lost days of his memory, and he was frantic and confused. He saw his mom looking down at him from the same spot she'd been sitting for the past four straight days.

With his eyes, Max implored, "What the hell is going on here?"

Max was clearly confused and couldn't stay calm. He had no real notion of what was going on, but he needed to get out of there as soon as he could. Eventually, Michelle, Father Sean, and the attending nurse calmed him back down and subdued him enough to pin him back onto his bed and put him back under sedation. It was clear he was not ready yet.

Father Sean became the spiritual totem on which the family learned they could lean. At the onset of this experience, Stan and Michelle didn't even realize the emotional chasm into which they had been cast. It was Father Sean's unassuming support which carried their grieving souls into a new state of hope for Max. He claims to have become the family's "Prayer Guy," personally taking responsibility for their spiritual healing.

"I was happy to do that," Father Sean remarks. "It was a real gift."

The days of waiting seeped dangerously toward becoming a week. While the Gordons settled into the constant uncertainty that had become their lives, they wondered how long they could live like this with their son's fate in complete limbo. They made the CCU their home in this time, and they had even laid claim to a couple of couches in the waiting area. During the day, a moment never passed when Max could wake to find himself unaccompanied. They went in shifts to Dorothy's old home, still in her name, to take quick showers before returning to the hospital to watch over him.

One week into the waiting game, Max's doctors were pleased enough with his head pressure and body temperature to attempt to bring him out of the coma permanently. Although his oxygen levels were still reading a little bit low, they made the determination that it was time.

This was the moment the Gordons had hoped and prayed for for seven agonizing days. The doctors removed his ventilator and pressure monitor, cranked down his Versed, and waited. Max gradually came to, and then he began coughing violently. He hacked and hacked in obvious discomfort. He

Nick, Stan, Michelle, and Max (left to right) on a hike at Lake Tahoe while visiting Stan's side of the family.

was conscious, but he had contracted pneumonia in the process of relieving his brain of the constant pressure.

"What the hell happened?" He uttered, his voice hoarse and weak. He clearly had no memory of the first two times he'd been awakened from the coma.

"Where's Nick?" Max asked frantically, immediately risking that his body might overheat and do him serious harm. He had a strange hint of awareness, as if he could somehow hear some of the information being passed back and forth between people in his room while he was unconscious. He could sense somewhere deep down that his big brother was gone.

"Well, we'll tell you that," Stan responded, knowing this was not the time for them to have this particular exchange. However, Max was obstinate and was putting himself into enough of a frenzy that he posed a danger to himself.

"Where is he? Where is my brother?" Max shouted again and again.

Needing to quell his outrage, Stan and Michelle finally realized that news as horrible as this would never be welcomed no matter how or when they chose to deliver it. They told Max the truth.

"Your brother … didn't make it, Max," Stan spoke softly as tears welled up in his eyes and began cascading down his cheeks. He looked his son in the eyes as he told him. The three sat, weeping together as they took on the news as a family for the first time. Max struck his bed in anger before falling back, spent and defeated. He stared helplessly at the fluorescent light and the white plaster of the ceiling, wondering how he would ever be whole again.

"It was one thing when Coach K and Grampy passed away, but it was just so much different to take away the only person that I ever really knew," Max painfully recalls.

"That was really frustrating. I thought, 'Everybody just keeps dying.' I was done trying to handle it."

But he wasn't done trying. Max Gordon was far from done trying.

CHAPTER 7

Get Well Soon

After breaking the news to Max, the Gordons talked very little about Nick's passing. They focused on making sure Max got better. But "better" was both a moving target and a relative term. There were some things about him which would never be the same: he suffered a severe concussion and as a result, he would experience permanent short-term memory loss. His spleen was lacerated, which posed a lasting threat to the rest of his vital organs if not treated properly. He had lost a lot in the accident, but he had gained a resolve the strength of which no one yet knew.

Just when it seemed like everything good in Max's life had been taken from him, his doctors sat him down to take one final thing away.

"Max, you can no longer play contact sports," they told him.

"Okay, well football season is already over," Max said. "I'm going to play baseball, though."

"If you get hit in the head, it could be life threatening," they explained, "and you can't dive or slide, because if you open up your spleen further, you'll bleed out internally and you won't even know it. You wouldn't wake up the next morning."

Of course, as a teenager, Max didn't fully appreciate the gravity of his injuries. He wanted to play sports with his friends again; it was all he'd ever known. But it was more than just petulance which determined Max to compete regardless of the danger he incurred. As soon as his brother's Subaru had been sent spinning through that snow-covered night, something inside Max changed forever.

"I'm on borrowed time now." Max took an honest inventory of his circumstances. By his estimation, little in his life had been left up to him thus far; from moving the family from Etna to Ashland, losing his coach, his grampy, and his big brother, and now being told he couldn't compete as an athlete. He reckoned he'd had just about enough of letting his circumstances be dictated to him. He was uncertain of a lot of things as he thought about facing this next stage of his life, but he knew one thing about himself for certain. He was a ballplayer, and he would once again play the game he loved.

58

"All that happened to me made it much easier to sell my soul to baseball. I'm tired of being told how things are going to be," Max recalls thinking. "I'm going to make it my own way."

He nodded along with the doctor's orders about contact sports, but he knew in the back of his mind that baseball season was just a handful of weeks away. Even with his more-than-healthy resolve, the facts of Max's physical situation made it feel like he might be up against insurmountable odds. As a result of leaky breathing tubes while in the coma—a common complication—Max suffered through persistent pneumonia. It was impossible for him even to draw a deep breath of air into his lungs. Attempting such a thing brought only agony.

When he was still in his coma, the medical staff attempted to relieve the liquid in his lungs, but they could only do so much. They would use a syringe to drain yellow discharge from his lungs until his airways could reopen. Occasionally, he could take deep, peaceful breaths for a time before the viscous fluid would again begin to fill his lungs.

The trauma and ensuing week-long coma had left Max's body incredibly weak. He could not walk, nor could he do much of anything on his own. If he wanted to go to the bathroom, Stan had to walk him in and physically hold his body up as he peed. Doing pretty much anything on his own was impossible for a few days. As soon as he was out of the coma for good, Max was inundated with visitors eager to see his condition for themselves. Coach Hall and Father Sean were regular visitors, seemingly always hovering in the corridors of Rogue Valley and ushering visitors in and out. As Max felt the first touch of strength returning to his body, an unexpected visitor poked her head in the door.

Trish Kitchell, Coach K's widow, strode into Max's room and could see she had surprised him with her unannounced visit. As soon as she entered, smiling, Max could see something in her hand. He recognized it as the hat Coach K always wore on the sidelines during his years coaching at Ashland High. She explained to Max that she wanted him to have it. After all the years by her husband's side as he fought his own medical battle, Trish was no stranger to long nights in hospital rooms with bad news looming around every corner. She knew better than anyone the fight that Max had in store now. The gesture left Max uncharacteristically speechless.

I have a lot of work to do, Max realized in that moment. *There are three important people that aren't here, people I have to make it right for. I have to make something for myself.*

It was the first time Max was able to put all that had happened into context with the rest of his life. On some level, he was realizing how his life and the decisions he made had a ripple effect on all the people he knew, all the people who cared about him. He recognized that when he suited up to compete, he carried with him pieces of all those who had gotten him there in the first place. When he played, he had never been playing for himself. He had never even been playing only for the team. He did what he did, everything he did, for love. Over the course of less than two months, three men whom he loved were taken from him. Three men who had shown him by example how to live with honor, and how to prevail against the cruelest of conditions. He was determined. He would play for them now. Above all else, he would play for Nick.

It was from these thoughts that Max drew his energy in the early stages of his recovery. As soon as he could muster any lasting strength, he started trying to walk around his floor of the hospital. At first, he would only manage to stagger a few rooms away from his own before coughing and collapsing into a heap. His legs, so severely atrophied from his time in the coma, would give up on him after a handful of steps and the nurses would have to wheel him back to his room in a chair. He was relentless, trying this out several times a day whenever he found the energy to get up from his bed. At first there was little noticeable progress, but after repeating these trials for a few days he had improved incrementally.

Hitched to his rolling IV stand, tubes in arm, Max triumphantly completed one lap around his floor. It must have been the 15th such attempt in the matter of a few days, and he was exhausted, but it was a major milestone for Max. He had set a goal and willed his body to accomplish it, and now he knew such a thing was still possible for him. The way he saw it, he had nowhere to go from here but up.

Max wasn't the only person thinking about his baseball future; one day he was visited by Don Senestraro, Ashland High's varsity baseball coach. He wanted to check on Max, but he also wanted to get a look for himself and see what the odds were that he'd have his starting center fielder in the lineup in two short months.

."We're having our first team meeting tomorrow," Senestraro informed Max, "spring baseball is starting to come around the corner, so is there anything you want me to tell the team?"

"Just tell them I'll be there, Game 1 in centerfield," Max told him with a look of determination on his face.

Senestraro chuckled, though it was clear that Max was being serious. Determined or not, he was nowhere near receiving clearance to compete, and the season opener was set for March 11, two months from the day of their meeting.

"The doctor told me you can't play contact sports anymore, because a hit to the head could kill you," Senestraro continued.

Max didn't care about that, but he didn't say anything to cause any more concern in his coach.

The coach knew his team captain meant every word he said. If anyone could pull off the sort of comeback they were talking about, it was Max. But that didn't change the sheer unlikelihood of the boy being able to follow through on what he had said he would do. Senestraro didn't want to relay an empty promise to his team, and he could not guarantee that Max would be on the field for Game 1 like he'd sworn. Still, he trusted Max. Before any of this, Max had been awarded the Coach Dave Kitchell Award for being the football team's most inspiring player. Even without the tragedy he had just faced, Max was the type of young man around whom his peers would rally. If Max said he'd be ready, something deep down told Senestraro that Max would be ready.

Max battled countless nagging ailments and symptoms from the crash and the week he spent unconscious. Constantly, he was awakened to take a pill or receive an injection, each of which addressed one of those ailments and symptoms. Despite the poking and prodding, things were looking up; after his second week in the hospital, he graduated from ice chips and could finally eat real food again. His father was so enthused by his progress that he told his son he would get him any food he wanted, when he wanted it.

"I want a steak," Max requested, craving some protein. He had always been a steak guy, and now he put his father's pledge to the test.

Stan did not disappoint. He went to Porters, an upscale steakhouse in nearby Medford, and got his boy a steak with all the trimmings. When he returned, Max was mesmerized by the look and smell of the thing. This must have been a $60 steak. All Stan cared about was indulging his son and doing anything to help him get his strength back. Max took up his steak knife and sliced easily through the perfectly cooked piece of meat. It cut like butter as he prepared himself several small slices, mouth watering. He had not had a bite of real food in weeks and he didn't know if he'd ever taste something this good again. He put the first small piece delicately on his tongue, languidly savoring the first drippings of flavor as he bit down. The second his teeth touched the meat, he dropped his utensils and howled in pain. His parents remember him trying a similar maneuver with what remained of his mom's breakfast burrito, and he had the same pain, keeping him from eating the much-needed protein.

The pain medication had kept him from realizing how much was wrong with his front teeth until he tried to use them. One was completely sheared from the force of the blow to his head on the dashboard. Looking straight on, one wouldn't even be able to tell, because it was split so finely down the middle. It was as if someone had taken a chisel to the very point of his front teeth, and then brought a hammer down onto it. This left nerves exposed and made it extremely painful to eat anything. This ruled out steak for sure, but also pretty much everything except for oatmeal and milkshakes. There were no oral surgeons at the hospital, so Stan and Michelle added that to the list of things to take care of once the Gordons finally were able to go home.

Max had several reasons for anxiously wanting to get back to full strength; sure, getting back out on the diamond was reason enough for him personally to take his rehabilitation seriously. There was something else nagging at him, too: his mom and dad. He knew that until they could put this crisis fully behind them, his parents would not be able to properly grieve the loss of their oldest son and return to some sense of normalcy. He was unconscious for the week following the crash, and the trauma left him with no memory of those seven days. He knew, however, that his parents would remember each waking second of those days for the rest of their lives. He couldn't imagine what they were going through, having suddenly lost a child and having come so close to losing another. He wanted to get himself back to full strength for them, so they could get back to living the life they had. What he couldn't yet recognize was that the life they would come to have would be centered entirely around their only surviving son.

The entire rationale behind Max's extended stay at Rogue Valley was his comfort; however, all the tests, pills, injections, and nurse visits impeded his ability to get much restful sleep. Before long, he found himself restless, exhausted and irritable. It was obvious he was feeling cooped up, and Michelle took notice. She decided that enough was enough. "You know what, we need to take him home," she insisted, "He's not getting any rest here. We need to take him home."

Thus it was time for the Gordons to return home, where Max's rigorous rehab would continue in what the family hoped would be relative comfort. He had not seen the house since he and Nick had set out for Bend less than two weeks before, and there was one stop left on the list before he would see it again: a visit to the oral surgeon. It was time for Max's teeth to be repaired, but there was just one little problem. He had been on so many painkillers over the past week and a half that his body had built up a resistance to them, and his mouth wouldn't numb properly.

"Are you numb?" the surgeon asked before poking the inside of his mouth.

"I can feel that," Max said.

After being carefully stabbed in several strategic points along his gum line and feeling every successive stab, Max cried a desperate appeal to the doctor. "Dude, I just wanna go home," he said. "Just pull this thing out. I don't care anymore, it's going to hurt either way."

Max was a tough guy, and even more impatient than he was tough in this situation. What was a little mouth pain compared to what he had been through? One sharp tug and he'd be on his way home. That was the teenager's expectation. In reality, the process of removing a tooth is rather barbaric. Max didn't realize that this was the case until the surgeon selected a crude pair of dental pliers, pulled his mouth open wide, and started tugging at the tooth with reckless abandon. He pulled and pulled with all his might until he finally managed to jar the tooth out of its spot in Max's mouth. He ripped it out, roots and all, and held it up in the light before Max's pale, sweaty face. He was moaning in pain, and his mouth overflowed black with thick, dark blood. Through all that he had endured over the past couple of weeks, this was the most physical pain he could remember feeling. However brutal it had been, Max was satisfied. The tooth was gone, and he was one step closer to being healed.

Acting true to form, Max was difficult to manage as soon as he returned home. Even though it was normalcy he said he was after, his parents saw his frantic efforts to recover as only more reason for concern. They knew their son, and they could tell he was trying to do too much too soon. It worried them greatly, and they ordered him to stay in the house and rest for a while before doing any more physical activity. Of course, this sort of decree only served to make Max more stir crazy.

It was basketball season in Ashland. Shortly after Max's release from the hospital, the Ashland High basketball team hosted its rival, Crater High. The showdown between the two squads always turned out a riotous crowd of classmates and parents. It was one of the events that students of the two schools looked forward to attending every year. Max could not imagine missing it. He knew convincing his parents to let him go would be a tall order, so he began his appeal in earnest.

"Come on, let me go to the game," Max begged his parents. Uncle Ron, his dad's brother, was also over at the house. He had been checking up on Max when he was in the hospital, and on this night, he was staying for dinner.

"Absolutely not," Stan said, wearing a stoic expression. "You're not going to the game, no."

"Well, I'm going," Max responded impishly, goading his dad to slip up in their negotiations.

"No, you're not," Stan held firm.

This stalemate continued for several minutes until Uncle Ron, clearly pitying his injured nephew, came to his aid.

When Max pleaded, "But it's Crater, dad!," Ron turned to Stan and backed him up.

"Yeah, come on, it's Crater," he reinforced Max's point, even though he had no idea what the significance of "Crater" was.

"No, Ron," Michelle chimed in from the kitchen, backing up her husband and refusing to put Max in harm's way.

"Tell you what," Uncle Ron countered. "Let me and Stan take him to the game. We'll watch the first half and then we'll take him back."

The conversation didn't end right then and there, but Uncle Ron's was a compromise everyone could get on board with, and both Stan and Michelle agreed it might be good for Max's spirits. They would allow Max to go to the game, but not without restrictions. He was to stay with his dad and uncle at all times, no matter what. No matter how tempting it might become to go down and join his friends in the student section, that was expressly forbidden.

The trio arrived at the high school and paid for their tickets, walking through the front atrium into the competition gym. They were greeted by the thundering racket of basketballs bouncing off the hardwood floor and banging into the rim and backboard in random intervals. The auditorium was raucous with the chatter of fans from both teams as the pre-game buzz reached full force. Then, as Max and his chaperones made their way to a spot in the bleachers, he noticed that the persistent sound of the basketballs had slowed, and then stopped entirely. The conversations around him shrunk to whispers, then to silence. He could feel the attention shift onto him, and as he heard the first claps slowly echo off the rafters, he felt their eyes bearing down on him. Before he knew what was happening, the few claps had transformed into uproarious applause. The crowd rose to their feet, a standing ovation forming as the loudspeaker in the gym crackled to life.

A jubilant PA announcer's voice boomed over the hundreds now on their feet, "We'd like to welcome the Grizzlies back home … and we'd also like to welcome back Max Gordon!"

The arena erupted. Most couldn't believe what they were seeing. Less than two weeks prior, they had sat in the hospital lobby waiting to see if Max was going to make it through the night. Now, right in front of them, he was standing on his own two feet. The hair on the back of Max's neck stood up as he took in the applause. He couldn't process the whirlwind of emotion coursing through him as the surge of support from his community washed over him. He was not the only one; Ron and Stan had to step out past the same doors through which they'd just walked. There, away from the crowd, they began to weep.

Composing themselves, the two men re-entered the gym and joined Max among the Ashland faithful in the stands. It was now abundantly clear just how much was riding on Max's recovery. After all of the pain and loss which his community had suffered over the past few months, he had become the symbol of a small town's hope. If he could be okay, maybe they could be, too.

Ashland wasn't the only place in which Max's survival had an immediate impact; word of his accident reached all the way to Japan, where Atsu Hamada, the organizer for the Pacific Rim Bowl's Japanese All-Star Team, was devastated. He was still reeling from the loss of Dave Kitchell, his American colleague, with whom he had worked for many years organizing the game. Now, one of the players who had done the most to signify this great competitive rivalry found himself in serious medical peril. Atsu felt he had to do something. He began making calls around Japan. Since his team was made up of all-stars, the players from the 2007 team that visited the United States were in different parts of the country.

In Japanese culture, it is a tradition to make 1,000 cranes to mourn a tragedy. As he made his calls, more and more families responded, saying they would make cranes by hand to send back to Atsu. He planned a visit to Ashland with two goals in mind: to pay his respects at Dave Kitchell's grave, and to visit Max with a surprise from his community of supporters in Japan. Upon arriving in Ashland, Atsu first tended to business with his old colleague and friend, Coach K. After saying his piece and wishing Dave Kitchell a peaceful rest, he set out to visit the Gordons.

Accompanied by Charlie Hall, Atsu arrived at the Gordons' home with a simple hanger in hand. When the family greeted him at the door, they saw the 1,000 elegant, handmade cranes cascading down on a series of threads from the hanger in the Japanese coach's hand. They were simply beautiful.

"That was really, really special," Max recalls. "We still have them in the house. I was pretty shocked; I didn't expect them to fly halfway across the world to give those to me."

It became clear that the Ashland athletic community was not the only one rallying around Max; 1,000 paper cranes had flown across the Pacific Ocean to tell him as much.

Just a few days after Max, Stan, and Ron watched Ashland notch a huge victory against Crater, all was quiet at the Gordon house. As Stan strolled down the hallway, he passed Max in sweatpants and a hoodie. It wasn't cold in the house, and Stan immediately sensed something fishy going on.

"Hey, I'm going for a run," Max said inconspicuously before slipping out the door into the abrasive northwestern winter. He made such a quick exit because he knew this announcement would not fly with his folks.

"Hey, whoa, whoa. God damn it!" Stan cried out in frustration, racing to pull his shoes on. "Michelle, Max is going for a run."

"But it's snowing outside," she answered, confused.

"I know it is," Stan said as he ran out the door.

He hopped into his truck and followed the fresh trail of footprints Max had left in the snow. He only got halfway down the block before spotting his son and pulling beside him, cruising slowly as he rolled down the window.

"Get in the truck!" Stan demanded.

Atsu Hamada (left) delivers 1,000 paper cranes created by Japanese football players to Max in the aftermath of his accident in 2008.

"What?" Max answered, pretending not to know why his dad was upset.

"You've got pneumonia!" Stan yelled.

He gave Max the obligatory lecture on the short ride home and told him that he was only thinking of his safety. He was angry, but he also understood implicitly what had Max so intent on making this comeback.

He's working for two now, he thought. *He's working for himself and his brother.*

Having one son clinging to life in the hospital put arrangements for the son the family lost on the back burner. That being the case, once Max returned home safely, they arranged to have Nick cremated. Before his brother went into the incinerator, Max kept Nick's toe tag. H78959. He wore it around his neck like a pendant. It always hung directly over his heart.

In the months following the crash, Stan would often have to pull over while driving, because the tears would blur his vision so badly. When Max's life was still hanging in the balance, it was easier for him to remain strong because he had something to hope for. Now with Max at home and stabilizing, the loss came crashing back down with the force it had the moment the highway patrol knocked on his door. Stan broke down, while Michelle stayed strong in the immediate aftermath of the tragedy.

"You could break every bone in my body and add it all up and it still wouldn't be one millionth of the pain losing Nick was," Stan recalls. "Michelle held me up. I was coming home crying on her shoulder all the time."

While Stan finally grappled with the crushing loss facing his family, Michelle and Max both still found things to stay focused on and determined about. For Michelle, it was Max. She made his care and well-being the only thing in her world that mattered. Everything revolved around the son she could still take care of. For Max, it was getting back out on the field to do Nick, his grampy, and Coach K proud. As far as he could see it, if he honored the men he'd lost, he wouldn't have to mourn them. This might work for a while, but only the forces of time could reveal to Max that this strategy would be unsustainable. The reality—he would one day find—was the exact opposite: only once he had properly mourned them would he be able to honor them fully.

He still had a long way to go. He wasn't even cleared for contact sports yet, but soon he had a doctor's appointment lined up for a week before the team's first practice. If all went well, he would be cleared and ready to go with one week to spare. As his physical wounds healed, he kept a reminder of what he had been through to get to this point. Max had been wearing an Ashland Conference Champions football sweatshirt the day of the crash that killed his brother. EMS had to cut the sweatshirt off him, but he regained possession of the hoodie after he came to. Instead of throwing it out, he poked holes in it and tied it back together with a shoestring. It was a fashion statement to be sure, but Max wore the mangled mess as a badge of honor.

Stan recognized the worn-down sweatshirt for the symbol it was, and it helped inspire him too. But he still wanted to make sure that he and the baseball coach were on the same page about Max's priorities going into the season. He knew that regardless of what any doctor told him, his son would try to get out on that field. So he paid coach Charlie Hall a visit at Ashland High one night on his way home from work. He just wanted to be sure that Coach Hall, who was an assistant with the varsity baseball team, would not even think about letting Max on that field one day too soon.

"I don't want him here," Stan said firmly, sitting in Charlie Hall's office.

"We're not going to let him practice, Stan," Charlie reassured him.

"I don't want him here, Charlie," Stan reiterated as if he hadn't even heard what the coach said to him. "It's cold out here and he still has pneumonia. Until the doctor gives him the okay, I don't want him out here."

It was clear that on this point, the two agreed. They both knew Max's nature by that point, and they knew that even if he wasn't technically participating, even being present at practice would lead Max to push himself beyond his limits. It would start with running down foul balls to be helpful and gain some stamina, and then it would be playing catch to warm up the pitchers, and before he knew it he'd be puncturing a lung diving head-first into home plate. Being careful was not Max's way, and although that is what made him a fierce competitor, it is also what made him a danger to himself. "Until you hear from me or Michelle, just tell him he's not wanted, not allowed ,and he needs to leave," Stan told Charlie, his decision final.

Max had lost virtually all of the muscle he'd ever put on through athletic training in the matter of a week and a half in the hospital. He knew that aside from getting onto the field, if he wanted to have any success when he returned to baseball, he would need to get at least some of that muscle back. So Max set out to hit the gym and start getting his strength and physique back.

He threw a 45-pound ring on each side of the bar and tried to squat. As soon as the weight came off the rack, Max collapsed under it and folded onto the floor. Several weeks after suffering the initial injuries, he was still incredibly weak. With every lift he would try, he experienced the same result. He had virtually no functional strength to speak of, and he was starting to feel extremely discouraged and frustrated. He didn't want to be better in weeks, he didn't want to be better in months, he wanted to be better right now. But, as he was learning, that just isn't how life works. It was obvious he wasn't where he needed to be physically, and it was also becoming obvious that no matter how determined he was, this recovery was not going to happen on his own personal timetable.

One week from the start of spring baseball practice, Max finally got to see Dr. Delgado, who would tell him whether he would yet be allowed to step onto the field. Holding back coughs and wheezes, Max immediately began making his case to the doctor.

"Am I going to be ready to play?" he asked desperately.

"I don't know, Max," Dr. Delgado said doubtfully. "Your pneumonia is still really bad."

Hearing the doctor's tone, Max's heart sank. He thought he'd been doing a good job masking his symptoms, but a trained physician could see right through him. It also remotely dawned on him that his parents might have been right and running in the snow had not been wise when trying to get over an intense bout of pneumonia.

"I'm still concerned about your spleen as well," Dr. Delgado told his patient. He was trying to let Max down easy. Although the family's primary concern had been his pneumonia, Max's lacerated spleen was actually the biggest immediate threat to his athletic future. His internal bleeding risk was high enough to rule him out of contact sports indefinitely. If the doctor made the determination that that risk was still too great, it would dash any hope Max had of getting back out on the field.

The team's first practice was set for the following Monday at 2 p.m. Max set a follow-up appointment for 1 p.m. that same day. He knew what he was doing. A week passed, and Max's pneumonia did improve marginally; however, he still had to stifle a cough any time he breathed in through his mouth.

"I'm fine, man," Max told Dr. Delgado, downplaying his condition. "I have no problems."

"I feel like you're going to go anyway," Dr. Delgado said after a short back-and-forth. A mischievous smile crept over Max's face. He knew the doctor was right. Note or no note, if he could find a way to get past his parents, he would be at that practice.

It wasn't as if Dr. Delgado made the decision on a whim. After much careful consideration, he determined that Max's spleen no longer posed an immediate threat. If Max were hit in the head, he could still be seriously injured or killed, but that risk was only marginally higher for him than any other kid playing baseball. Max had managed to convince him that his pneumonia had improved far more than it actually had, so he was fairly certain that the lungs would also be safe for action. Finally, Max had what he wanted since he woke up in the hospital: a second chance. Dr. Delgado scrawled out a note that he himself was shocked to be writing. He signed it, and just like that, Max was cleared. Less than two months prior, doctors had told him with a fair degree of certainty that he would never play a contact sport again. He had already proved them wrong. He just hoped others would doubt him in like fashion. He had acquired a taste for proving people wrong.

Max raced from Dr. Delgado's office to Ashland's practice field. He hurried to pull on his cleats and get onto the field before the baseball gods changed their minds and took his legs and lungs back for good. If he was weary of obstacles, he was onto something, as he saw his dad step into his path along the fence. Stan had a feeling that note or no note, he would find Max lacing up his cleats to take the field for Ashland's first practice. When he saw his son eagerly suiting up to go, he stepped in front of him and grabbed him as Max tried to push past his father and get to the field.

"I got a note," Max announced in an attempt to bypass his dad.

"Come back here, you have to talk to me," Stan said, bewildered.

Max gave his dad Dr. Delgado's note, clearing him to play. Stan surveyed it up and down, not believing what he read. He never thought the doctor would clear his son in time for the first practice. Once he was satisfied that the note was authentic and not some last-resort forgery by Max, he relinquished the paper back to Max and looked his only boy in the eyes.

"Okay, I want you to take it easy," Stan said, his voice full of apprehension

Max nodded dismissively before sprinting out toward the practice diamond.

Max savored the familiar feeling of his cleats digging into the grass, a feeling he wasn't sure if he'd ever feel with his own two feet again. As he neared his team, he entered a new mind-set which he would carry with him on the next leg of his journey to recovery.

"I made it a point to myself that I was going to push myself in base-ball," Max says. "I knew that was what I was most passionate about and that's the area in life I wanted to be successful."

As he strode up to his teammates, crushing the infield dirt under his spikes for the first time since everything in his life had changed, Max knew that the time had come for him to do something extraordinary. His eyes locked onto those of his teammates and his coach, and he could see a clear path lit up before him. It was time for him to do what he was meant to do.

"I wanted to be successful in baseball to honor Coach K, Grampy, and Nick," Max says. "I needed to show them that what they taught me and what they gave me was worth a damn."

CHAPTER 8

State

Max gasped for air, throwing his hands over his head in an attempt to open up his lungs. Warmups had just begun minutes before. No matter how much he could downplay it to his parents and doctor, the pneumonia was still a major obstacle to his aerobic capability. He didn't care; he knew the stakes set for this season were high. No one would be happy with less than a conference title and a deep playoff run. So Max huffed, puffed, and wheezed his way through drills he'd talked and laughed through hundreds of times in seasons past. He took the occasional brief break to gather up more air, but he finished each and every drill. As they got into practice, Coach Hall had finally seen enough of Max torturing himself. "All right, Gordo, You need to sit down for a minute," he said to his starting center fielder, still not totally able to believe that he had made it out here for the first practice.

Of course, Max protested. But he recognized how fortunate he was to be out on the practice field at all, so he quickly capitulated. He sat and watched practice get in motion. With each second, the urge within him grew. When he could take it no longer and had sufficiently caught his breath, he hopped up and jumped right into the flow of practice. He had a second wind now, and he wore a clear look of jubilation on his face. He was back at it. "I was overjoyed," Max says. "I was like a golden retriever chasing a tennis ball, having a blast."

Sam Gaviglio was enjoying it, too. He had his friend back. Naturally, the two hadn't seen much of one another during Max's rehab process.

"We had to take a step back," Sam remembers. "It wasn't that same relationship we had before. It wasn't 'Oh, we're in high school, we can mess around and have fun,' it was to the point where he was recovering and his family was grieving over the loss of Nick."

Once Max stepped back onto the diamond, though, it was as if their friendship hadn't missed a beat. Sam was the firepower, and Max was the dazzling defender in center field. Now, Max served as the team's inspiration as well. Everyone wanted to win one for Max, for Nick, and for the entire Ashland community.

Though Max's role as motivator was immediately clear, the dazzling defense took a little while to shore back up. Only a few weeks from opening day, it was clear that Max was struggling in the outfield.

Even Michelle took notice. She attended a few practices early on to make sure Max was taking care of himself. "I got really scared, because a ball got hit out there and Max tripped over his feet and fell in the outfield," she remembers. "Another one, he misjudges it and it goes way over his head. At that point, I realized he wasn't doing great."

"Normally, when the ball was hit to center field, they were out, no question," Stan adds.

When his mom expressed concern, Max told her it was his spikes that were causing the issues. Although it seemed to his parents that time away from sports and his weakened physique were probably responsible for his hard time in center, they wanted to do anything they could to get him back to where he needed to be. He got a new pair of cleats, and within a few practices the frightening episodes in the outfield seemed to go away. Of course, it was the spikes. Max knew his body failing him couldn't be responsible for the hard time he was having.

Just when Max started to feel a hint of comfort that this baseball season might go off without a hitch, a fateful moment at practice reminded him what a dangerous tightrope he was walking by being on the diamond. He was standing in foul territory with Matt Dierks, who played quarterback for Ashland's football team. They stood to the left of the protective screen meant to shield them from errant foul balls. Facing away from the plate, Max heard the loud crack of a bat from where some Grizzlies were taking batting practice. He turned his head just in time to register a screaming line drive hooking his way. It skipped the screen and whirred right toward Max's temple. He leaned back at the last possible second, contorting his body like Keanu Reeves in "The Matrix." Crisis averted. Max stood back up straight. His heart was thumping furiously in his chest. He realized with shock that such a blow to his head would probably have killed him. This was the exact sort of thing he'd been warned against, and yet here he was, after everything he'd gone through, still feeling like nothing bad could happen to him. He was still a teenager. He still had that unspoken sense that he was invincible, even though life had made a point of showing him that nobody is.

The ball didn't hit Max. It did, however, connect squarely with Matt Dierks' face. With Max's body screening him from view until the very last instant, Dierks didn't even know what was coming until he felt the impact and was leveled to the ground. He screamed out in pain. The team would soon learn that he had broken his orbital bone and several other small bones in his face. It was a gruesome injury that would put him out of commission for months. The team was despondent, but they knew that their goal had not changed. With the number of players returning for their senior season, the Grizzlies had high hopes that they could ascend to the top of Oregon high school baseball.

Finally, after weeks of practice, the regular season began in Klamath Falls, where a young Norman McPhail's train had pulled into the station over 50 years hence. His grandson's Grizzlies were set to take on the Hornets of Henley High School in the season opener. Wind and hail pervaded the scene. The cold was the only thing on anyone's mind. Ashland wore their pants long and their sleeves longer. They donned their new red, white and blue-accented uniforms for the first time ever, but the effect was dulled by the low visibility and heavy layers of outerwear.

It had been barely more than two months since Max's accident, and now here he was, in the starting lineup. He had butterflies, but not about his own performance. This was not his junior year. No more was he focused on becoming a one-man wrecking crew. All he wanted was to be a key cog in the winning Ashland machine. As first pitch approached, the teams were introduced and stood on their respective foul lines for the national anthem.

As the song started, Max began his practice of pre-game visualization, something taught to him by Coach K during those post-practice sessions on the football field.

His mind wandered, snatching up the best plays of his career one by one as if to reassure him there were more to come soon.

Eyes closed, he watched his first-ever high school home run sail out of the park as his mind's eye perfectly relayed every detail back to him, his memory serving as a reminder of his prior feats on the diamond. He could see his team gathered around home plate waiting, cheering him on as he touched every bag before jumping into their arms.

Diving catches, lots of them. Each of his favorites flashed through his mental rolodex as he imagined just how much he could elevate his defense in his senior season. Then, suddenly, the visualization stopped. He couldn't seem to summon any more memories of baseball accolades. He was busy remembering *what* he had done, but in that moment, he moved on to remembering *why* he was still doing it. The visions started anew.

Coach K's obituary picture popped into his head, followed by Grampy Norman. Two smiling faces. Faces of two great men who had a hand in shaping the competitor who straddled the foul line in Klamath Falls.

Nick's obituary picture was as clear as day. As "The Star-Spangled Banner" built to a fever pitch, Max kept his eyes shut tight. He didn't just see Nick, he actually felt him there with him. His brother was a part of him now, and that was the only way he could exist. The only things Nick would ever do now were the things Max brought him along for. As his father had said, he was playing for two now.

Max says a prayer before an Ashland baseball game just months after losing his brother, Nick.

Max reached down under his jersey, grabbing the one piece of jewelry he would wear for the rest of his life.

The crowd and players applauded the rendition of the anthem softly. Max pulled his brother's toe tag, attached to a necklace, out from underneath his shirt. He kissed it gently, looked up to the sky, and to himself said, "Here we go, boys."

Game on.

Sam, the Grizzlies ace, was on the mound for Game 1. He had to turn his shoulders away from the wind, trying to keep the hail and sleet from pelting him relentlessly. It would be a miserable day for the outfielders; with Sam on the mound in conditions like this, they weren't going to get much action. On a cold day with a bracing cross-wind like the one that pounded Max's cheeks, a ball hit to the outfield was the only hope of warming up at all. Max and his fellow outfielders stood around in the freezing cold as they watched their ace mow his way through the Hornets' order. The winter weather served to exacerbate Max's lingering pneumonia symptoms. When he drew a sharp breath in through his mouth, it felt like ice cold pins and needles filled his weak, narrow lungs. The pneumonia would hang around and make problems for Max well into the first month of the season. Thankfully for everyone involved, the Grizzlies scratched across a run on offense and headed for their heated bus, 1–0 winners in the season opener.[1]

That game's weather was all that was cold at the start of Ashland's season. The opening day victory was the beginning of an incredibly hot start for the Grizzlies. They allowed just three runs in their first five games and showed no signs of slowing down. Through the first month of the season, they lost to just one team from Oregon, cruising to an overall record of 12–2. Over that span, they outscored their opponents, 87–29. Then came a doubleheader with Eagle Point, a major rival. This would tell the team just how good they could be.

Max's pneumonia was finally starting to subside, and he was hitting his stride, playing some of the best baseball of his life. He set the tone for the rest of the team, which was virtually unstoppable whenever Sam Gaviglio was on the mound. Whenever Ashland made a pitching change, Max would do push-ups in the outfield to stay warm and loose. Most players would do something like that for show, but it was more than that to Max. There was something about the way he played the game and led his team that made shenanigans like that just, well, Max. Not to mention, he took every chance he could to build his strength back up. The Grizzlies' tiny lefty strolled to the box in the first inning to face the Eagles' starting pitcher. He got his signs, stepped in, tapped his bat against home plate, then raised it to the sky. He looked up the barrel and once again said to himself, *Here we go, boys*. It was a new in-game routine he had developed, and he would use it between every pitch in every at-bat for the rest of his career. He didn't just keep the ones he'd lost close. He kept them there, with him in every moment.

The winter weather of the start of the year had given way to true spring as mid–April presented the two teams a beautiful day to play two. Max upped the tempo by slashing a double to open up the inning. He eventually scored, and the team refused to stop there. After bringing across a few more runners, the Grizzlies lineup rolled over, and for the second time in that opening frame, Max strolled up to bat.

With the bases loaded, he stepped back in, *Here we go, boys.* He was locked in. As the pitcher set for his windup, Max locked eyes with him, daring him to give him a pitch to hit. The lanky Eagles pitcher obliged, delivering a straight fastball right in Max's wheelhouse. He turned on it, unloaded all of his 140 pounds into the ball, and launched it, high and far. Climbing, climbing, the ball soared out of the park for a grand slam, just about icing the game in the very first inning. Max couldn't believe how well this was going. They practically still had two full games to play. By the end of two innings, it was 12–0 in Ashland's favor, and most of the team's starters were removed from the game to give them time to rest.

The Grizzlies' focus shifted from winning to tanning. Starters on the bench, cheering on the hard-working reserve players getting some of their first significant game action of the season, rolled up their sleeves and pants and tried to eliminate some of their baseball tan lines. They clowned around for the rest of the game, a 20–3 win. Clearly they were not satisfied with that result, as they improved upon it in the afternoon game with a final score of 21–1. They didn't just win, they didn't just dominate; they embarrassed their opponent. Before this doubleheader, the Grizzlies knew they were very good. The results they earned against Eagle Point, however, were the first indication that maybe they had a chance at something more. Maybe, just maybe, they could be great. "We started walking onto people's fields and just staring right at them," Max recalls. "There was zero fear."

And with good reason. After all, they were 14–2 and had just one loss in conference play. After the massacres at Eagle Point, they had run their active winning streak to six games, only their second-longest winning streak of the season after their sterling 7–0 start. There was no shortage of confidence in the Ashland dugout as they neared the home stretch of the season. When they walked onto the field and sized a team up, they usually knew right away that victory was almost certain.

"We'd just look at the other team warming up, playing catch down on their side and we'd think, 'Man, you guys are in for a long day,'" Max says. "'We're going to pound you and we're going to enjoy every minute of it. It

Max makes his leap for a diving catch at Ashland High School during the 2008 season. His diving catches would become his trademark.

isn't going to be hard for us. We're going to have a lot of fun beating the piss out of you.'"

Had the Ashland team's pride evolved into hubris? Most likely. But whatever it was, it did nothing to slow the boys down. Thanks to "hit pills" provided by Grandma Cook, a woman whose love for those Ashland boys was exceeded only by the boys' love for the game, the team seemed unstoppable. Those hit pills consisted of red licorice sliced into smaller, bite-size pieces, and the way Ashland was playing, nobody denied their potency. Grandma Cook called the members of the team her "kids," and she was along for the ride wherever the trip would end for the red-hot Ashland Grizzlies.

They trounced through the rest of their regular season competition, not losing another game. Doubleheader sweeps became the norm with the Grizzlies mowing down opponents, allowing no more than two runs in nine of their final 11 games. Ashland took a 17-game winning streak into the playoffs; over that period, they had scored more than seven times as many runs as their opponents.

Riding the wave of momentum, Ashland extended the winning streak to 18, rolling through St. Helens, 4–0, in the first round of the playoffs to advance to the quarterfinals. Just three wins separated the Grizzlies from a state title; it was apparent, however, that they could not just walk over inferior conference foes to get there. Now they were facing off with the best teams in the state; to reach the semifinals, they had to go through North

Eugene on the road. The Highlanders, after stumbling to a mediocre 7–5 record to start the year, had recovered nicely, winners of eight out of 10 entering the quarterfinal match-up.

The game was a tense, back-and-forth affair. Max was an offensive force, notching hit after hit. He was raking off a lefty, which was unusual. He ate up right-handed pitching, but normally floundered against southpaws. That was not the case against North Eugene. The way he was seeing the ball, it might as well have been a beach ball floating across the plate. Down 4–3 in the sixth inning, Max strolled up to face the same lefty against whom he'd already had so much success, this time with the bases loaded. He was licking his chops. A base hit would give the Grizzlies the lead, and even a sacrifice fly would tie things up. Just as he was ready to dig in, the Highlanders called for a pitching change. A right-hander was summoned from the bullpen.

Awesome, I'm already red hot and now you're bringing in a righty, Max thought.

Watching from the on-deck circle while the new pitcher warmed up, Max had no doubt in his mind that he was about to break this game wide open for Ashland. He stepped up to the plate. *Here we go, boys.* The first pitch went by, and he didn't want it. Second pitch, now, that was exactly what he was looking for. He got a fastball over the inner half of the plate. It was so juicy looking that it took Max an extra split-second to react, and he rolled over the ball, spiking it right toward shortstop. Just like that, it was a 6–4–3 double play and the inning was over. Ashland was three outs from elimination, and Max and the rest of the Grizzlies were stunned. Michelle and Stan, who had found solace in Ashland's incredible season, gritted their teeth, knowing how much that double play was eating at their son.

Knowing the Grizzlies needed a shutdown inning to have any prayer in the seventh, Coach Senestraro summoned Sam Gaviglio on in relief. He was able to get out of the inning unscathed, setting up a top of the seventh inning, which would see the heart of the Grizzlies' order come to the plate. Through three batters, all the Grizzlies managed to produce was a runner on second base. However, Sam Gaviglio was coming to the plate with a chance to tie the game. A base hit would tie it, but an out would end Ashland's season two games short of its ultimate goal.

Sam Gaviglio was already a big deal in the state of Oregon by this time. He had signed to play with Oregon State, the very team he and his Ashland teammates had watched win the national championship in each of the past two seasons. Everyone knew how dangerous he was on the mound, but he was also a dangerous hitter. With first base open and weaker hitters following him, some teams may have opted to walk him intentionally. The Highlanders chose instead to pitch to him, not wanting to put the go-ahead run on first base. He immediately made them regret that decision. With the season hanging in the balance, Sam clobbered a ball into the next area code. The groans of the North Eugene players were drowned by the roar of Ashland fans as they jumped to their feet and watched the ball easily clear the outfield wall. Miraculously, the Grizzlies had the lead, 5–4.

However, they did not yet have the game. Ashland still had to hold North Eugene in the bottom half of the inning. With Sam still on the mound in relief, it was as good as done. After playing the hero for his team in the offensive half of the inning, he reprised that role from the mound. He struck out the side to send the Grizzlies into the state semifinals. The Gordons and the rest of the baseball families in Ashland let out a collective sigh of relief. They weren't ready to stop this incredible ride.

Stan's days of pulling over while on the job to weep weren't over. Neither were Michelle's days of wondering what was next while providing the support her husband needed. But each was able to put those feelings on hold, at least for a couple hours, to watch Max play the sport he loved. They weren't ready for the magic to run out. All they needed were two more wins.

The first one came easy. The Grizzlies punched their ticket to finals on their home field, beating Pendleton, 8–1. In four days, they would play for a state title. Their opponents: the 24–5 Thurston Colts. Like Ashland, they had been dominant all year long, more than doubling their opponents' scores. Something had to give. The Colts entered with a 16-game winning streak, while the Grizzlies had won 20 straight. Neither team had lost a game in six weeks, and each featured one of the best players in the state on its roster.

Sam Gaviglio was the Grizzlies' star, headed for Oregon State in the fall. His counterpart on the Thurston squad was Darrell Hunter. He was headed to the University of Oregon, the first Ducks signee since they reopened their baseball program ahead of the 2009 season. Hunter started for the Colts, while Gaviglio would come out of the bullpen for the Grizzlies. They had already leaned heavily on him throughout the playoffs.

Hunter was mowing through the Grizzlies' order, so when the Colts clawed out a run in the fifth inning, it seemed like it might be the difference. With Ashland's bottom of the order up in the fifth, things looked bleak. Two guys got on, though, bringing Hayden Miller to the plate. He had been solid for the Grizzlies all year, but his was not the number the team prayed would be called in this moment. He had sort of an awkward swing, and he rarely hit for much power. With runners on first and second, Hayden Miller became an unlikely hero for Ashland. He smoked a ball to the gap, which scored both runners, handing the Grizzlies a 2–1 lead.

The game went on, tension building in both dugouts and in the stands. As the game neared the final inning, Ashland led 3–2. One of Max's good buddies on the team, Luke Jannusch, walked up to the plate. He had never hit a home run in his entire baseball career, but in the final game of his senior season, he changed that. He cranked a ball so far that nobody saw it land. To hear some tell it, the ball is still rolling down the I-5 freeway to this day. The home run was long, and it was also crucial as it gave the Grizzlies a big insurance run. Now leading 4–2, Ashland called once more on its star pitcher, Sam Gaviglio, to close the game out in the seventh and final inning and bring the state title home.

Unlike North Eugene, who had sort of rolled over after Sam's crushing go-ahead home run in the quarterfinals, Thurston still had some life going into their last at-bats. They scratched one run across the plate with one out. Suddenly, the Colts were just a base hit away from potentially sending the state championship game to extra innings. There were runners on first and second, still just one out. Trying to get to third base so he could score on a sacrifice fly or a softly hit ground ball, the runner from second took off, trying to steal. The whole Grizzlies bench screamed to alert Ashland's catcher, Lewis Sebrell, who popped up and turned to fire to third base. Unfortunately, he lost hold of the ball and bobbled it slightly. He had no chance of retiring the runner at third. Luckily for the Grizzlies, Lewis had a very high baseball IQ. Thurston's right-handed hitter was so occupied with watching the play develop that he did not bail out of the box to allow Lewis a throwing lane to third base. Knowing he had no chance at the runner and recognizing the position the batter put him in, Sebrell started a throwing motion before ramming into the batter, not even attempting an actual throw.

Everyone on both sides was shocked. For the first time all game, the crowd was silent. Sebrell knew exactly what he was doing, and he looked up expectantly at the umpire.

"Batter's interference!" the umpire shouted.

Chaos ensued. The Colts couldn't believe what they were seeing. It was very clear what Lewis had done, and he himself knew it. But he sold it really well, and, at the end of the day, he knew he was entitled to the area which the batter occupied. On paper, it was the right call. After the umpire made it clear there would be no appealing his decision, the Colts players and coaches went ballistic. The tying run was destined for third base moments ago, and now that baserunner was trotting off, a victim of his teammate being called for interference. After that drastic swing, the Colts now had a runner on first base with two outs. Sam needed just one more out to seal the deal.

Fittingly, nothing would come easy for the Ashland squad as they drew painfully near their program's first state title. Sam threw a ball that got away from Lewis behind the dish, allowing the runner to move up to second base. Now, once again, a base hit could send the game into extra innings. To make matters worse, the best hitter in the state stood in the on-deck circle in the form of Darrell Hunter. His imposing stance crept into Sam's peripheral vision as he prepared to face the batter at hand. If Hunter got to the plate, he was capable of putting the Colts ahead with one swing of the bat. Pitcher and hitter both dug in as Sam labored through the at-bat, allowing the count to run full with Hunter waiting in the wings, taking practice cuts. He knew he was one strike away from being swarmed by his teammates and fans, but one bad pitch away from the most intense showdown of his career.

Sam, cap pulled down low, partially covering his face, came set, looked over at second base, and turned his attention toward the batter's box. He rocked and fired a fastball floating way up in the zone. It was high heat, and he knew it had no chance of coming into the strike zone. He was already preparing for a harrowing sequence against Darrell Hunter when he saw the look in the batter's eyes. He wanted it. The high fastball can be the most enticing pitch in the game because it's the only pitch that allows the hitter to see the entire baseball at once. As the ball rose through the zone, Sam watched the batter rear back, take a huge swing, and then look back at Lewis Sebrell behind the plate. He had the ball in his mitt. Sam was the first to see it, jumping up and down on the mound and throwing his mitt in the air. The rest of the Grizzlies weren't far behind as they swarmed from the field and raced from the dugout toward Sam on the rubber. The crowd was in pandemonium. A cacophony of cheers rose up above the baseball diamond. The Ashland Grizzlies were state champs.

"It's one of those things you don't think will ever come true," Sam says. "But then it does."

Max raced in from center field, hopping onto the mass of bodies celebrating a state title and ending the season on a 21-game winning streak. That very winter, he had lain unconscious in a hospital bed, wondering if he had any life worth returning to. Now he had achieved the one goal that had mattered to him since returning home. It had been his relentless spirit and team-first attitude, paired with a superstar season from his friend, Sam, which had turned this promising Ashland team into one destined for greatness. Max and Sam shared a knowing look as they embraced at the center of the diamond; with Sam headed to Oregon State in the fall and destined for the Major Leagues, the boys had every reason to believe that this was the last time they would ever stand on a baseball field as teammates.

The boys continued to celebrate on the field as parents cheered them on, still in awe at the drama they had seen unfold. Stan and Michelle were among them, reveling in a moment which neither of them had truthfully believed could ever come. There they were, celebrating arm in arm with the same community which had lifted them up months ago when they needed it most. They looked out at their son atop the dogpile, knowing it was the greatest moment in his life so far. As they looked, they knew he was

Max triumphantly waves the AHS flag in the back of a pickup truck as part of the team's victory parade through town in June 2008.

not alone. Max had been playing for two the whole season, and they had a strong sense that both of their sons were rejoicing in this victory.

It had been month after month of bad news, waiting and wondering. Finally, Max had brought some good news home. Less than five months after his entire world was torn away from him, here he stood, being crowned a state champion. He let go a breath that it felt like he'd been holding in since he left the doctor's office with the note clearing him to play. *We did it.* He looked up to the sky. *We did it.*

"That baseball season saved our lives," Michelle says with certainty.

The Gordons weren't entirely sure where all of this left them; the season had given them all something to focus on and to hope for. Now that it was complete, they would have to go back home and figure out the next piece of life after loss. Neither Stan nor Michelle was certain where the family would go from here, but they knew that baseball had been a major part of the healing process for Max. As long as he could do something that he dedicated to his brother, his coach, and his grandfather, he could still grow. Even with the gaping hole that was still left inside him. Although Max didn't have that sort of self-awareness at the time, there was one thing he knew for sure: his baseball dream did not end nor fully come true with the state title. There was still work to be done.

Here we go, boys.

CHAPTER 9

Juco

Fun in the sun and one last adventurous summer awaited Max and his buddies, fresh graduates of Ashland High School. Sam was getting ready to head to Oregon State for his first season as a Division 1 athlete. Josh was hoping to play football at a junior college. Those summer months were the quintessential "last hoorah" for a group of boys who had been together forever, before everything inevitably would change in the fall. The local American Legion team, the Medford Mustangs, weren't yet aware of Max's prowess, and their lack of tryout advertising left Ashland's scrappy lefty out of the loop. He was without a Summer League team heading into his freshman year at Sierra College.

He had a late birthday, not turning 18 until August. Officials for the local men's baseball league he was trying to get into with his friends didn't need to know that. You had to be between 18 and 40 to participate in the league, and all of his friends were legal adults. On one of the forms, he placed his birthday three months sooner than it actually was. Together with some All-State players from nearby Crater and Phoenix high schools, they assembled a squad that gave middle-aged men fits. Sometimes Max would even play shortstop, which is a true rarity for a lefty.

The team might only have seven players for a particular game and be forced to play with two outfielders. They could still cover the area much more effectively than most of Southern Oregon's finest 20- and 30-somethings could at full strength. Max was having a blast playing low-stakes baseball that summer as he prepared to try to win a job on the Sierra College baseball roster.

Max also got his first-and-only tattoo when he turned 18 that August. He had played summer ball for his buddy's dad, who was a power lineman in Ashland like his own father. During Babe Ruth League ball, his coach would give out three-leaf clover stickers to players for various feats on the baseball field. Soon, they proved good luck as the team continued to win state title after state title on the summer circuit. Going into his magical senior season, Max and the team decided to put the three-leaf clover stickers inside their hats as good luck. As the season wore on, Max insisted he would get a three-leaf clover tattoo if the team won the state title. It didn't dawn on him until weeks after they had won that he should keep his word. He had the perfect design in mind.

He went under the needle, this time by his own choice, and gave his tattoo artist specific instructions. When he was done, he had the same three-leaf clover the Grizzlies had seen as good luck, etched in his skin. However, his design had a twist. In the first leaf was the letter "K" for Coach K. The second leaf had "N" for Nick. And the third leaf had "G" for Grampy. It was a physical and permanent reminder of three of the men outside his own father to whom he owed his past success and future inspiration.

As quickly as the ink set in his new tattoo, a summer full of memories was behind him, and it was back to business as Stan dropped his son off with Doug and Julie, his parents' friends. They lived 45 minutes from Rocklin, California, where Sierra was located, and they offered to put Max up during the fall term.

When Max stepped onto Sierra's field for the first time as a prospective player, the odds seemed steep. In Junior College, nobody can be turned away instantly; it's simply an elective class you sign up for, and then slowly, but surely, the cream rises to the top and coaches make cuts leading up to the spring season. This makes for a vast field of players for the coaches to whittle down. Max saw more than 100 kids on the field, all of them competing for just a handful of spots. "I thought: 'I'm in big trouble,'" Max remembers. "Everybody looks huge. I'm just some 5 '7" guy out of Oregon."

He was the only player there from Oregon, vying for a spot on the team that had just won the California State Junior College championship. Then again, he was also likely the only one who had been in and out of a coma in the past year. He had made surmounting unfavorable odds his calling-card.

Everyone wanted to be a part of the repeat effort. Of course, just because there were a lot of players trying out doesn't mean a lot of them were good. In fact, Max had no way of knowing right away just how good everyone was. He did know that he would have to continue devoting his heart, mind, and soul to baseball in order to succeed at such a high level. He didn't have the overwhelming size or talent level to rest on his laurels and still make the team. "I have to really dig my heels in and go to work," Max remembers thinking. "Because this could go very wrong very quickly."

He had his work cut out for him after he and his dad assured head coach Rob Willson that he was capable of playing at a competitive junior college program like Sierra. While most others were in class or taking care of other obligations, Max was grinding away. He stacked his class schedule so that he would be done by late morning every day, and he would head to the practice field right when he was done. Then he would make his daily voyage to "The Gap."

The Gap was the space between the dugout and team equipment shed, which was fenced off, with a little bit of space left between the two buildings. It's where the Wolverines put all their buckets of balls, tees and other equipment after practice. Hours before the day's practice would begin, Max would start scaling the fence of The Gap in order to get the equipment he needed. Luckily for him, there was a small person-sized opening at the top of the fenced enclosure. Even more luckily for him, he was small enough to fit through it.

Therefore, he was able to climb the fence, hop over, and grab what he needed. The entire process was a labor of love. First, he stacked the buckets of balls on top of each other, so he would be able to pull other buckets up. Once he climbed on top of this precarious, man-made stool, he would toss buckets of balls as well as a tee on top of the team's dugout, where he could later fetch them. After that was over, he would squeeze back into the space between the dugout and The Gap before tossing the tee off the dugout and into foul territory on the practice field. In the final and most daring maneuver of the ordeal, which really was more for Max's own entertainment than anything, he would take a bucket in each hand and jump off the dugout, trying not to spill a ball from either one.

Over the course of the first several weeks of fall camp, Max went about this routine every day. He hit off the tee until both buckets were empty and then run out into the field and pick every single one up. He was on the field by 11 a.m. most days, though practice didn't begin for another three hours. If more could have been done to prepare for this next trial, it probably wouldn't have been medically advisable. Just as Ashland's 2008 state championship season had, the quest to make Sierra's roster became more than a lateral goal; it was a way for him to turn the well of loss in his heart into a bottomless pit of desire for greatness on the field. The events of the past year weighed heavy on him, and he missed the men he'd lost every single day. Especially Nick. He knew that no matter what he was doing, they would be on his mind, so he did something all day everyday that would at least make his constant ruminating a productive venture.

Coach Willson, who taught classes during the day, had a flag football class nearby one day when he heard an unusual noise.

"Ping! Ping! Ping!"

It sounded like someone taking batting practice in the cages. They were close to the baseball field, but it was still late morning and practice didn't start for a few more hours. All the equipment was locked up. He peered around curiously as his students ran around, frantically pulling at each other's flags. All he saw was Max. He was taking cut after cut after cut in the left-handed batter's box on the field. Nobody was pitching to him. After every swing, he would hold the follow-through, lean back down, pick up a ball, and place it on the tee for the next rep. Coach Willson watched the rhythmic routine repeat itself countless times.

"Ping!" and then the same silent beat: one, two, ball in hand, one, two, ball on tee, one, two, "Ping!" the same every time, as if he'd been doing this every day for a while.

Occasionally, he would even see Max square around to bunt as quickly as he could, over and over again for 20 minutes, before he even touched a baseball. Max didn't care much for bunting; he loved to swing the bat and was rarely called upon to lay one down. Nonetheless, he knew that as a short, scrappy outfielder, he would need to add effective bunting to his repertoire if he had any chance of getting onto the field at this level. Doing all of the little things right was the only way he was going to compete with bigger, stronger, faster competition.

This guy is mentally insane, Coach Willson thought. It was also a beautiful sight to behold for a JuCo coach struggling to find players with heart. He knew he could field a team of pretty talented guys, but that didn't mean it would be a team worth a damn.

The first couple of times he saw Max doing this, he was slightly perturbed. After all, the equipment was locked up for a reason, and the boy was trespassing, using things that didn't belong to him. But once he saw that day after day, Max was there doubling the work that was asked of him, he felt a growing sense of admiration for this wiry newcomer. Finally, he decided to intervene.

After weeks of watching the same show every day, Coach Willson approached Max. His prospective freshman outfielder half-expected to be reprimanded or worse for his antics, and he feared that the jig was up. That is until he saw the coach lift his hand in the air and noticed the glint of metal reflect off the afternoon sun. In Willson's hand was a key. "Hey, I'm going to leave this here," he told Max. "I've watched you climb this fence every day for three weeks. Here's the key, so you stop trying to hurt yourself."

In the ensuing weeks, they meticulously hid the key where Max could find it. They finally decided to just put a lock with a number combination on it and let the team know what the combination was. If they wanted to use the equipment during non-practice hours, now they could. This was a privilege that hadn't even occurred to the coaches before Max came along. Nobody before would go to such dangerous lengths just to get in extra reps. Once the right was extended to the entire program, still nobody took advantage more than Max did.

Beyond his work ethic, not much got Max noticed early on. Until the fall scrimmages, there weren't many good ways for unknown players to stand out. Players who had redshirted in 2008 had priority since they had sat out one season in order to play the following season. However, their spots were far from locked in. In a densely competitive tryout environment, no one could afford to be complacent for even a single day. Each group of roughly 40 players got only 11 days to play during fall scrimmages. They could play for as long as they wanted on those 11 days, while the coaches watched and evaluated.

Lineups would get switched around, and players would get swapped in and out. The coaches shook things up however they could in order to differentiate some guys from others in the short time afforded. Although he saw limited action during these scrimmages, Max apparently showed enough to impress some coaches; when the first Fall Ball roster was announced, his name was on it. This group would travel and play other junior colleges in an opportunity for coaches to get a much closer look at specific guys before narrowing down the roster to the one they would take into the season. Essentially, Fall Ball equated to an extended tryout for the guys vying to grab the few loose spots on the team. With a few amendments based on fall performances, this roster would carry Sierra into the regular season come spring.

Seeing his name on that roster was the first concrete piece of validation Max had gotten since starting the junior college process. Coaches rarely offer much feedback to individuals during tryouts beyond mechanical pointers, so Max had little to no idea where he stood compared to his competition until finally seeing his name on that list. When Sierra went on the road for its first official fall game, Max got his second piece of validation. He browsed the lineup card from the bottom up and was surprised not to see his name until he got to the very top slot. Not only had he earned a spot on the fall squad, but he would bat out of the leadoff spot and play center field in their first contest. *Oh shit*, Max thought. He was just excited to be on the roster and travel with the team.

He was not yet privy to the fact that he was slowly becoming a favorite of the coaching staff. With his visibly impressive work ethic, it was only natural. He was simply the type of guy with whom coaches fall in love. With his head down, just focused on making the team, though, Max wasn't sold that he was a shoe-in to land a spring roster spot. His first at-bat saw him chop a ball into the ground and sprint to first base. He was thrown out, but he made it a close play rather than a routine groundout. He would run just as hard down the baseline every chance he got. His college career had unofficially begun. His bid to replace several returning redshirt players looked promising since many of them started the game on the bench, while he led the team off and captained the outfield. Still, he couldn't be sure until just before Winter Break, when the coaches decided that it was time to reveal the final roster.

Sierra's coaching staff had kept roster decisions close to the vest; only returning starters were given any assurance that they would be on this year's team. Coach Willson, a fiery, old-school baseball guy who loved hard work and hustle, used one of his famous post-practice speeches as a stage. These speeches would sometimes go on for more than an hour. Sometimes the subject matter wouldn't grip the players, or Coach Willson might find himself talking in circles a little bit. This was not one of those occasions. That day, he had a clear message he was looking to deliver before looking at his new team for the first time.

"You guys need to understand what it means to work hard and why guys play and make this team," Coach Willson said. "You guys need to understand that you are the ones who write the lineup, it's not the coaching staff."

Wolverine players nodded along as his speech built toward its climax.

"You guys are the ones who are or aren't putting in the work everyday," Willson continued. "It really doesn't come down to the coaching staff. You guys are going to make the decision for us about who is going to play and who is going to make this team."

He had made his point, though many still wondered which category they fell into in his eyes. There was only one guy in the crowd who knew for certain which category he'd put himself into, regardless of whose eyes were watching. He almost felt like the coach was speaking about him directly.

He was.

"That's why Max Gordon, that little guy, is going to be playing center field for us this year." Willson pointed at Max, and all eyes were on him, like that day in the Ashland auditorium when the basketball team took on Crater High.

Max quickly wiped a grin starting to grow on his face. His stomach rolled over and filled with butterflies, the kind of feeling you get when you actually hear words that you only ever thought lived in your imagination. "He's going to be wearing all the gear, he's going to be in the trenches with us working his ass off, because this guy has been pouring his heart and soul into everything," Willson finished.

After practice broke for the evening and everyone started going their separate ways, Max was greeted with several handshakes from players who still didn't know their own fate. It was only Max's name that had come up in the post-practice meeting. "That's awesome, man. Congrats," they would say, just hoping they could call him a teammate come spring.

Max did revel a little in the good reception he seemed to get from the guys he'd been competing against, though being liked was never a factor to him during this time. In fact, he had gone out of his way not to socialize and make connections. Anything like that had the chance to distract him or compromise him before he achieved his goal.

"I'm not here to be your friend. I'm here to take your job," was his mantra. That was the ideology behind every interaction Max had during the late summer and fall at Sierra College. He only had one thing in mind: success on the diamond.

From his 45-minute drive every day to and from campus along the Sacramento River, to his time spent in his room doing homework, to passing up invites to parties with his teammates so he could get back on the field and work, every little sacrifice he had made finally paid off. He had made his first college roster. The first call he made was to his mom and dad.

"Yippee!" his mom yelled over the phone. Stan and Michelle had lived in Sacramento and knew how big a deal baseball was down there. Max kept them mostly in the dark about how the fall had gone, so they knew even less about his chances. That's why it came as such a great relief to receive this call and know that everything he had done, not having him home, worrying every day was worthwhile. Their son would be coming home for Christmas with the best present of all: a roster spot.

Following the holidays, it was time to get back to work. Max had made the roster, but there was no guarantee as to how much he would play. For the center field job, he was in a one-on-one competition with Kareem Campbell, a player like most who was bigger, stronger, and faster than Max was. Just as he'd practiced in the fall, Max knew that doing the little things right would be his way onto the field. On Opening Day, he checked the lineup card, posted just minutes before first pitch, and there was his name. Kareem Campbell was his backup. Max had become accustomed to seeing his work ethic put him above players with more pure talent.

He would check the lineup card religiously, before every game, and he kept seeing his name penciled in. Coach Willson decided to snap him out of it.

"Max, don't worry," he reassured him. "I'll let you know when you're not playing, but until then, you're going to be playing every damn game."

In his first real action as a junior collegiate athlete, Max strolled to the plate as a freshman starter. He dug in, tapped his bat on the plate, raised it to the sky, looking up the barrel as he said, "Here we go, boys," and bore down. Nick's tag was tucked under a Wolverines jersey. He battled in his first at-bat, eventually fighting a pitch off into the opposite field. It was a slicing line drive that cleared the sprawling shortstop and tucked into the left-center gap. He rounded first base hard as the ball dribbled into no-man's land, but he also saw the center fielder quickly closing the gap between himself and the ball. Max thought better of it and returned to first with a leadoff single.

"First hit, first inning, I don't need to get thrown out trying for second," Max wisely decided. It was exactly such a miscue that could quickly

Max (right) looks for signs with first-base coach Brett Hemphill during a game at Sierra College. The black arm band on Max's right arm was from the AHS football program, and he wore it all year at Sierra College as a tribute to the three men he'd lost. The band covers the "K" Max has carved into his forearm for Coach K.

steep a young player in skepticism from the coaching staff. Max called on wisdom within him that was well beyond his 18 years. He had a few older guys he took a lot of his cues from, and he looked up to the sky as he stood on first base, thanking them.

Although he hadn't necessarily been trying to, Max did make a handful of friends on the Sierra squad once he finally felt secure enough that he'd be on the roster for a while. Just as the season kicked off, he moved into a house with several teammates. It was a stately, beautiful building which boasted a market value north of $1 million. Somehow or another, this gaggle of rowdy college ball players got to call it home. Max was in his element there. Having so many teammates around helped him relax and branch out. He even managed to make friends with some guys he knew might be competing with him for time on the field. That was never easy for the cutthroat competitor in him to abide, but Max just enjoyed the spot he was in.

Being as nice as it was, Max's house became a prime party destination for students of Sierra College. Even though he didn't drink, those parties helped Max to cut loose in a way he'd never experienced before. For most of his life, the only way Max cut loose was to play games and sports with Nick and the neighborhood kids. Playing games that didn't count was the most free-spirited activity he could think of for a long time. But now, his new teammates and friends were showing him other ways to blow off steam. Suddenly, he could be silly and raucous, and there was a setting in which that sort of thing is not only acceptable, but often encouraged. He had promised his mom that he wouldn't drink until he turned 21, and he intended to keep that promise. He didn't need to drink, mostly because he was so entertained watching his friends and guests get wasted and tromp around.

He still played beer pong, and he was a dead shot. His partner would have to drink double, but it was seldom hard to find someone willing to take on that proposition. Eventually, no matter how much fun he was having, the night would get sloppy and rowdy. Around 2 a.m., Max would have had just about enough. He knew he wasn't going to sleep anyway as the parties often raged on at full volume into the early morning hours. The way he figured it, these were hours his teammates weren't taking advantage of; they were all at his house, getting ready to fight hangovers and make it to practice or class. So he started using this time to get an extra workout in. He would toss up a peace sign to his friends and slide inconspicuously out the door, hopping in his car and driving to 24-Hour Fitness. Confused party-goers might look around and say, "This is his house. Where is he going?" but before long, the word was out. This Max Gordon kid was cut from a different cloth.

He would grind until nearly four in the morning before returning home to find every surface and piece of furniture lined with passed-out bodies in different states of undress. He would pray there was no stranger passed out in his bed, grab a shower, and fit in a few hours of sleep before getting back to the task at hand. He always fell asleep with a smile, knowing his decisions were giving him a subtle edge that would strengthen with each passing day.

As Max worked harder and harder, he began to party harder as well. The house parties were reaching full swell every weekend, only getting rowdier and better-attended as time went on. Max recalls one party getting way out of hand. The parties were getting so notorious, it became hard to control the guest list. Friends of the team began inviting their friends, and that second layer of friends just brought everyone they knew. Max saw more strangers' faces among the sea of guests than he did familiar ones. The keg was in the kitchen, servicing the nearly 100 people occupying every inch of the house and lawn. When all the guys who actually owned the place were too drunk to pay attention, someone stole the tap from the keg to try and exchange it for cash at the store.

One of Max's roommates, Sam Montgomery, noticed the small pack of guys trying to slip out the front door unnoticed.

"Hey man, what the hell?" Sam beckoned to the thieves.

The pack of kids got spooked quickly by being confronted, and before he knew it, they had descended on Sam. One of them registered a forceful punch to his jaw, and as Sam staggered back, the beating began. The whole group went in on him, brutalizing him in a very short burst of senseless violence. By the time they were done hitting him, an outpouring of people fell onto the lawn. Friends quickly helped Sam inside. His face was bleeding profusely, his ribs were bruised badly enough that it agonized him to breathe, and his eye was blackened and swollen shut. All this was over a keg tap. The attackers were loading into their car, trying to make a clean break from the scene, when Max and a group of guys went after them. They were seeing red after watching their friend's assault, and they wanted retribution. Then, with a chilling nonchalance, the driver dragged the hem of his t-shirt up past his waistline, exposing a shiny black handgun. That gave Max's group second thoughts about a conflict. They backed down, shouting a few obscenities, and let the car peel away down the road. They were one keg tap short.

This display of violence didn't slow the party scene down one bit for Max and his teammates. The parties raged on, and by the time baseball season was in full swing, Max was a regular part of that tapestry. He had gotten in the habit of acting like he was drunk without actually having a drop to drink. While at a house party at Chico State University, he turned in the performance of a lifetime. "I would just walk in, find a beer bottle, and then act like an asshole," Max sums it up. "It's super fun, because you get into a character and then you can do whatever you want, because you're actually sober."

He was acting tipsy and having a great time when another guy at the party took exception and got in his face. Never one to back down from a fight, Max stepped up and started jawing with him. By that point, he was acting cartoonishly drunk, slurring his words and stumbling around like an idiot. Before he knew it, he had a bouncer on each of his arms, picking him up and kicking him out of the party. His acting career had reached its pinnacle.

The only performance more entertaining than "drunk Max" at Chico State was the real Max in center field. He had crazy range in both directions, and he consistently produced web gems on the run. He soon blipped the radar as one of the toughest defensive players in the whole conference. Since he was just a small boy running down balls in the backyard, Max was hard-pressed to see a ball he couldn't haul in.

To hear Stan Gordon tell it, "When they hit it to center field, they were out."

Just a few games into the season, Coach Willson already knew that Stan had been right in lauding his son's ability to be a junior college competitor. "Mr. Gordon, you wouldn't believe how many parents tell me their kids are Nolan Ryan or Willie Mays when they ain't worth a shit," Willson told Max's dad. "But you were right. Max can play at this level."

"Well, I just call them like I see them," Stan responded wryly.

Max was becoming a difference-maker on the field. His nonstop energy and tenacious style made him someone people stopped to watch. He was getting fans.

His biggest fan always remained his mom. She knew there was something special about what her son brought to the competition. "Whoever Max plays against, I always picked out my favorite on another team," Michelle explains. "It's usually the guys who are fun to watch, the kind that when they come up, they change the energy *just a little*...Max is that person."

His teammates liked watching him, they liked being with him, and most of all, they liked that his consistent level of production helped keep them in the hunt down the stretch of the season. One time, Stan even brought Grandma Cook's "hit pills" from back home in Ashland for Max to have and share with teammates. One of his cohorts was mired in a long slump when he popped some of the licorice "pills," and just like that, he got back on track at the plate. If he kept hitting and inspiring others to elevate their game, Max was more than all right with his coaches and peers. While the Wolverines weren't as dominant as they had been the previous year, they still put together a playoff-worthy campaign, which saw them draw Fresno City in the first round. It was a three-game series, and the first side to win two would advance to the Super Regional tournament. After a stale, uninspiring effort in the first game, Sierra found itself down 1–0 in the series and facing elimination. Saturday afternoon held the Wolverines' fate. If they won the first game, it would become a double-header and the two sides would square off again immediately after in a winner-take-all finale. If they lost, their season would be over and Max's freshman campaign at

Sierra would come to an end. In his mind, even with all he had personally accomplished, he would consider the whole season a failure if they fell
short in this fashion.

Much in the same spirit as the Ashland High team from the previous spring, Sierra relied on late-game heroics to survive elimination; down
to their last out and down one run in the ninth, in stepped right fielder
Abel Alcantar. Down two strikes in the count, Alcantar watched a borderline fastball that easily could have sent him packing on strikes. The umpire
sided with him, calling a ball and giving him new life. He choked up on
his bat and fought the next fastball off, spraying a base hit into shallow left
field. He stood on first base, providing the first small spark for the Wolverines. It was all the spark they would need. A few pitches later came the
explosion. A walk-off home run ended it, and as the Wolverines mobbed at
home plate to celebrate the epic 7–6 victory, they also silently assessed their
team's condition going into the decisive game of the series.

After the first two games grinding out the way they did, the coaches of
both teams found themselves with few personnel options. They had both
exhausted all of their top pitchers, and there was a sense that game three
would be a brawl in the mud.

That sense was spot on. In a game that saw each team reach double
digits in the runs column, and a couple of position players completing brief
stints on the mound, Sierra emerged victorious. The Wolverines would
advance to the Super Regional, which would be played, strangely enough,
at Feather River College. It was the team Max had momentarily thought he
wanted to play for, but eventually turned down. Led by Terry Baumgartner, a man Max already admired a great deal, Feather River was having one
of its best seasons in recent memory, among four Super Regional finalists,
joining Sierra, San Joaquin Delta, and San Mateo. This reaffirmed to Max
that he made the right decision in choosing Sierra. As he looked back over
the surreal freshman campaign he was about to finish, he could not guarantee that he would have had the same level of opportunity for success at
Feather River.

That Super Regional was loaded with traditional powerhouses, of
which only one would advance to the state tournament. Ultimately, Sierra
was beaten rather easily by the powerhouse San Joaquin Delta, but not
before the team pulled off one of the most surprising comebacks in the history of its program. In the opening salvo against Feather River, Max faced
off against the team which would have been his if he had chosen to play for
head coach Terry Baumgartner. He was happy where he was.

Sierra was traditionally the stronger program, but when 2009 rolled
around, Feather River looked poised to give them a run for their money.
They rolled into the first game of the tournament with a sterling 42–3

record. Sure enough, they jumped out to a convincing 8–0 lead over the Wolverines, making their hopes at advancing slim.

Having no shortage of resolve, Sierra slowly chipped away at the deficit. Having erased a once-momentous lead with steady, strategic hitting, they drew the game even at eight runs apiece as they reached the final frame. They managed to squeeze a single run across the plate, and it proved to be enough as Sierra's bullpen shut Feather River down in the bottom half. The Wolverines had pulled off a monumental comeback, embarrassing the Golden Eagles by stifling them on their own field. While Sierra notched its first loss to Delta in the next game, Feather River lost yet again on their own diamond, this time to San Mateo, ending their promising season abruptly. After Sierra dispatched San Mateo the next day, the stage was set: once again, they would have to beat a team who had previously beaten them, and they would have to do it twice in a row.

San Joaquin Delta would face Sierra with a trip to the state tournament on the line. Unlike other big moments Max had played in, this one didn't provide much drama. It was simply clear that Delta was the most talented team in their Super Regional, and they were destined for a run at the state title. They made quick work of Sierra, ending Max's season on their way to a loss to Orange Coast in the state title game the following week.[1]

His first collegiate season behind him, Max returned home more determined than ever. He had tasted success with Sierra and wanted more of it. While he graded out as just a slightly above-average high school player, he was determined to play Division 1 baseball. At a junior college, the only way to do that is to play well the first two years and hope to transfer to a bigger school. His buddy, Josh Scarminach, the first friendly face he saw when he got to Ashland four years prior, was looking to continue his football career as well.

Josh was recovering from wrist and ankle injuries that had held him out of football the previous fall. This year, he was determined to play at Shasta College. Both he and Max had a lot to play for in 2010. Their training regimen together was unlike the previous summer, when they worked out to the point of failure nearly every day.

Mostly that summer, the two just hung out. They could often be found in Josh's basement, playing XBOX 360. They ran out of controller batteries one night, so Max took the Scarminaches' motorized scooter up the road to his place to grab a few spares. As Josh waited for his friend to return, he heard shouting in front of his house. Max had hit a raccoon with the scooter and was flung off, sliding across the concrete. He was seriously hurt with road rash down to the bone near his ankle. A hint of deja-vu wafted through Max's consciousness in between sharp bursts of pain. The pain was made worse by the fact that he hadn't just wiped out as he arrived at the

Scarminaches, as it may have appeared at first; he wiped out moments after leaving home, still in sight of his house. Too afraid of worrying his parents, Max walked the entire way to Josh's house and dealt with his injuries from there.

"It would've scared my parents shitless to see me like that," Max explains. "Instead of walking back home, I walked to Josh's all bloody."

To the hospital Max returned, this time with a lot less suspense hanging in the air, but there was an eerie familiarity about the whole scene that made his skin crawl.

After a 10-hour boat trip with no sunblock a few days later, Josh suffered some serious skin irritation, too. Stan and Michelle walked inside the house one day when the two were hanging out, and they looked like mummies, each wrapped with gauze seemingly from head to toe. They were enjoying each other's company, but more importantly, each valued the other's drive to compete and keep pushing forward.

Max continued pushing his limits that summer as he had ever since recovering from the accident that killed his brother. Physically and emotionally, he had put up walls and kept his head down as he moved from goal to goal, accomplishing nearly everything he had set out to do. As the summer wound down and he prepared for the most important season of his career so far, he found it wasn't possible to keep the walls up forever.

Baseball had become the outlet into which Max poured every ounce of uncertainty and inner turmoil since the moment he was cleared for his first high school practice after the accident. Up to the end of that summer before his sophomore campaign at Sierra, the sport had been adequate in keeping the pangs of loss and anger at bay. Deep down, though, Max knew he was still running from something. With every long fly he chased down and every time he hurtled down the baseline at full speed, he put distance between himself and the part of himself that would allow him to feel the full weight of everything that he had been through. As he would soon discover, however, running from the past only works for so long; one look over your shoulder, and you won't see the brick wall right in front of you.

CHAPTER 10

Walking Away

Max hobbled to the trainer's room, having sprained his ankle yet again. As it turned out, the scooter crash had rendered him an injury that would nag him for an indeterminate amount of time. Alarm bells blared in his head as he again sat on the trainer's table, watching as his swollen ankle and foot got wrapped. This was the make-or-break season in JuCo ball. He was basically getting a second shot at his junior year of high school, as this was the season when Division 1 scouts would give him one last look. If he didn't distinguish himself this season, junior college would be as high as he ever got in the baseball hierarchy. In fact, his baseball career was at risk of coming to an end entirely. He was only allowed two years in a junior college program before he had to move on to a Division I, II, III or NAIA program. Getting just two years in a junior college program would be enough for many athletes. Not for Max. He fancied himself a Division 1 athlete, however far-fetched, and he could visualize no other outcome for himself.

The pressure he put on the season and the moment pervaded his performance on the field. He didn't do as well at the plate as he wanted early in the fall. He would slam his bat in frustration, knowing with each missed opportunity, his chance of jumping to a larger school was further diminished. When he fell into these spells of negativity, he wasn't nearly as fun to be around. His coaching staff at Sierra took notice. Head coach Rob Willson had seen this before, an ultra-determined player feeling the desperation of the sophomore season. It was especially disturbing seeing it from Max, though, who had been a force of both positivity and productivity during his freshman campaign. Most of the time, when a player did this, they would calm down and rely on their talent to get them over the mental hurdle. Willson waited and waited to see Max turn that corner. He saw no such turn happening.

His concern was not yet palpable, but he kept his center fielder close on his radar. He could sense that this might be about more than just Max's on-field performance.

Privately, Max had been wondering if he should still be playing baseball at Sierra College in his sophomore season. Those thoughts went away, though, after his performance at the Sophomore Showcase hosted by Sacramento State University. All of the most prestigious collegiate baseball programs were there, including Florida State and Oregon State, two teams constantly vying for NCAA titles.

The Sophomore Showcase is a scrimmage of sorts, set up to allow coaches and scouts at top schools to see as many kids in action in as little time as possible. Most players would get in about two innings and step to the plate only once. Before stepping into the batter's box, the PA would announce your name, so coaches and scouts could mark you down in their notes if they liked (or disliked) you.

After waiting and watching so many other players get their turn at the plate, all the time taking practice swing after practice swing, Max finally heard, "Max Gordon from Sierra College, outfielder," crackle through the public address system. The 5'7", 170-pounder strolled toward the box. He dug in, getting ready for one of the biggest at-bats of his career. Nothing that had happened to that point in the fall mattered anymore. If he impressed the right coach at the Showcase, his career would never be the same.

"Aaron Jorgensen, pitcher from the College of the Siskiyous," the announcer called out. Max's ears perked up immediately upon hearing the name. His eyes darted toward the mound, where the pitcher wore the same bespectacled look of recognition. They looked at each other in stunned silence for a few seconds. They had played in Little League against one another in Yreka, California, when they were kids. Max hadn't seen his old counterpart since they were nine or ten years old. Now, they were grown men going toe to toe, ready to do their damnedest to stand apart from the field of talented competitors around them.

Hell yeah, Aaron, let's go! Serve one up for me like the good old days, Max thought to himself, recalling the time he homered off of him in Little League. As he settled into the box and set into his stance, he hoped for a similar result this time around.

Here we go, boys.

He was ready for battle. It was dramatic, but within seconds, the drama was over. Max made good contact, grounding a screamer to the second baseman which was easily handled, and he was thrown out at first by a step. Although concern set in for Max as he hustled back to the dugout and grabbed his glove, he knew all along that his offense was not necessarily the thing to set him apart from the competition. If Max had any truly exceptional talent in the game of baseball, it was his defense in the outfield.

In Max's one inning in the outfield, he positioned himself in center, hoping he would get an opportunity, any opportunity, to make a play on a ball in front of the contingent of Division 1 talent evaluators. Even just camping under a routine fly and making a mechanically sound play would make him feel a lot better about his position in their eyes. Michelle and Stan were as nervous as their son was as they watched the showcase unfold. Where they sat in the stands, though, they had the advantage of being surrounded by the scouts and hearing bits and pieces of their conversations. If any word of Max surfaced, they had a chance to hear it. Unfortunately, Max had not exactly given them any reason to talk yet. That is, until the crack of a bat sent a shot to the right-center gap.

As he often did, Max got a great read on the ball, and his first step was perfect. He covered ground with impressive speed, but as he closed in, the ball continued to carry. Its path looked certain to clear Max's sprawling body and drop into the gap for an extra-base hit. Max had already sold out for the catch rather than trying to play the ball off a bounce and cut it off, so it was almost sure to be a triple if it escaped his grasp. Sensing that he had reached the point of no return, Max sprawled out with a leap, contorting his body while in mid-air to reach behind his head for the ball.

It truly didn't look like he would get it. Stan and Michelle winced as they watched the paths of the two projectiles—the ball and their son—raucously collide a few steps from the warning track.

Max had jumped a little too far, and as he reached back behind his head, he actually saw the ball coming across his face. As he plummeted toward the earth, he watched the stitches of the ball rotate end over end one more time before dropping hard into the webbing of his mitt. He crashed hard into the outfield grass and lifted his mitt up for the umpire to see. He held his pose long enough to catch a glimpse of the umpire a few steps out from the infield, as he raised his arm up and signaled "Batter out!"

A small roar coursed through the stadium as coaches and scouts who had been quiet for most of the afternoon exploded. Some stood up and cheered.

"Did he catch that? He didn't catch that, did he?" Stan and Michelle were close enough to hear the incredulous murmurs emanating from the scout section. Michelle took special notice of the Oregon State scouts. They had jumped to their feet the moment Max initiated his dive. She was overjoyed for her son. She knew that was the school he had his heart set on for years, and she had been watching her boys' games long enough to know that that play would get him noticed.

Like every junior college baseball player, all Max really wanted was to get noticed by a Division 1 program, any Division 1 program. He had made the most of his couple innings of exposure and now, all he could do was sit and wait to see if the phone would ring. He didn't have to wait long.

"Hey, I really liked what I saw from you at the Sophomore Showcase,"

Max lays out for a diving catch at Sierra College, where he quickly became a team leader during the 2009 season.

Max remembers the voice on the other line telling him. It was Buddy Gouldsmith, the head coach at UNLV, a Division 1 program not too far from home. This was the phone call Max had been waiting for his whole life. A Division 1 coach was interested in him.

"I'd love to get you down here on a visit one of these days," Coach Gouldsmith went on, "We have a senior outfielder leaving and I think you could fit us really well." Max was dumbfounded. He continued listening to the coach as much as he could, but his heart and his mind started racing out of control.

"I know you're a tough player," Gouldsmith said, "I talked to Rob about you and I like how hard you work." Nearly speechless on the other end of the phone, Max expressed interest in the program and, keeping his composure, he told Coach Gouldsmith he would love to visit campus and see what they could do about getting him in a Runnin' Rebels uniform. "Just send me over your transcripts and maybe we can get the ball rolling on this," Gouldsmith said, leaving Max ecstatic before he hung up the phone.

As quickly as he could, Max sent over his transcripts and waited to hear back. He and Buddy Gouldsmith never spoke to one another again. At the end of the 2010 season, Max would come to learn, Gouldsmith had been fired by UNLV following another lackluster year.[1] From a recruiting standpoint, he didn't have much power in the final months of his run as manager, since he was halfway out the door.

After the Sophomore Showcase, Max's hopes were pretty high. After his highlight-reel catch and with his reputation as a gutsy, determined player, he figured he would at least generate a decent amount of buzz from scouts in a few programs. Now, with the major recruiting period drawing to a close and the one coach who had expressed interest out of the picture, Max was feeling antsy. More weeks passed, and antsiness turned to a sense of defeat. The way he saw it, he had missed the boat. For the first time since taking his initial steps out of the Rogue Valley hospital bed, Max Gordon had come up short of a goal he set for himself. It was the big one, too.

His route to playing Division 1 baseball seemed gone. Interest in school waned, and even interest in baseball waned as something deeper ate away at Max's identity on and off the baseball field. The game that had been his answer for everything over the past two years was suddenly bringing up nothing but more questions. The Sierra outfielder whose aim in competition had been truer than any player to come through the program in years abruptly was aimless. "His effort was the same, but he lost a bounce in his step," Coach Willson remembers. "He lost that a little bit and I could tell his mind was divided."

As he had his junior season of high school, Max put entirely too much pressure on himself. It was like he was stuck in quicksand; the harder he struggled, the deeper he sank. The facade was finally starting to dissolve, and he had to come to grips with the reality that his life was not going to be a heroic baseball story. The story of his life would be much darker and less flashy than that. He was eventually going to have to face reality head-on: Nick is gone. He had been strong for his parents when they needed him to be. Then he jumped right into baseball mode because he thought that was what he needed. He got out of Oregon because it reminded him of what happened, and it was easier not to think about it in a totally new place without his family around. But now, he was homesick and ready to admit that he had never taken the time to grieve his big brother.

He confided all this to Coach Willson one afternoon; the coach was concerned, but also relieved to finally know what had been eating at his most energetic, positive player. He knew this would be a process, and he was glad Max felt that he could come to him. He wanted to help Max get back to his old self with the season right around the corner. What he didn't yet realize, however, was that the type of player he wanted back was creating the problem for the young man sitting across from him now. It isn't healthy to dive into something the way Max had, with no regard for self-preservation or well-being. The player Max had become was a by-product of the person he hoped never to become: one who has to face up to his true feelings and overcome them.

"Coach, I don't know if I'm mentally right to play here in the spring," Max told him, looking him in the eye and nervously folding his hands in his lap. Coach Willson was shocked, but he was calm and tried not to panic. He knew Max would snap out of it in time for the season. He asked him not to decide anything this second, and the two made arrangements to meet again and talk about it in a couple of weeks.

As those two weeks went by, Willson could see that the Max Gordon he'd deeply admired during his freshman campaign was gone for good. The joy he drew from the game was no longer apparent in his play. If anything went wrong, he took it out on himself, and he wasn't as warm a teammate as he had once been. He acted selfishly, and the shift in his demeanor signaled a significant blow to team morale. His coaching staff met with him at the two-week mark to find a solution together.

"We know something is up," they explained. "We don't like seeing you like this, and we know how hard it's been getting the short end of the stick every time. It's starting to really show on the field by your actions and the way you're carrying yourself, how you're going about everything. You've been getting more and more flustered. I think a lot of it has to do with what you've been through, and we think you should seek some help."

Sierra's coaching staff outlined various resources for him on campus, including people he could talk to about what was going on mentally and emotionally. Finally, Max grew tired of acting strong. He bowed his head into his hands, let out a sigh, and began to sob. In front of nearly his whole coaching staff, he let the emotional toll of the past couple years wash over him all at once. He knew what he had to do. Deep down, he wanted out of Sierra, and what his coaches had hoped would pull his heart back onto the field actually put him in the head-space to be able to move on.

"Baseball wasn't fun anymore. That whole lifestyle was really tough," Max explains. "I was pulling and pulling on something that wasn't going to give. The harder I pushed, the worse it got. So, when leaving became an option where I could still be in everybody's good graces and not look like a total coward for walking out, I was relieved I had that option."

He told Coach Willson he would mull the decision over Winter Break, but his mind was already made up. Baseball was no longer fun, and he wasn't going to put himself through the grind anymore. Max was depressed and he was done with baseball. With one month left in the fall term, he routinely skipped class. Of his four classes, he might attend one or two and took F's in the others. He didn't care anymore. His sudden apathy was alarming; Nick's death brought up heavy questions about his life. He had no idea what really mattered. While he was still seeing great success on the baseball field, he didn't have to ponder these things because the answer was simple: baseball matters. Now that that was in question, everything was in question.

Max was satisfied to simply run out the clock on his fall semester. He and his roommate, Dave Wagner, a player cut from the baseball team, spent a lot of time together over the last month or so before Winter Break. Most of their time was spent doing nothing, and Max was fine with that. It was what he needed for the final month of the term since he was no longer going to baseball practice. They would stay home, get a Redbox movie, order a pizza, and just sit, eat, and stare at the TV all day long. Dave kept going to class, while Max stayed home, but the two still allowed themselves to go to a dark place, doing whatever they wanted whenever they wanted. They had two other roommates, but they had a little more going on than Max and Dave, the homebodies.

The fall term was drawing to a close, and Max's depression was only getting worse. He was ready to get back home and figure out a plan of attack. Baseball was out the window, and he needed to go home to get better. What could possibly make him feel better? His guess was as good as anybody else's. A few weeks before the end of the semester, Stan and Michelle dropped off the pick-up truck and took Max's car back to Ashland. That way, he could load up all his stuff in the pick-up and not worry about having enough space.

Emblematic of his eagerness to get out of California, Max got a speeding ticket just over an hour into his drive home. The rest of the drive seemed to take forever, and the last thing Max wanted was to be alone with his thoughts. Reflection, however, was what he ultimately needed. Part of that reflection led him to look back on his baseball career to that point. What he had already accomplished was relatively uncommon for a small outfielder with no power and an average throwing arm. Reminding himself of that did little to make him feel better. Predictably, he was not satisfied with how things ended up. But ultimately, it had been his decision to leave. For the first time, he broke down and began to feel sorry for himself.

It was as if he had been just close enough to taste his Division 1 dream multiple times, only to have it snatched away from him. UNLV's declining interest in him, plus his own depression bubbling just below the surface, had come up just in time to dash his baseball dreams. He needed something encouraging, a light at the end of a new, long, and narrow tunnel. A vague idea popped into his head, prompting him to call up the hero of the 2008 State Champion Ashland High baseball team.

"I'm moving home, and I want Pat Casey's number," Max told his buddy, who was gearing up for his sophomore season at Oregon State.

Pat Casey was the Beavers' legendary head coach, who took the program to new heights, winning back-to-back national championships just three years prior. After Max asked for it, Sam Gaviglio, being the friend that he was, gave him Casey's number, and that was that. Max had no idea what he planned to do with this information, but he had a Division 1 baseball coach's phone number. At this low point, that felt like progress.

The moral victory was short-lived as more negativity filled Max's psyche. He felt a growing anxiety with every mile he erased between himself and Ashland. When he got there, he actually had to start over. The notion was paralyzing. All the progress he had made since Nick's death had essentially been erased. When he pulled up to the house with his dad's pick-up truck, he could hardly contain his emotions. He was starting from scratch, and he was terrified.

Baseball had been Max's entire identity since the moment he found out that his brother wasn't coming home from the hospital with him. It had been his main fixation since even before that, when he lost Grandpa Norman and Coach K. He had accomplished so much, but now he had no discernable identity. One way or another, he was setting out to discover who he really was in this new life without a few of the men who had contributed so much to who he was.

"He had anger management issues," Michelle recalls of her son. "He'd blow up over nothing. You could try to talk to him about anything and if he had to think about it or didn't initially like the idea, he immediately blew you off."

It was a tricky situation to handle as a parent. Michelle and Stan had to discern between which aspects of his behavior came from the growing pains of becoming a young adult, and which ones stemmed from the damage he'd suffered to his brain along with the strain of the loss he experienced. "I didn't know whether I needed to backhand him or hug him," Stan says.

The injuries Max suffered in the crash had left him with permanent short-term memory loss as well as PTSD. This, the family already knew. But the depression had only come to the surface in the last few months. This complicated things; if he saw a therapist, the process would naturally begin with debriefing about the initial trauma, the car crash that killed Nick. It had been two years since the crash, and there were a lot of things crossed up in Max's brain. For a very long time, he refused to see any professional. He insisted that it would do nothing to help him.

It quickly became clear, however, that he needed help. A vivid example was the day Stan asked his son to do him a relatively simple favor while he was at work: "Hey, when you have a chance today, go out there, and put a coat of paint on these baseboards," Stan told his son. "I have paint, there's a paint brush on the shelf. Then, probably just put one more coat of paint on it tomorrow night."

"Yeah, yeah, okay, whatever," Max shot back dismissively.

Stan had the baseboards set up on the sawhorse, he had already sanded them, and all he needed Max to do was walk out to the garage and administer a simple, solitary layer of paint on a few boards. He returned home expecting the easy job to be finished.

"Hey, did you get those baseboards painted?" Stan asked.

"No," Max said, immediately growing visibly exasperated. He looked angry, and before long, he was on an expletive-laden tirade around the house.

He proceeded to stomp out to the garage and upend and break more of the Gordons' things. During his tirade, he kicked over a piece of equipment that made a loud noise which Stan could hear from outside the garage. He rushed in, opening the door and getting in Max's face.

"Hey, what's your problem?" Stan asked his son. Max was seeing red.

Michelle stood several feet behind Stan in the doorway, apprehensive. She could plainly see that Max was not well, and neither she nor her husband had the answer. "It's not that hard, just paint the damn baseboards," Stan lashed out in frustration. "It will take you 10 minutes."

It was not a very tough task, but Max's mental state was weakened and deteriorating. He didn't have the energy to wrap his mind around even the most menial of tasks. He finished the outburst by spewing a few choice obscenities in his dad's face as he stormed out of the garage. Stan and Michelle could do nothing but look helplessly at one another, left in the wake of Max's self-destructive episode. They had never seen their son lose his composure like that. One thing had become abundantly clear: they had let him try to find his own way for long enough. It was time to seek professional help for their son.

For Max, getting out of bed was a nightmare. By the time winter was in full swing, he was swirling in a darkness that surrounded him in every direction, swaddling and smothering him until he had neither the strength nor the will to do anything at all. When his parents asked if he was thinking about going back to school, Max got uneasy because he didn't know what his future held and he felt a great deal of anxiety over it.

He awoke the morning after his blow-up in the garage and just wanted to put it behind him. He had calmed down, after all, and his memory of the event was fuzzy because of his issues with short-term memory. The impression it left on his parents, however, was something different altogether. For the first time since he lay unconscious in the emergency room, they were deathly afraid of losing a second son. The time had come to broach the subject of Max seeking a healthcare professional to help him through the grieving process. "I talked to your father and we think you need to get help," his mother calmly told him.

He could see the fear in her eyes, and although he knew that it was mostly fear for his well-being, he sensed a note of something else, too: for the first time, a small part of her feared him. He had shown anger, violence, and a total lack of self-control lately, and he saw it in himself too. He had zero faith that psychology could offer him anything, but he agreed to go. It was the least he could do, and he genuinely wanted to stop hurting his family. His parents had been through enough.

Even going in with an open mind, Max had a hard time making any sort of connection with the psychiatrist, "It went horribly. It really was a waste of my time and the doctor's time," Max recalls.

A general air of paranoia and defeatism pervaded Max's world-view by this time; in his eyes, everyone was out to get him. He had found work with Ashland Public School's maintenance department, mowing lawns beginning in the spring. He viewed his semi-weekly therapy sessions as merely a way to cut into his paycheck. His cynicism made it unlikely from the beginning that he would gain anything worthwhile from the experience. Nothing worked. His doctor tried every treatment option he could think of, and nothing was compatible with Max's profile. He was struck by Max's sheer callousness and how demonstratively he displayed the crushing depression in his demeanor. There was no shot at productive dialogue; Max was closed off completely.

"Let's talk about your brother," his doctor would say.

Max always knew this was coming, and he was always ready to deflect by acting like it didn't have an effect on him.

"Nothing to talk about," He'd say, "That's not the problem."

"Do you miss him?" the therapist would ask.

Do I miss him? What kind of question is that? Of course I do, he would think to himself, but he would just grumble some non-sequitur to keep the doctor at a distance from his true feelings.

Max was angry, and he didn't expect anyone to understand him, much less some therapist to whom he'd barely spoken. He was sabotaging his doctor's efforts to help him, because he was scared that they would be futile in the first place.

Max managed to find a few meditative moments throughout all of this; one such moment would arise when he was mowing lawns for work with his headphones in and his music blaring. In the spring, he helped coach the Ashland High School varsity baseball team he had helped lead to state title just two years prior. It was his first foray back into the sport which had brought him so much joy, but which also plunged him into so much anguish. Either way, being closer to the sport and a school he'd left as a champion was the closest he got to feeling normal again while sorting through his psyche. When he returned home from the practice diamond, though, he still faced the pit of despair to which he had grown accustomed in the recent months.

Max had only one more appointment scheduled for counseling with the doctor he'd been seeing, and neither had any confidence that a break-through was on the horizon. Even the doctor was discouraged as week after week, Max persisted in his stone-like demeanor and shared very little. But the psychiatrist still had one more card left to play...

"Listen Max, we need to talk a little bit before we get started," his preamble began. "I feel like I'm failing you right now in this adventure we're going through. It's not doing anything; I'm not helping you. You're extremely detached from your emotions and feelings, but I want to try one more thing. If this doesn't work, I'd like to refer you to another doctor to start helping you, because I don't know if I can."

Max couldn't believe what he was hearing. He felt like he was being given up on. He had no plans to try this whole process again with another doctor who would eventually just tell him he was hopeless.

"I want to try something called brainspotting," his doctor explained as Max listened tentatively.

Brainspotting was a relatively new therapy at the time; it was designed to help people access, process, and overcome negative emotions and pain associated with trauma. Dr. David Grand invented it less than a decade prior, and many mental health professionals find it to be an effective way to treat a myriad of mental health concerns. Dr. Grand's creation sprouted from the idea that where one looks affects how one feels. During a brain-spotting session, the therapist helps his patient to train the eyes in ways that allow them to target sources of negative emotions. Then, using a pointer, the therapist slowly guides the patient's eyes across his field of vision, find-ing appropriate "brain spots"—an eye position that activates a traumatic memory or painful emotion—along the way. It is usually a measure of last resort when a doctor finds it impossible to get a patient to open up about the trauma at the center of the affliction.[2]

Therapists using this technique believe trauma lurks undetectably in the body, altering the way the brain works. Since trauma affects how people feel physically and emotionally, as well as recalling events from their past, advocates of the practice say it activates the body's innate ability to heal itself from trauma. Max's therapist believed in the therapy enough to use it as a last-ditch effort to get through to him. He had made no progress to this point, so Max figured he had nothing to lose by trying.

After being walked through the basics of the procedure, Max was directed to train his focus on a specific spot on the wall opposite him. His therapist sat diagonally across from him in the warm room. Max traced his finger over the textile of the sofa chair on which he sat, breathing uneas-ily and not knowing what to expect. Headphones were placed over his ears, eliciting a drone of soft, simple music, soft enough so that he could still hear his therapist. Max zoned out on the wall, just as he was instructed. After a few moments, he felt himself slipping into a sort of trance. He still registered the soft music playing and his therapist speaking slowly and softly, moving from topic to topic. Max's consciousness gradually became less secure. He was slipping in and out of attention when he felt something tug him back toward the doctor's words. "I want you to welcome your brother into this room," he told Max. "Welcome him into this moment right now."

Max continued sinking further and further into his chair, staring at the wall. Upon mention of Nick, he intensified his stare into the blank white wall until he could sense a vague sort of pulse coming from it. It was ephemeral and bizarre. Gradually, the pulsing spot began gaining texture and bubbling between one non-distinct form and the next. He felt like he had been slipped a hallucinogenic drug of some kind and that now he was having some kind of trip. He knew that Nick was in the room with him. He had allowed him there. Before he actually saw him, it was just a feeling. But he knew it was true the moment it came over him. Once he saw whatever he saw in that bubbling vibration, everything else melted away. Music ceased playing, and his doctor's words faded into distant silence. He couldn't hear or see a thing other than the heartbeat on the wall in front of him.

His doctor's mouth was still moving, he could see that much in his peripheral vision, but he was existing in a moment outside of time as he sat transfixed, feeling not only his own heartbeat but two life forces present between him and the white drywall. Without warning, Nick's voice echoed through Max's head. He hadn't heard that voice in years. Of course he had revisited childhood memories since the accident, but this was different. This wasn't a memory or something happening in the past. His big brother was talking directly into his ears.

"I'm good, man, it's fine," Max heard his brother's warm, firm voice reassuring him from a realm just outside of his reach. "I'm fine, man. We're all good. You don't have to worry about me anymore." He listened to Nick, languishing in his voice as if it were countless rays of life-rendering sunshine. Then, suddenly, the wall stopped its pulsing, and the energy that had perforated the room moments before completely dissipated.

Just like that, Nick's voice was gone, but Max had heard all he needed. His psychiatrist didn't know what to make of all that he had just witnessed. Brainspotting could get intense, he knew that, but from what he could tell, he had just watched a young man go through a full out-of-body experience. He would have to wait to do more evaluation to understand what had gone on while Max was in his trance, but it was clear that whatever he experienced had an immediate, profound effect on him.

Without realizing it, Max started to tremble, and he let out a soft cry. It was so soft, his doctor couldn't even hear his crying as tears almost silently streamed down his face. He shook lightly, like a feather delicately resisting being swept up by the passing wind. He had been broken for such a long time, but he didn't feel that way anymore. Nick was okay. He knew that now, and he knew it more certainly than he'd ever known anything. Slowly, he wiped the tears away and gathered his emotions. Gently, he removed his headphones and set them down. Then he stood up and shook his doctor's hand.

"Thanks, man," Max told him. "I'm good."

"What?" his doctor was at a loss for words. He had never seen anything quite like what had just transpired, and obviously a breakthrough like this one would have to be documented, analyzed and monitored. This could be the beginning of real, outstanding progress for his young patient who had just recently seemed utterly hopeless.

"I'm good, dude," he said again. "I'll see you later," eliciting another blank, confused stare from the psychiatrist. Max placated him with a warm smile, the first genuine one he had issued anyone in months. "Thank you so much, that was really helpful," he told the doctor. "It's all going to be fine." He really believed it.

Unable to provide further explanation of what had just happened—and seeing no real point in trying—Max left the clinic, never to return again. He was in a hurry; he had to get to Ashland baseball practice. After months of turmoil and looking for purpose, suddenly Max had inner peace. He also had direction again. It's no surprise which direction he found himself pointing. Baseball had taken so much from him physically, mentally, and emotionally up to this point, but he decided he still had some soul left to sell to the game.

As he threw batting practice to a bright, hopeful new group of Ashland ballplayers, the Oregon State High School champion and former Sierra College outfielder had a new plan crystallizing in his mind. When an idea came as clearly to him as this one did, then for all intents and purposes, it was already a reality. He was turning back toward the sense of conviction which his grandfather and big brother had ingrained in him long ago as he came up in the shadows of Etna's solitary water tower. He hadn't been able to count on that conviction to propel him to achieve new heights for some time. He had stagnated because he was afraid of the future and was unwilling to let his brother go. But now that he knew for certain that Nick had moved on, he could, too. It was time to make his own way.

Max served up pitch after pitch into the wheelhouse of each respective hitter, greasing them up with a round of BP to close out practice. He thought about the little card in his wallet, the one onto which he had written Pat Casey's number, courtesy of Sam Gaviglio.

I know exactly what to do with that thing now.

Chapter 11

A New Way Forward

Max stared at his phone screen blankly. He swiped through his contacts until he landed on the name he was looking for, "Pat Casey." Sam Gaviglio, who was in the middle of a rough sophomore slump, had given Max his coach's number simply because he asked. Max was finally turning a corner with his depression and was ready to do something for himself. He decided to see what he could do, if anything, to make some impression on the Oregon State program he grew up watching.

As the line started ringing, Max realized that the coach wouldn't recognize his number and would likely screen it to his voicemail; he had to be ready with what he wanted that message to say. As he started running through possible greetings in his head, he was stopped dead in his tracks.

"Yeah, this is Pat Casey," the voice of the legendary skipper crackled onto the other end of the line.

There was no time to prepare. It was showtime.

Max jumped right in, his heart pounding, "Hi, my name is Max Gordon, I'm a friend of Sam Gaviglio, and I'd really love an opportunity to come up and talk to you about playing baseball for Oregon State."

Coach Casey was moved by how badly Max had always wanted to be a part of his squad. Max detailed to the coaching legend how he had watched in awe as the Beavers won two straight titles a few years prior. Although he was a fan of Sam Gaviglio and knew his vote of confidence was worth something, Casey still couldn't make Max any promises since the Beavers were in-season at the time. There was also the simple fact that Max was an undersized player who had limited power. That was not generally the type of player who fit into a powerhouse program like Oregon State. If he went down this road, it would be fraught with adversity. Coach Casey told him that he could call back in a few weeks, and they would at least set him up a time to visit the campus.

Coach Casey thought back to when he had briefly seen Max play for the Mustangs, an American Legion team that was always a state power in Oregon and which always had a couple of players with Division 1 upside. *This guy is very, very aggressive*, Coach Casey remembered thinking as he watched Max in the outfield and on the bases. *He loves to play the game, he's a spark plug, dirt dog. This is a guy who loves to put on the uniform, play and get dirty.*

When Casey saw Max and the Mustangs play, he ran into Michelle Gordon in line at the concession stand. Michelle already knew who he was and very much wanted Max to play for him some day.

"What does Max have to do to be able to play for you?" Michelle had asked.

"He has to be just a little bit faster," Coach Casey had replied. "Just a little bit faster."

Max wasn't going to hit home runs, and he didn't have a cannon of an arm in the outfield, so his superior speed had always been his only tangible physical edge; now, as he pondered taking on the game's next level, he knew he would need to find even more of it.

Years after that conversation took place, the stage was now set: Max had spoken to Coach Casey, and the first semblance of a plan began to take shape. His parents no longer had to ask about when he planned to go back to school. He casually brought it up at the house one day.

"I'm driving up to Corvallis to meet with Coach Casey," Max mentioned.

"What? Did he call?" Michelle asked.

"No, I'm going to meet with him," her son replied.

Stan and Michelle shared a look. They had seen this before.

"Doesn't he need to have some type of conversation with you first?" she asked.

He explained to his mom just what was going to happen, his demeanor rock-solid and his tone matter-of-fact. While he didn't know where his conversation with Coach Casey would lead, he knew it was somewhere better than where he was now.

That's just how Max broke things to his parents. He wouldn't say anything until all the details were dialed in perfectly, and then he'd drop the news on them. It had been that way since he was little and had unilaterally committed himself to play Midget Football 30 minutes away, no small amount of time for his parents to spend dropping him off and picking him up five times a week. But Max always had the logistics figured out and so, even having their doubts, his parents held their tongues, trusting that he at least had a plan. They were, however, mildly skeptical; they knew how little was guaranteed, especially for a player like Max at a program as prestigious as Oregon State. He seemed so determined and sure of himself, they just didn't want to see him run himself into another brick wall with his vigilance. They still remembered vividly how close they'd just been to losing him again.

Max could sense his parents' hesitation, and he used that as extra motivation. When someone told him he couldn't do something or he thought someone was doubting him, he would do everything in his power to prove them wrong. He wasn't upset that his parents weren't totally enthusiastic about the plan right away; he knew as well as they did how steep the odds were, but after everything he'd been through, he knew ultimately that he held his fate in his own hands.

Josh Scarminach was back in town working on his apprenticeship, and the pair hadn't been able to see much of one another recently. Not yet knowing any details of his hoped-for meeting with Coach Casey, Max turned to the only thing he knew how to control fully: his work ethic. He and Josh were reunited and started training for an Iron Man, waking up at dawn to go running, biking, and swimming. It was therapeutic for both of them as they reached a critical juncture in their lives. Josh was done playing football and was entering the working world, finally focusing on making a living for himself. Max was done playing at Sierra College and had only one major lead to follow at this point in his life.

After a while, the pair could no longer confine their workouts to early mornings. Each would follow up with work all day and then would do more power lifting at night. It was just like old times, with each friend pushing the other to squeeze all he could out of every rep. "He'd always look forward to seeing me and I'd look forward to seeing him," Josh remembers. "It was amazing having a partner that boosted morale so much. His character was inspiring, because he was still hurting for his brother. But I never talked to him about it."

Max was ready to put that behind him and write his next chapter. He still thought about Nick constantly, but it was in a much more healthy and accepting way. He knew that his brother would be with him on some level for the rest of his life, but he also knew that the only way to honor him was to let him go and live a life which they both could be proud of. For the first time in years, he felt he was the author of his own fate. Finally, he was able to iron out the details with Coach Casey and they scheduled a meeting on campus, where they could chat about Oregon State and what next steps he could take.

Max was never the type to relax when he had something big to look forward to; a heavy undertaking or major event only made him more vigilant and laser-focused. The three-hour drive to Corvallis for his Oregon State visit was no exception. He spent the entire time in the car looking out the window, ruminating over how the first interactions with Casey and the Oregon State program would go. He was torturing himself, but there was nothing that would slow his train of thought for more than a few seconds at a time.

Max had no idea what to expect as he headed north on I-5 toward Goss Stadium, the Beavers' home field. He thought back to his first interaction with Rob Willson, a coach rather similar to Pat Casey in style and attitude. Max remembered being intimidated by Willson the first time they met, and he expected another meeting along those lines when he met with one of the most accomplished head coaches in college baseball.

Luckily, Max left early, because he got turned around the instant he arrived on campus. He walked into the administration building, wondering if he had found the right place. He looked lost, and he was. After the woman at the front desk managed to figure out exactly what he was trying to do, she helped him find Gill Coliseum, where the Beavers' basketball team played and where all athletic department employees were quartered. It was also clear on the other side of campus from where Max currently stood.

Max hopped back in his car and tried navigating over to the athletics section of campus, finally stumbling upon his destination. He saw Goss Stadium, parked, and began walking. He strolled in and paced through the different sporting departments until he reached the area devoted to the baseball program. When he found it, he did not walk in right away. Instead, he took a moment to breathe, visualize, and energize before one of the biggest meetings of his life.

"Well, here we go," he thought, sensing that very soon he would know whether Oregon State was a possibility or a pipe dream. Max knew what he was about to attempt was an extremely improbable feat, but Oregon State was the only worthwhile program with whom he had any sort of inroad. For all he knew, Coach Casey was simply taking the meeting as a courtesy to him. He paid no attention to these possibilities which were outside of his control. He had wanted an opportunity to tell his story and make a case for himself to Pat Casey, and he had it. Everything that happened from here out was on him.

Just don't say anything stupid, Max chided himself as he made his final mental preparations.

Finally, he pushed his way through the doors of the baseball area and asked to see Pat Casey. After a short wait, he was summoned back to Coach Casey's office. As he headed back, he could see in through the open door. Over Casey's shoulders, he saw two national championship trophies and a slew of Pac-10 titles. Instantly, Max knew he was in the presence of a winner.

Here, right before his eyes, was the man he had watched lead Oregon State to back-to-back national championships. He thought back to legendary performances shepherded by this icon in the baseball world. He had watched those games with his Ashland High School teammates and with current Beavers pitcher Sam Gaviglio, and he had discussed those improbable championship runs with his brother, Nick. Now he stood in the presence of greatness. After a moment, it spoke to him:

"Hi, Max. Have a seat."

CHAPTER 12

Legend

In the early 1960s, in the quiet town of Newberg, Oregon, a young Patrick Casey could be found romping around the playground of St. Peter's Catholic School. It was the dawning age of modern sports, and he could not get enough of them. He played anything he had—or could figure out how to make—the equipment for. He was insatiable. His grade school was extremely small, and it placed an emphasis on athletics. Sports were a way to teach discipline, but also a way to have fun. From a very young age, he didn't just love to play, but also loved to grind, battle and win. He was an incredibly intense competitor as far back as he can remember.

"I just wanted to be in athletics," Casey recalls. "I wanted to be around competition, be around people, and be around winning. That always seemed to come naturally to me."

Baseball ended up winning his heart, though he was also an excellent basketball player. As he matriculated through Renee Junior High and Newberg High School, he started catching the attention of college scouts. In the end, he elected to stay in Oregon, the state in which he had lived his entire life. He did so by way of a commitment to attend the University of Portland and, of course, join their baseball program. Casey knew, however, that he wasn't going to stop at Division 1 ball. He had his sights set on the majors, and he soon found out he had the skill set to see his dream through. He developed into a pro prospect and was selected by the San Diego Padres in the 10th round of the 1980 MLB Draft.[1]

The ebb and flow of pro ball caught him off-balance for a while. His small town in the Pacific Northwest hadn't offered him the same resources as major programs in states like Texas, Florida, and California. Although he had traveled small distances for tournaments and showcases, he was now competing against young men who had been representing national programs and traveling the country for years. He had some apprehension about fitting into the road lifestyle of a major league club. Thus, it came as a bit of relief for Casey when he found out he'd be able to stay in the Pacific Northwest for one more year, playing his first minor league season in Walla

Walla, Washington, with the Padres' Low-A Ball affiliate. After one season of home cooking, it was on to the true grind of minor league baseball. He played in four cities in three years, moving from Reno, Nevada, to Salem, North Carolina, to Amarillo, Texas, and finally to Beaumont, Texas.

After four years of trudging through the minor league system, Casey found himself playing Double-A ball; gradually, the first cracks started forming in his psyche as he wondered if he would ever get the shot at the majors which he had made his life's goal. One day, his fortune seemed to change. He was called into his manager's office and informed that he was part of a trade with the Seattle Mariners. He would be sent back to the Pacific Northwest in anticipation of the 1985 MLB season. Instantly, he was optioned to the team's Triple-A affiliate in Calgary, one step away from the big leagues. Had he been ready to perform in this moment, Casey thinks he could have taken that final step. "I certainly feel I had the talent to make it to the majors," Casey says. "But I never really understood what I should be doing in the off-season. I never lifted weights or did anything that is just common in today's game."

As so many do, he struggled to make that last leap, the one that would land him a big league roster spot and a chance to prove himself. While the road warrior life was tough, Casey was also having the time of his life along the way. Throughout his minor league career, which included one Winter Ball season in Colombia, he cherished the relationships he forged. These experiences also helped him realize just how much instruction young ballplayers need. He felt that he could have used a little bit more hands-on guidance from his coaches during his pro ball journey, and he had a feeling that he could offer that to the next generation of players. He had always been someone to whom his teammates came for advice and pointers, even though by the time he reached pro ball, he was rarely the most physically gifted on the team. He had a deep love and understanding for competition itself, and he respected the game of baseball as competition's shining example. One could say he was born to be a baseball coach.

He still had some playing to do, however; Casey put up very good numbers in his two seasons in Calgary, posting slash lines of .265/.375/.469 and .307/.408/.539 respectively with a combined 31 homers and 120 RBI. Seattle finished the season 67–95 in 1986, but the man getting the majority of playing time at Casey's first base position was Alvin Davis, who had won the 1984 American League Rookie of the Year Award. The organization made it abundantly clear that they would be sticking by Davis, regardless of his diminished numbers in his sophomore campaign of 1985.

Casey got called up to play in a Spring Training game for the Mariners along with Danny Tartabull. They reported to Hi-Corbett Field in Arizona to take on the Cleveland Indians. In his first at-bat in a Mariners' uniform,

Casey smashed a home run off of Vern Ruhle, a pitcher who would win 67 big -league games. It showed Casey that he could play at the highest level, but it became increasingly clear that he would never get that chance with the Mariners.

With nowhere to go in Seattle, Casey signed with the Minnesota Twins for the 1987 season. Immediately, he felt the pressure to perform with Minnesota. He was now 28, and if he didn't do something to distinguish himself from the pool of minor league talent soon, his time in organized baseball would be over. Casey knew he had the connections and the longevity to have a career and provide for himself for several more seasons at the Triple-A level, but the fierce competitor in him couldn't fathom doing that. It was all or nothing. Either he would crack a major league roster or he would find something else to do with his life.

After 48 games with the Portland Beavers, Minnesota's Triple-A affiliate, the Twins released Casey, who was hitting just .215 with three home runs. A week after he was released, he got a call from Paul Berry, the athletic director at George Fox University, an NAIA school. Berry asked if Casey would be interested in a coaching position with the George Fox baseball team; the school is located in Newberg, the town in which he grew up. Quickly, Casey told him he was not. He understood that his playing career had probably run its course, but he also had his family and quality of life to consider.

Pat Casey was married with two kids and had no desire to coach at a small school in his hometown. It was time for him to make some real money. His dad was a sole proprietor in real estate and had suggested that his son get his real estate license, so he did. He started piecing together the first image of his life after baseball; he would sell properties and secure a solid living for his family. Then Paul Berry called again. Berry asked Casey if he would at least visit campus, meet the president, and look around the facilities. Having been born and raised in Newberg and not having forgotten his manners, Casey obliged. In his mind, it was a formality; however, it ended up being the decision that changed his and his family's lives forever.

The job paid $3,000 a year, hardly enough to make a living at the time. His first call was to his best friend, Ron Northcutt, whom he had wanted to join his staff.

"Hey, I don't know what you're doing, but are you making any money?" he asked.

"No," Ron replied.

"Perfect. I have a job for you where you're not going to make any money either," Casey laughed. He had found himself a pitching coach.

Once he got used to life as a baseball coach, everything started falling into place for Pat Casey. He was still selling real estate on the side, but his job at George Fox took up the majority of his time. As an NAIA program, George Fox left its head coach to do it all; from coaching to recruiting to building cages, manicuring fields, organizing fundraisers, and more. He was their GM, maintenance supervisor, and disciplinary officer. If he had said one too many prayers, he would have become their priest. The hours were long, the days were grueling, and the pay was lousy. But Casey was having a blast.

Some part of Casey knew this lifestyle wouldn't be sustainable forever. He was working way too hard for way too small a paycheck. He needed extra income, but he refused to give up on the job and the program he loved in the town where he had spent most of his life. The solution was to sleep less and find a second job. The Abby's Pizza near campus often hosted baseball recruits, and in need for extra cash, Casey took a job there. He was the pizza parlor's janitor; he woke up at 5:30 in the morning to head down to the parlor and clean. Back home, he would shower and change clothes before heading down to his baseball office and getting everything in order for the long day ahead. Occasionally, the team took morning batting practice, and he had to facilitate that too. He checked with the proper authorities to make sure all his players were attending class and earning passing grades before heading out to the real estate office for a few hours of work before afternoon practice.

During practice, he gave every ounce of energy he had left, teaching lessons and doing anything in his power to drain every ounce of effort out of his players. After practice, it was back home for dinner, to spend a couple of hours with his family before heading to bed and doing it all over again. The 16- to 18-hour days would not be sustainable forever, but Casey was earning the respect of his players and was seeing results on the field.

He assumed he'd spend the next couple of years of his life coaching just to get rid of the competitive juices left over from his professional playing career. The more immersed he got, though, the more he realized it wasn't a passing fancy. He began to understand that coaching could be his life's vocation.

"You start to realize how important leadership is and how much kids need direction," Casey explains. "I enjoyed how much of a struggle it was. It inspired me that kids at that level really wanted to be good and to win. I'd been in professional baseball where development and moving up in the organization, to a lot of people, is more important than winning. To all get to where our whole common goal was to win and do that together, that was truly inspiring."

Pat Casey viewed his first job as a trial by fire. He was never an assistant, never a scout; from the very beginning, he was the skipper and was responsible for the fate of the entire program. As it turned out, George Fox was the ideal incubator for his competitive spirit as a manager. He was allowed to take risks, to be bold and make mistakes as he honed his leadership style and re-learned the game from a new perspective. His Bruins experienced steady progress year by year, improving from a 15–14 record in his maiden season to 31–13 by 1994, his seventh year in charge. They had won themselves a District championship, knocking Linfield from its perch. That very achievement was something Casey had made the onus of his team's last several campaigns. He found he was very good at finding what truly motivated a group of young men and leveraging those things to generate their most impressive performances. Still, after the 1994 season, he felt restless. He cherished his experience at George Fox and felt great pride at what the squad had accomplished with him at the helm. He knew, however, that the school was not a platform from which he could hope to launch a serious professional coaching career. It was time to make a change.

In his mind, he thought it might once again be time to do something different with his life. Now with three kids to take care of, he had to make serious money. Once again, it appeared that his time in the baseball world was up. He had proven to himself and others that he could coach at a high level, but that NAIA grind wouldn't be sustainable for much longer.

Sixty miles south of George Fox's campus, Oregon State's head coaching job opened up ahead of the 1995 season. Casey didn't see much use in applying; the consensus was that they would promote one of their assistants, Kurt Kemp. However, after seeing that Casey hadn't submitted his name, Oregon State administrator and Pac-10 North Commissioner Jack Rainey called him, wondering why. "I really think you should apply," Rainey appealed to him. "I'd really encourage you to apply."

Rainey also mentioned that longtime head coach Jack Riley, whose stepping down opened the position in the first place, had given Casey a nice endorsement before he left the program. Those endorsements truly meant something to Casey, plus he reckoned he had little to lose, so he put together a resume, drove down to Gill Coliseum, and dropped it off at the athletic department office. He handed his application to the athletic department secretary, and that was that. Casey walked out the door and drove home.

If I could just get an interview, Casey thought, *this thing could really be mine.*

He kept telling his wife, Susan, that if he got an interview, he was confident in his ability to make a strong case on his own behalf. This put the writing on the wall when he got the call that he was one of four finalists selected to interview for the position. It would be him, Bill Kinnenberg, Terry Pollreisz, and Kurt Kemp competing for the head coaching job.

In preparation for the big interview, Pat and Susan went to Portland's

Washington Square to buy him a sport coat, a new shirt, a new tie, new slacks, a new belt, a new pair of socks, and a new pair of shoes.

"Keep the receipt," Pat told his wife. "If I don't get the job, we're taking them back."

In his interview, donning his brand-new suit, Casey laid out his vision for the future of Oregon State baseball. He drew on his experiences working for an underfunded program. He knew they would have to raise funds to build better facilities if they wanted to attract top recruits to the Pacific Northwest. Just as he had always wanted to reach the next level of competition as an athlete and coach, Casey could sense that Oregon State was a program which wanted desperately to break into the next echelon of collegiate competition. He truly felt that he was the guy who could get them there. He outlined his belief that only once they were a regional staple, competing with the likes of UCLA and USC, could they become a legitimate contender for national championships.

The Beavers had reached the College World Series just one time prior to 1995, and they hadn't competed for college baseball's top prize in 43 seasons. They had stagnated and needed firm, forceful direction for their program. Casey's ambition and lively manner of delivering his message was striking to the hiring committee. "We can not only compete in the conference, but I think we can compete on the entire West Coast and eventually nationally," Casey told them. "I think we can build a huge facility and really do anything we imagine. I'm going to be honest with you, it's going to take hard work. It's going to take commitment."

"Most of all, it's going to take the right players and the right people," Casey closed before telling them his philosophy of developing a student-athlete, not just a baseball player. He walked out of the room knowing he had done all he could to put himself in position to get the call he really wanted.

In Dallas, Oregon, three of the four finalists were at the Summer American Legion State Baseball tournament scouting: Pat Casey, Kurt Kemp, and Terry Pollreisz were all there, and each had been told to expect the decision on the Oregon State job to be handed down sometime that weekend. Mike Corwin, the chairman of the selection committee for Oregon State, was the home plate umpire for the American Legion games they attended. As a result, a bizarre tension wove itself into the fanfare and liveliness of the whole affair.

Not everyone liked the calls Corwin made on the field that first day, but the following morning, Casey got the only call that mattered.

"Would you accept the Oregon State head coaching job if it were offered to you?" he was asked.

"Well, of course I would," Casey responded dumbfoundedly. "That's why I applied for it."

The pair went out to breakfast that morning, and Pat Casey was formally offered the position of head baseball coach at Oregon State University. He accepted, still unsure how his career could make such a momentous leap from George Fox to Oregon State so instantaneously. The first thing he thought to do was call his wife. Safe to say, she could go ahead and throw away the receipts for his new suit.

Casey's tenacity and determination became apparent from the moment he accepted the job; he hit the ground running, fundraising as hard as he coached, which, if you ask his players from that first season, was pretty damned hard. He knew that one of Oregon State's biggest challenges was that Corvallis did not have the same appeal as Palo Alto, Phoenix, or Los Angeles. That meant that if he hoped to attract the nation's best talent, Oregon State's facilities and resources had to be far superior to the likes of those upper-echelon Pacific-10 programs. His pitch to potential donors was simple. "I hope you know how passionate I am to help our program, student athletes and university grow," Casey would tell them. "You could be a part of that, and you could help young men who will go on to make people's lives and futures better."

He noticed early on that convincing people was far easier after befriending them, and making new friends was something for which Casey had always had a knack. He had an agreeable way about him, and everyone he met in the baseball world seemed to take an immediate liking to him. Before long, he had established a solid network of connections which he hoped would translate into donation dollars for his baseball program. He cemented himself as an asset to Oregon State University before he even had a real chance to prove himself on a baseball diamond. His progress surprised his superiors because he had achieved it with minimal institutional support.

When he took the job, they had been very up-front that their priority was to turn around their struggling football program. That afforded Casey far more freedom in his fundraising efforts than at other programs, but it also meant very little formal support from the university. Once he came back to them with handsome sums of money he had raised himself and was ready to spend on the baseball program, that got the ball rolling.

It took Casey just four years to help plan and fund Goss Stadium, the Beavers' new state-of-the-art facility, which vastly improved the baseball field which had opened in 1907. The stadium improvements debuted in 1999.[2] On March 12, the team fell to Barry Zito and his USC squad in their home opener. For the home fans at Goss Stadium, however, the game itself was not the true spectacle; the amenities of the new facility, featuring a dazzling new jumbo scoreboard, were impressive enough to grip their fascination all afternoon. Goss Stadium's opening was a testament to the athletic department and its commitment to baseball in the Pacific Northwest. It was also a sign of the progress they could achieve with a competitor like Pat Casey as their champion.

In the previous two years, 1997 and 1998, the Beavers had good seasons, but since teams in the Pac-10 South wouldn't play them, their RPI wasn't high enough to qualify them for a College World Series regional. Frustrated that those teams' refusal to face his team was keeping them from breaking into the upper echelon of Division 1 competition, Casey spearheaded an effort to combine the two divisions into one unified conference.

Not wanting to play the four teams in the Pac-10 North on a regular basis, the Pac-10 South teams tried to appease them (mostly Casey, the only one passionately pursuing the issue) by playing each team a combined nine times a season. However, the games wouldn't count on their record. Well, in 1998, Oregon State went a combined 7–2 against UCLA, Arizona, and USC, sweeping the Bruins and Wildcats before taking one of three from the Trojans.[3]

"You know, if you guys get to a Regional with that team, you have a chance to get to Omaha," USC head coach Mike Gillespie told Casey after their 1998 series.

Coach Casey was floored. Of course, the Beavers didn't get to a regional in 1998 and were never given the chance to compete on the national level. USC, meanwhile, won the national championship. After he saw that, Casey was convinced that perhaps Gillespie had really been onto something in his assessment of the Beavers' potential. There was a shift happening in college baseball, especially in the Northwest. It was one largely ushered in by Casey, and USC was simply the first program to seize the shift and cash in on it. Casey had a new determination; if Oregon State had proper facilities and a commitment to baseball, they could do what he had just watched the Trojans do.

Finally, in 1999, with Goss Stadium opening, the Pac-10 officially combined the North and South to play one another in games that counted. Nobody in the South outside of Gillespie was in favor of it. Gillespie didn't like the idea of it for his program's sake either, but he thought it would be good for the conference. Coaches and administrators from Pac-10 South schools warned that North schools were in for a rude awakening. The way they saw it, they had the weather, facilities, and tradition on their side. For the most part, they were right.

After a 1999 season which saw the Beavers limp to a 7–17 finish in conference play, Casey began to suspect as much. Had he made a mistake by helping force the Pac-10 South teams to play them? He realized he couldn't give in to the fear that 1999 could have brought out in him and his program.

The way for Oregon State to start competing with the Pac-10 South teams was for members of his program to change the way they thought, change the way they walked, change the way they talked. They needed to change the way they did everything. Each player and coach needed to change his attitude toward the environment. It wasn't the environment that was the problem; it was the attitude.

Pat Casey took it upon himself to be the barometer for change. If he was going to ask talented young men to follow him in his vision for the program, he had to lead by example. As much as he could do himself, he would expect from each of his players and staff. He hoped that with a bit of momentum, the program could build each year upon the progress and energy of the prior one. The road was still rough, as the team finished 9–15 in its second full season against the Pac-10 South. A marginal improvement saw them go 11–13 in 2001 and reaching the cusp of their first-ever regional appearance. All they needed was two wins against USC at home in a three-game series. In the opener, Mark Prior shut them out. In Game 2, the Beavers rebounded for a 6–0 win. In devastating fashion, they fell 1–0 in Game 3, which knocked them out of Regional contention. They had given up just one run in 18 innings, but fell heartbreakingly short.

The team fell back to 10–14 in 2002. Again in 2003, the team slipped to 7–17 in conference play. In Casey's first four seasons in the Pac-10, the team had a conference record of 44–76. The pressure was on, but Casey and his team stayed the course.

Behind future MLB All-Star, Jacoby Ellsbury, the Beavers started to feel differently going into the 2004 season. Although they still played little brother to their competition in the Pac-10 South, they could feel that they were on the verge of a breakthrough. After five full seasons in the conference without recording a single winning conference season, some wondered whether the new attitude was simply a foolhardy optimism; but everything was about to change. Those who had continued to believe in the team's vision, including Ellsbury and teammate Darwin Barney, knew they were on the cusp of something special. The next three years would change the program forever.

In 2005, the team went from having never finished above .500 in true Pac-10 play to dominating their competition, going 19–5 in the conference.[4] After winning seven of eight conference series, the Beavers were league champs. Breezing through their Regional, the road to the College World Series ran through Corvallis, with the Beavers hosting the Super Regional where one team would advance to Omaha.

It came down to Oregon State and none other than USC for a berth in the College World Series. After the Beavers took Game 1, the Trojans had to win two straight to end Oregon State's season. They overcame a five-run deficit in Game 2 to force a decisive Game 3, with the winner moving on to college baseball's biggest stage. In a slugfest, Andy Jenkins hit for the cycle, and star closer, Dallas Buck, sealed the deal in a 10–8 thriller that sent the Beavers to Omaha for the first time in 53 years. In his 11th season, Pat Casey had delivered on his promise to make the Beavers a national contender.

While they fell short of their ultimate goal in 2005, it merely set the stage for the heroics of 2006 and 2007, when the team took home back-to-back national championships, the first in school history. As a high school baseball player, Max Gordon watched those teams. He was the first generation of Oregon kids who saw baseball as a fixture in his region, and it was due almost entirely to the steady, heroic efforts of coach Pat Casey.

Casey had learned what it was like to steer a team toward a title. He had taken three straight Beavers teams to the College World Series and had won twice. With the help of his vision and enough players buying into it, he had reached the mountaintop he had promised in his meeting with the hiring committee more than a decade prior. There was no doubt baseball was now the most popular sport on Oregon State's campus, and with winning came culture and talent. All of a sudden, the best players in the country were seriously considering playing their college seasons in Corvallis.

Well into middle age by this time, Casey was connecting to his players on a much more personal level and took as many lessons from them as they did from him. "I not only inspire my players," Casey explains, "but I'm inspired by them. The more trust I put in my players, the more I got to know them. It's common now for a player to say, 'Hey Coach, I love you.'"

It was his intimate connection to his players that made Pat Casey such a beloved coach over the decade and a half leading up to the 2011 season. He was now tasked with getting a team back to Omaha after a three-year drought, one that seemed long based on the standard of success he had taken 15 years to build. As he prepared the 2010 squad to be the one to do it, he received a phone call from a young prospect from Ashland. He listened to him explain how he'd grown up watching the Beavers, how their national championship runs inspired his Grizzlies to win their first state title, and how it had been his dream for as long as he could remember to play baseball in Corvallis.

"When you have a guy come in whose dream has been to play for the Oregon State baseball team," Coach Casey says, considering the state of the program when he came on board in 1995, "that's pretty inspiring to have kids like that."

As this Gordon kid, whom Casey vaguely remembered seeing in an American Legion tournament years ago, stepped into his office, he wasn't sure where he fit into the mix. He certainly wasn't a scholarship player, but perhaps he could show him something in the fall. With Oregon State now long-established as a college baseball power, Casey had plenty of talent coming in; getting talented players was no longer the challenge it once was. He needed players with heart, with passion, who could drive up the needle of his entire team just by being in the dugout. He thought back to his professional baseball days, remembering how he had wished the right person would take a chance on him. One of the things he cherished most about the position in which he found himself now was the ability to be the one taking that chance on young men he found particularly special.

After hearing Max's story, Casey got the type of feeling to which his decades as a coach had taught him to pay attention; Max Gordon was the least of his considerations when he outlined everything he would have to do to get his team back to Omaha in the coming season, but as he looked across his desk, he saw a man who had gone through Hell to be sitting there. If the Beavers were going to make it back to the promised land, Casey knew they would need to bring a few fighters with them.

CHAPTER 13

Trailer

Max settled into his seat in Pat Casey's office as he listened to the legendary coach speak. He could immediately tell why Casey was so effective, what made him a winner: the man spoke with such confidence and certainty that he instilled it in whoever listened to him. It was no wonder he had built the Oregon State program up from nothing. Each came into this meeting with a separate agenda. Max wanted to make a great first impression on the coaching staff, while Casey simply wanted to share some of his own stories and discuss the ways Oregon State could be good for Max's well-being, not just his baseball career.

"I really enjoyed that conversation," Coach Casey recalls. "Max wanted somebody to give him the opportunity to climb the mountain nobody thought he could climb. I thought it was important to let him know I'd give him that opportunity and that life isn't easy for everybody."

Whatever time it took, Max assured Coach Casey that, if he were given an opportunity, he would ride it out and would continue working until the coaching staff told him he couldn't do it anymore. He still felt a twinge of regret over not finishing what he had started with Sierra, even though it was ultimately the right choice for his health. He would never leave another team without finishing what he had started. That struck a chord with Casey, who could tell that Max wasn't one to simply talk the talk. His story was intriguing, and the coach thought that perhaps a chapter of that story was meant to be written in Corvallis, even if that only meant spending the fall with the team as he tried out.

"You almost never go out and recruit a guy of his size," Casey explains. "In our sport, you measure power, arm strength, and speed. I didn't feel he had the arm strength, the power, the bat, or flat-out raw speed at his size. But there's one thing you can't see, and that's the size of a man's heart."

Pat Casey is aware of the existence of MRI machines; of course, he was speaking about the great depth of Max's competitive spirit. The two talked for close to an hour and a half as practice time approached. Casey leaned back in his chair, feet up on the desk, while Max continued to sit with his hands cupped nervously in his lap. "Well, you know, Max, I have to get ready for practice," Coach Casey told him. "We're doing some early work. Why don't you get some lunch, come back and come out to practice. I'll introduce you to Pat Bailey, our outfielders coach."

Max shook Coach Casey's hand, took his advice on where to grab some lunch, and joined practice to meet with more coaches. He couldn't be more thrilled. When he went to the meeting, part of him suspected that it would be a brief formality and that Pat Casey would smile, thank him for making the trip and wish him luck, and that would be the end of it. He did not expect the conversation to be all that productive, and he certainly didn't expect the invitation to audit the Beavers' practice. He was getting an up-close look at his dream, and it got the blood pumping just that much harder through his veins.

While awaiting further instruction, Max chatted with Sam Gaviglio as well as an ex-junior college teammate who was on the team. Then Coach Casey, whom Max quickly learned was referred to by the whole team affectionately as "Case," called him over and introduced him to Coach Bailey before heading back to his drill.

The two shook hands and made small talk, Bailey telling Max a little bit about what the program was about and walking him around some of the facilities. Bailey was in his third year as a Pat Casey assistant, and he knew that the program didn't invite just anyone to fall tryouts, so when he asked Max what his plans were for the following season, he was listened closely to the answer.

"Are you going to be here to try out in the fall?" he asked. Max was beside himself.

"Absolutely. I will be here without a doubt," Max answered emphatically. He was overjoyed. This was one of the best invitations he'd ever received, without question. Just like that, he had the chance he needed.

After everything through which Max had to persevere to get to this opportunity, he was slightly surprised at how easily it had been presented to him. He wasn't used to having the character and story speak for itself. "I was prepared to do this whole 'have to prove myself' thing, having to keep communication going and all these different odds and ends," Max remembers. "I was prepared to put myself through all that in order to give myself a chance, and then they're just like, 'Hey, here's an opportunity, want it?' It caught me off guard, but it was really exciting."

The drive back to Ashland had a completely different energy from the drive up. Max was thrilled that he had secured the opportunity he needed, but he also felt the renewed pressure and urgency of facing unfavorable odds.

> I fell back into who I became months after the accident. It made me really happy that I could be that person again. I had something to look forward to, something

to hold onto. I had hope. That really was what it was. That whole drive back, I thought, "I can't wait to get back because I have work to do. I can't waste a single day, a single second, because I have something to be ready for." If this was going to happen at all, I literally couldn't waste any sort of time.

He hadn't played organized baseball in several months and was currently in no shape to try out for a roster spot at Oregon State. His body was still in good shape, but the baseball muscle memory was a little rusty. If he wanted to be prepared come the fall, he had to play for a Summer League team. He had been out of the game for so long, though, that he didn't know where to turn. Feeling like he was out of options, he reached out to the man whose junior college squad he had spurned in favor of Sierra College.

"Listen, I know I never played for you and you don't have to do this," Max said to Terry Baumgartner, the head coach at Feather River College, whom he had met years ago and was now calling out of the blue. "But do you know of any summer teams that I could play for? I'm getting ready to play at Oregon State and I need to see some live pitching."

"Let me look into it," Baumgartner responded, "and I'll get back to you as soon as I find something out."

Terry Baumgartner was the embodiment of what a college baseball coach ought to be. He cared for the players he recruited as well as coached, and he had a special place in his heart for Max. He loved the way the small, scrappy outfielder played the game, and although Max had chosen not to play for him, he could tell that in Max, there was something unique, something different about the way he played the game. His motor ran more uniquely than most of the other players he'd seen come through the junior college level.

"I didn't want him to get lost in the shuffle," Baumgartner remembers. "I just wanted to help him out, help him get back on his feet, and I knew people."

Baumgartner used those connections and reached back out to Max a few days later. He had found an opening, which was no easy task given how late in the spring he was looking. "I found you a team in Portland," he told Max. "It's a small, four-team league, and they'll take you up there. I'm not sure if they're going to keep you or not, so you're going to have to play your way onto it."

That's all Max needed to hear. Again, he had an opportunity. Much like Oregon State, there was no guarantee, but he would take things one team at a time. He had to earn playing time in order to continue getting live at-bats that summer. Max never forgot what Coach Baumgartner had done for him, and it helped forge a relationship that would only grow in the years to come. With a place to play for the summer, the Gordons now had to figure out where Max would stay in Portland over the next few months.

"Oh, I have this girlfriend, Leslie, who lives in Gresham," Michelle realized. "I'm just going to call Leslie." Gresham is on the outskirts of Portland metro, near where Max's home games would be that summer. Max had never heard of Leslie in his life. Who were these people his mom was talking about? "Oh, Chad and Leslie, they're awesome," his mom assured him. "I was in their wedding."

This was news to him. Leslie and Michelle had met in the early 1980s while working at Bearings Incorporated in Tigard, Oregon. Michelle had gotten into the business through her dad, Norman, and the two worked together for a couple of years. Michelle was Leslie's boss and the pair got along great; by the time Michelle reached out on Max's behalf, though, the two hadn't spoken in years.

Leslie was thrilled to talk to her old friend again as she explained Max's situation. Michelle told her she was the first person she thought of, partly because the two had played softball together all those years ago. "Who better than a good friend who's a good softball player to call than you?" Michelle asked playfully.

"Give me a day or two to think about it," Leslie told her friend. "I need to talk it over with Chad, and I'll give you a call back and let you know."

Leslie and Chad had no kids of their own. They had decided they didn't want any. Would bringing a 19-year-old with such an intense situation into their home be a good idea? They went back and forth as Chad was wary of interacting for months with a teenager they'd never met. In his eyes, they could do it, but if things went south fast, they would have to pull the plug. By the end of the conversation, they thought that it wouldn't be too much of an imposition, and it might be nice to do something good for an old friend in need. Plus, they both loved baseball, so they figured going to games and supporting Max when they could might actually be sort of fun. Ultimately, after days of consideration, Leslie informed Michelle that the pair would love to host Max as he attempted to get playing time with this new summer team in Portland.

Max began his drive up toward Portland and called Leslie to figure out where to meet. They decided on Mount Hood Community College, where Max's summer team would play its home games. They met there a few hours later, introducing themselves and exchanging a few words before getting back into their cars. Max followed Leslie home, where Chad was waiting with everything set up for his stay.

He could either stay in the couple's guest room or in the motorhome right outside the house. Since the motorhome had WiFi and cable, it was a no-brainer to Max. He'd stay in the motorhome, his own little apartment for the summer.

Leslie made dinner for the three of them that night, and the summer was officially under way. Max was now living with two people who, until roughly a month before, he didn't even know existed. This was the most important summer of his life, and he had no familiarity or comfort to fall back on. He was out on his own, the way he saw it, and he had just one goal.

Both Leslie and Chad understood that Max was a 19-year-old kid and wanted his privacy. They were laid back and let him be independent. Leslie would text Max when dinner was ready. He could come inside and join them, or he could stay out in the trailer if he preferred. The arrangement went swimmingly for both parties, and after a short time Max had settled into a quaint, unassuming life with Chad and Leslie which gave him the comfort and reliability he needed in order to do everything he could on the field with his new team.

The couple made it out to several of Max's games and watched him interact with his teammates. Their favorite part was watching him point up to the sky between pitches. As Christians, it touched them to know that he believed in something. He never took them up on their offer to join them at church, but they smiled each time they saw him practice faith in his own way. Of course, none of their initial concerns about taking in an unknown teenager ever came to fruition. They actually loved having Max around.

"We never wanted kids, but Max made me at least think, 'Man, did we make the right decision by doing that?'" Leslie recalls. "And I know we did, but we just really enjoyed having him around, because he always thinks of others first."

The couple was struck by Max's politeness and respectful conduct. This was not how they expected a 19-year-old kid to act, especially not one who had been through what he had. Chad felt that Max had a very calming effect on them. He was always smiling and asking what he could do to help. He was a far cry from the Max of a year ago who had practically accosted his own father for asking him to do a simple chore. "We have some good friends who don't suck the energy out of the room," Chad explains. "They're just easy. That's how I'd describe Max. He's easy."

As the summer wore on, Max worked hard enough to secure a permanent roster spot for the season. Slowly but surely, his team emerged as the best of the four in the league. With each week, he, Leslie, and Chad learned more and more about one another. One thing they all learned quickly was that Max was not a "cat person." Their cat had a way of sniffing out people like him, and it tormented him in whatever ways it could. After a whole summer of torture, however, he even began to begrudgingly enjoy the cat by the season's end. He was sort of a sucker for pain. In time, Max was affectionately referred to by Leslie and Chad as their "Summer Son."

The good times off the field rolled right onto it as Max's team went on to win its league behind head coach Bryan Donohue, who was also the head coach at Mount Hood Community College, where they played their home games. "Hey man, if Oregon State doesn't work out, I want you back here," Donohue told Max. "I'll even try to find some scholarship money for you."

Max was very grateful, but he knew he was going straight to his friend Terry Baumgartner at Feather River if his dream of playing at Oregon State wasn't meant to be. Either that or he would be done with baseball altogether.

With the summer winding to a close, Max bid farewell to his "summer parents," Leslie and Chad, whose motorhome had been a much-needed place of refuge for him. He loved the solitude it provided. It allowed him to withstand the constant swirl of pressure and outside voices and just focus. On the drive back to Ashland, he thought about how much he would miss living that lifestyle. "We would have adopted him in a heartbeat," Leslie and Chad agreed at the end of the summer.

Once he arrived back in Ashland, the search was on for a place for Max to stay in Corvallis during the fall. It was one of many things he had to do in order to be squared away at Oregon State. Before his summer season, he had already received a letter in the mail telling him he was NCAA eligible, which was not a foregone conclusion. His grades had slipped at Sierra in the first semester of his sophomore year, and he wasn't positive that both the university and the NCAA would make him eligible right away. With NCAA clearance and the summer now behind him, he was ready to do the baseball part. But where was he going to live?

There was, of course, Sam Gaviglio, but he was already staying in a one-bedroom apartment with his brother, Gus, who was sleeping on the living room couch. "Dude, if you want to crash on the couch for as long as you need, that's fine," Sam told his pal.

Especially after his months in the motorhome, however, Max did not see this as a desirable living arrangement even in his desperate situation. Plus, if Gus was staying on the couch, that really meant that Max would be crashing on the floor. He couldn't imagine getting the training and practice done that he needed if he was stiff from sleeping on a hard floor every night. With a relatively tight budget, it was tough for the Gordons to find something suitable. Making matters worse was the simple fact that Max's actual chances of making the Oregon State roster were fairly slim. If they got locked into a one-year lease, they would still be on the hook, even if he left school after the first semester. After a long bout of consideration, Max finally conjured up an idea that might actually work.

"Hey, do you guys care if I take the trailer up there?" he asked his parents.

"That's not a bad idea," his dad replied, while Michelle quickly and sternly said, "No, you can't live in a trailer."

The Gordons had a trailer similar to the motorhome Chad and Leslie let Max live in for the summer. Max did some research and found a lot that was in their price range and which provided month-to-month leases. The family wasn't using its trailer much at the time, so it was available to him. In Max's mind, it was perfect, because he could leave nearly at any time and not be locked into a lease. Finally, his mom relented, and the family made plans to move him up to Corvallis in the Gordon family trailer. His solitary motorhome aesthetic was preserved, and Max was relieved to know where he would lay his head during the most trying months of his athletic career.

Stan hooked the trailer to his pickup and followed Max's car up to Corvallis. He cut bait on it, and Max parked right next to it. That was the extent of his initial set-up. He had picked out a corner lot with two big trees off to the side. There were pastures behind the trailer, and out his front window he could see rodeo grounds. It was a bit reminiscent of the Scott Valley, where Max had grown up. He and his dad set up netting between the trees where he could do tee work at home without disturbing the neighbors. He didn't need plumbing or running water, but he needed somewhere where he could do tee work. Stan built a rig that allowed the balls to slide down the netting and back into the bucket, so his son could be more efficient with his practice hacks.

Also parked next to the trailer was the only slightly flashy thing Max owned: his bike with a side hack. It was what he rode to campus after getting multiple parking tickets. Who wanted to pay for a university parking pass anyway? He and Josh had created the side hack two summers prior when they had a little too much time on their hands. Both Josh and his dad, Michael, are talented welders, so the family had plenty of equipment. The friends had talked about adding a sidecar to Max's bike before, but they didn't know what to make it out of since they weren't going to pay the steep price for high-quality metal.

Suddenly, a light bulb went off inside Josh's head: they could take a grocery cart and use the metal from that. Without their parents being privy to any of it, they nabbed a grocery cart from Shop 'N Kart, where Nick used to work. From the store, they took turns pushing each other in the cart up to Josh's house. After they got another bike tire and a fork, Josh welded the pieces together to make a legit-looking side hack on Max's old BMX bike. They rode it to Ashland's Fourth of July parade that year. It became the talk of Oregon State as Max would ride it to Sam's house near campus, leave it in the tall weeds behind the building, and go to class. He was not Oregon State's most conventional student, but he was not there to be conventional. He wasn't really even there to be a student. He only had one thing in mind at all times, and that was baseball.

Max lived in isolation in his trailer. He got only three channels, so he

The trailer where Max lived during his first year at Oregon State, the 2011 campaign. His sidehack sits in front, ready to be used at a moment's notice.

wasn't distracted by cable. He had WiFi, but it was just barely fast enough for him to do his homework. There were no streaming shows or movies to take away from his focus. Mostly, he just sat in the trailer alone with his thoughts. He would lie around, make himself food, do homework, and obsess about the next day's plan. He would visualize every detail of how he would attack that day on the baseball field. Much like two years prior, Max took a business-like approach to his interactions with the team and staff. He wasn't there to make friends; he was essentially there to interview for the job for which he had waited his whole lifetime to apply.

"I didn't hang out with a lot of teammates," Max recalls. "I'd go to the cage for a while and hit with a handful of dudes and then I'd go home. Once I was home, I was home. I didn't leave."

Early in the fall, Coach Casey arranged an appointment for Max to take a short-term memory test with the university. After verifying through this test that he did, indeed, have short-term memory loss, Max was able to register for classes sooner and be eligible for classes with smaller sizes. It would also make tutors available whenever he wanted help with classwork or test prep. Casey's involvement in developing his players and getting them whatever resources they needed to be successful both on the field and in the classroom became apparent to Max from the beginning. He had never even laced up his cleats for Oregon State, and there was no guarantee that he ever would, but nonetheless Pat Casey wanted him to have what he needed in Corvallis.

Before even taking the test, Max exhibited the profundity of his memory loss. His appointment was set for nine in the morning, and after going to morning weights, Max completely forgot about it. In an all-time display of irony, he forgot about his memory test. He showed up to practice in the afternoon, and minutes in, Casey walked over to him.

"Oh, hey, Max, did you go to your short-term memory test?" he asked. Max was pretty sure his coach already knew the answer to his own question. It was only in this moment that Max himself realized he had forgotten to go.

"I'm so sorry, I forgot," Max assured him. "I'll reschedule it. I'll make it happen."

"You're going to do this to me?" Casey asked, somewhat surprising Max, "I bust my ass and do all these things to get you out on this field and you're going to skip out on me?"

Max felt his heart start pounding, as if he was hearing Casey through the head of a pin. He wasn't even yelling, but it felt like his coach was bringing his whole world down on him with his accusatory tone. He felt like he was letting down the one great man that had been willing to take a chance on him. He knew he had to get his act together.

No more excuses. From here on, everything has to be perfect.

Later that day, in the middle of practice, fellow outfielder, Mike Miller, asked what all the fuss was about during warmups. "Hey, what was Casey yelling at you about earlier?" he asked in between pop-ups in center field.

"Dude, I forgot my short-term memory loss test," Max replied.

Miller burst out laughing, totally losing his composure and laughing hard enough to turn completely red in the face. "Are you serious? He blew you up for that?" he asked, recovering from a good chuckle.

"Yeah," Max sheepishly replied, realizing that jokes about this moment weren't likely to end soon.

"Dude, he was getting into you," Miller said, not telling Max anything he didn't already know. After all, he'd been there.

"I know," Max replied, stepping up to take another fly ball and hoping to put the whole episode behind him.

Later in the fall, with Max playing left field and Miller playing in center, he once again attracted some unwanted attention. A ball was hit in between the two outfielders, nearly perfectly between them. The coaches had warned the outfielders never to call someone else off unless you're sure you are going to catch it. Not wanting to commit that cardinal sin and come up short, Max continued giving chase, not sure whether he could make the grab. Mike Miller did the same thing. Both players dove at the same time, Max's forearm caned Miller upside the head, and both went down in a heap.

It was an intrasquad scrimmage, and Max tried to take attention from the miscommunication by popping up and throwing the ball into the infield as quickly as he could. The only problem was that his forearm was still freshly numb from nailing his teammate in the face. His throw sailed near right field in foul territory rather than reaching its intended target at second base. The whole scene elicited confusion from everyone else involved in the scrimmage as they looked on.

In another intrasquad scrimmage, Max was summoned to hit against Josh Osich, a power lefty who clocked 95–97 MPH with his fastball. Osich was coming off Tommy John surgery, which forced him to miss the 2010 season, and was just working his way back to facing live hitting.[1] Max had been struggling at the plate the whole fall, even against his friend, Sam, who was coming off of a rough season. If he couldn't hit Sam, whom he was more familiar with, he had little confidence he could do much against this fireballing lefty.

That fall, Max was 0-for-7 against Sam, who himself had something to prove entering his junior campaign. He was coming off a disappointing sophomore season and knew he had to put together a solid junior year to get back on the radar of pro scouts. The pair faced each other in the Orange & Black Scrimmage held between the starters and the backups/fringe players. Though Max didn't have any success at the plate against Sam, the fact that he was even facing off with him signaled a significant step. "It was surreal seeing him in the box," Sam remembers of those fall showdowns, "but he looked like he belonged there. He wasn't out of place."

Max and his Ashland buddies had been following Sam's journey at Oregon State. They considered him the superstar of the group. When Max was ailing the previous spring, he joined some friends in watching Sam pitch at Goss Stadium. This time, he was in the batter's box against one of his best friends. It was as if everything had come full-circle. Sam was still here, Max was still here, and they were both still fighting for the same thing.

"I was pretty aggressive that fall," Sam remembers. "I had a rough sophomore year, I needed to make some changes, and I wasn't taking it easy on him. I was going after him like everybody else. At the same time, it is your buddy. That's one of your best friends, so it was a challenge, but he wouldn't expect me to take it easy on him."

If Sam wasn't taking it easy on Max, Josh Osich certainly wasn't either. The coaching staff knew that Osich had to face a lefty at some point, so that's when Max was called upon. Max felt lachrymose; he was always excited at the opportunity for an at-bat that fall, but he also dreaded the power and control of which Osich had firm command.

Osich's first pitch was a heater right down the middle. Beavers coaches had been preaching plate discipline, so Max watched it go by for strike number one. The second offering was a knee-buckling curveball, and Max couldn't pull the trigger, 0–2. Max was impressed by the sheer force and movement which Osich was able to harness. Trying to put him away, Osich pumped a fastball in on Max's hands, but the tiny outfielder was able to get around on it, spinning and pulling a frozen rope out to right field. Unfortunately for him, the ball went directly to the right fielder, and it was handled for the out. However, the sound of the solid contact had resonated through the park, and the onlookers wore measured looks of surprise. They'd sent the little newcomer up just to give Osich a look at a left-handed batter, not expecting him to offer much resistance. Instead, he had shown surprising bat speed and asserted himself as a formidable opponent at the plate.

The Osich at-bat was a turning point in fall camp. It was the point after which Max started playing with a little confidence. While he would never be a power hitter, the ball jumped off his bat just a little bit more. His teammates took notice, but he couldn't tell if the coaching staff did. With no margin for error, Max had to make sure to do every little thing Casey told him he must do to make the team. He had become an excellent bunter thanks to hours and hours of practice. He was hitting the cutoff man and running the bases well, being aggressive without running into outs. As he had always done, Max made sure to do all of the little things perfectly.

At some point, Max realized that for fringe players like himself, a roster spot came down to who was least consistently noticed making mistakes. He would look around and watch other outfielders get chewed out by the coaching staff for making mental mistakes, and he would take note of what his teammates did wrong. His vigilance once again became one of his chief assets as he made perfectly sure that he would never duplicate a mistake for which he saw a teammate get called out. He knew that unlike some of his teammates, he did not have the sheer talent or physical endowments to afford any of those miscues.

His parents called frequently to see how he was doing. They were completely in the dark regarding where he stood among his competition, especially since they knew many of the players for Oregon State were on scholarships.

"How are the other guys hitting the ball?" Stan would ask.

"Dad, everybody hits the crap out of the ball," Max told his dad, "They wouldn't be playing here if they weren't."

The only way to get a lot of attention from the coaching staff during the fall was to hit for power, clubbing home runs and extra-base hits. Max simply did not possess a power swing, so he had to trust that if the coaching staff never had to use him as a negative example, eventually they would realize he was doing all the little things right. After the first couple months of practice, he got the first sign that perhaps his plan might pay off.

"You see this guy?" Casey asked his team one day after practice, "We have the smallest guy out here and he works his ass off." It was reminiscent of the speech Coach Willson had given when singling Max out for his extraordinary work ethic during his first season at Sierra College.

Pat Casey was using Max as an example for his star players, many of whom would go on to have successful major-league careers. He wasn't singling out those star players, because unfortunately the ones with all of the talent don't need to have all of the heart; at the end of the day, he was talking about Max Gordon. But was that all there was to Max? Was he the guy brought in to motivate and push the more supremely talented hitters on the roster? That started increasingly sounding like the role of a mascot, not a teammate. Self-doubt crept in as Max once again allowed himself to think of what steep odds he had to make the team.

"I'm sitting there thinking, 'Man, that was cool when Case talked about me after practice today,'" he says. "But deep down, I'm like, 'That doesn't matter, man. If I'm not good enough, I'm not going to be on this team.' That's all good and fun, it feels good and everything's cool, good for me. But at the end of the day, that doesn't matter. *Those guys don't play.*"

Max was not okay with just being the guy that motivated more talented players. He wanted to make an impact. At night, alone in his trailer, he stared at himself in the mirror.

Man, you better do something, because all these "atta boys" aren't going to get you on this team or into the uniform, Max said to himself. *You still have to perform.*

When he began to question himself, he would look at the tattoo he'd gotten as a reminder of Nick, his grandpa Norman, and Coach K, the three men for whom he continued to play. He also used Casey's advice that "if you ever have a question, the best person to ask is the man in the mirror."

As he looked into the mirror in times of doubt, Max simply asked himself if he could do it. He would sit there for 15–20 minutes and wouldn't leave until he knew that both he and the man looking back at him were on the same page.

I can do it, he would repeat over and over until he believed it. Once he convinced himself, he believed it 100 percent.

His nerves manifested themselves on a daily basis as he felt every bit of the importance of what he was doing. He would routinely dry-heave or vomit before taking the field or walking up to the plate. The coaching staff didn't see much of Max's pre-scrimmage jitters, but they were looking at everyone more closely. It was just about time to start making some difficult decisions. They had just 35 roster spots, and the majority of those were given to scholarship athletes. Max and a handful of others were competing among themselves for the handful of available walk-on spots. As he had expected, Max's biggest impression made on the coaching staff was a result of his work ethic, not his actual physical ability.

"Most of our conversations about him were about what an enjoyable guy he was to have around," Casey explains. "We talked about what an inspiration it was for us to see a guy who was going through what he was going through and trying to make our team. That part was the majority of what we were talking about as a coaching staff. He wasn't a guy that was wow-ing us with his play."

He was not someone the coaching staff was considering keeping in the program based on what he could do on the field at that moment. In the late stages of fall camp, Casey thought Max was a kid who might have a positive effect on the program, and on whom he thought the program may have a tremendous effect. But was that worth giving him a roster spot over some-body else he felt was more naturally talented? It was a very hard call, and it was a call he had to make soon. "Until you get somebody into the actual competition and they're calling balls and strikes with the lights on, people in the stands, you really don't know," Casey says.

They weren't banking on him making an immediate impact on the field, especially in his redshirt sophomore season, but there was no deny-ing that Max was a kid who fit into the program's family-first culture. There was something to be said for that. A few roster spots were still up for grabs by the second week of December. It was finals week at Oregon State, mean-ing there was no baseball practice. Max found himself in a desperately time-sensitive situation. If Casey and his coaching staff didn't let him know his fate with the Beavers quickly enough, he faced the prospect of being stuck at Oregon State for another semester and having no chance of trans-ferring to a junior college for the spring season.

"Am I going to be on the team? What's the deal?" Max pestered his coach, hoping to wear him down.

"Max, I can't make that decision yet," Coach Casey would tell him. "We still have a few weeks of spring practice when we get back after the New Year. Then I'll let you know."

That answer didn't satisfy Max. He didn't have that kind of time. He had come all this way, and he needed to know now whether it had all been for nothing. He continued badgering Casey, needing to know where he stood in the coaching staff's eyes.

"Case, come on man, I have to know," Max constantly pled with his coach.

"Max, I told you already that I can't let you know yet," his coach would respond, to his dismay. "We still have a lot of tough decisions to make."

Certainly, Max was on the bubble and was one of those hard decisions the coaching staff had to make one way or the other. It's a struggle coaches at nearly every level have faced more than once in their careers: is heart enough to outweigh talent?

With his impatience reaching a boiling point, Max arranged for a meeting with Coach Casey at his office at Gill Coliseum. Sam drove him there, and when Max hopped out of the car, he asked him to just wait, as the meeting wouldn't take long. Upon entering Casey's office, Max quickly jumped into his usual process of trying to pry answers out of his head coach.

"Look, if I don't make this team, I have to transfer somewhere and if I enroll in classes and try to transfer in late January, when final cuts happen, it'll be too late," Max explained. "I'll be stuck here. I want to play for you. That's the first and only thing I want to do, but if it doesn't work out, I still want to play. I appreciate everything you all have done for me in getting me here and helping me. This fall has been a lifetime experience for me."

Coach Casey looked at his outfielder, preparing to enter his usual spiel about the final decisions not being made and not giving anyone privileged information ahead of time. Max continued his plea: "This has been an incredible opportunity, but if this isn't gonna happen, I have to tell my parents, so they can come get the trailer and take it to a junior college, so I can move forward from there," he explained to the coach, matter-of-factly.

"You're living in a trailer?" Casey asked, stunned and a bit confused. Max had not made that information available to the coaching staff. He didn't want anything but his play to factor into the decision on whether to keep or cut him.

Wow ... the old coach thought.

Casey recalls:

> Him telling me that reinforced what I thought about him and his commitment. Our program was built on real people with a committed and dedicated heart. This told me everything I thought about him was true. He was there for the right reason and he would do anything it took to play. It shed some of my thoughts I had about someone who had maybe a little more talent, but wasn't as committed as he was as to why we do this thing.

At that moment, for one of the few times in his coaching career, Pat Casey made a roster decision without first having a full conversation with his staff.

"All right, well I'll tell you what," he told Max. "You're on the team."

"What?" Max asked, not believing his ears.

"You're living in a trailer, you've been busting your ass off all fall, I'll make it easy on you and your parents," the coach said with conviction. "You're on the team. We're going to take you."

Max couldn't believe it. This was it. It was a moment that at times he was certain would never come. Even in these months of trying to distinguish himself, he still felt as though his number might never be called. On the outside he stayed composed, not wanting to make a fool out of himself as he processed the news, but on the inside he was beaming with vindication.

"Wow, thank you," Max said modestly, hardly mustering the words. "Thank you, I appreciate you doing that. That's awesome. I appreciate the opportunity."

He shook his coach's hand and slowly walked out of his office, practically floating. Sam greeted him once he got outside.

"What was that about?" Sam asked his friend.

"I'm on the team," Max stared blankly at him and spoke softly, still in shock.

"What?" Sam asked, confused.

"Yeah dude, I fucking made the team!" Max yelled this time, his disbelief showing.

"Hell yeah, that's awesome," Sam replied as the two rejoiced in the fact that they were officially teammates once again. He had never questioned whether Max would do enough to land on the roster. "I was obviously thrilled, but there wasn't any thought in my mind that he wasn't going to make it," Sam remembers. "At the same time, we didn't get too excited or have some big party. We knew we had a season in front of us."

Calling his parents to give them the news was a major milestone for Max. His mom and dad had been put through more than anyone throughout this entire ordeal, and when Max no longer had the will to keep going, they had been the ones who pushed him toward healing. His mother had found him a place to live in Portland for the summer, and his dad had made sure the trailer made it up to Corvallis for the fall. In more ways than he could even count, Max had only gotten to this point because of them. Now, he got to tell them that he had once again defied the odds.

"Hey, mom and dad, I have some news," he told them on speaker phone. "I'm going to be flying to Arizona for the first game in the spring. I made the team."

They immediately made him glad that he didn't have the phone up to his ear, as the other line was filled with screams and cheers. They were overjoyed, in pure disbelief that their son had set such a lofty goal for himself and had accomplished it; he was officially a Division 1 athlete. "That was a really happy moment for all of us, especially after the past few years we had," Max recalls. "That was big, because we finally caught a break. We got a good distraction."

But as he'd thought to himself all autumn long, Max wasn't okay with

being a team mascot, someone around whom the rest
of the guys could rally, but
who himself would never
see action on the field. Now
that he had made Oregon
State's roster, he was not
content. He was not satisfied with merely being on
the team. He wanted to con-
tribute in a real way on the
field. He knew that this
would probably be a heavier
undertaking than just trying
to make the team. He knew
how much Casey had stuck
his neck out for him, and he
didn't want to let him down.
He had visualized playing
in games and roaming the
outfield with his teammates
that spring. The same way he
conjured hopeful images of
himself wearing orange and
black on the national stage,
he also had to try blocking
out all of the images of his

Max (right) and Sam Gaviglio bump fists in
business-like fashion. The former AHS teammates reunited at Oregon State during the
2011 baseball season.

coaches and teammates potentially realizing that they'd made a mistake by
having confidence in him.

"I was super pumped, but at the same time, if I just become a human
punching bag at home plate and I'm not able to play, they're going to be
really disappointed in me," Max remembers thinking. "They're going to
question themselves on their judgment, like bringing me on was a bad idea
or it was a waste of a roster spot."

As Max's first spring as a Division 1 athlete approached, the pressure
continued to mount. Just as he had been ever since the car accident that
almost claimed his life, Max was a man on a mission. But the stakes had
never been quite this big. "The coaching staff had done so much for me,"
Max says. "They held up their end of the bargain. Now, it was time for me to
go out and help them win games."

His coaches would look back on the decision to include him on the
roster not as Max feared they would, but as a turning point for a program

filled with future MLB talent and a storied history of success. His outfielders coach, Pat Bailey, would ultimately echo this sentiment in his summation of Max as a player: "You can't help but root for the guy," Bailey says. "With all the stuff he's been through, the car accident and losing his brother. I'm not sure if he was the last guy we put on the roster, but if he was, I tell you what, it was one of the best decisions we ever made."

Chapter 14

Sophomore

It was no longer a dream. Max was an Oregon State Beaver, and as the couple of months wore on before the season opener, he was already well on his way to earning the respect of his teammates and coaches. He came to practice every day and did more than his fair share of work, and he never complained. He played selflessly and tried to become a more compassionate teammate, but he would still never be the guy giving up a rep to somebody else. It grew increasingly likely that the ceiling for his redshirt sophomore campaign would be as a role player, because the talent on Oregon State's 2011 team was overwhelming. With a pitching staff boasting several MLB prospects, the Beavers were ready to get back to Omaha for the first time in four seasons. Their lineup was almost as imposing as their starting staff.

Max continued to show that he could bunt, work deep counts, and play solid defense in the outfield. He knew from watching plenty of Division 1 baseball that all of those would be key aspects of his game this season if he wanted to be successful on such a talented squad. He had to find his niche, and he hoped to find it in Northern California when the team made the trip to Fresno State to take on the Bulldogs from both Gonzaga and their hosts, Fresno State.

Ahead of the opener against Gonzaga, Coach Bailey sat down with the outfielders and went through each opposing hitter one by one, discussing where to play them in the outfield. Max took infield-outfield with the center fielders and just tried not to overthrow a cut or do anything to attract negative energy toward himself before the game could even start.

Warmups were over. At two in the afternoon, Oregon State and Gonzaga assembled along the foul lines, listening as the national anthem was played. As usual, Max took this time to go through his visualizations. He thought back to the great plays he had made at Ashland High School and Sierra College, but now he had to imagine what plays like those would look like in a Beavers uniform. As the anthem swelled to a finish and the crowd roared with applause, those same three faces flashed across his mind, before he kissed toe tag *H78959*, looked up to the sky and, to start his first game in black and orange, said, "Here we go, boys."

Just 250 patrons were on hand in the crisp, 52-degree air to see Max make his Division 1 debut.[1] He started the game on the bench as he would in most games his redshirt sophomore year. There he sat, rigid, still very nervous about playing time and where he fit on the team. That quickly changed when a teammate failed to get a bunt down in the early innings. The first pitch was bunted foul, and Coach Bailey turned and hit his clipboard against the bench. "Doggone it!" he yelled.

"That was an icebreaker for me," Max said, "because it was pretty ridiculous and Miller looked over at me and gave me one of those looks and I almost started laughing, because the whole day, I was like, 'Oh shit, this is real. This is really serious.'"

Having settled down a bit, Max pinch-hit for right fielder Jordan Poyer later in the game, striking out in his first plate appearance for the Beavers. He stayed in the game, playing left field. Sam Gaviglio started the opener on the mound and went 6 2/3 innings without allowing an earned run, setting the tone for what he hoped would be a bounceback junior campaign. He got stuck with a no-decision, but the Beavers won, 4–3, thanks to a Tyler Smith walk-off single in the 11th inning. Max finished his debut 0-for-3 with two punchouts.

He followed up that performance by coming on as a late-inning defensive replacement as Oregon State topped Gonzaga again, this time 4–2, to start the season 2–0. Next came two games against Fresno State and a fast-rising power hitter named Aaron Judge. Max started Game 1 and played left field, marking the first start of his collegiate career. Judge was held to a 1-for-3 day, but with Max running the beginning of his college career to an 0-for-7 mark, the Beavers weren't able to generate much offense and suffered their first loss of the season, 2–1.[2]

Down 4–1 to Fresno State in their second match-up, thanks largely to a 3-for-4 day at the plate by Judge, the Beavers stormed back for three late-inning runs, tying things up at 4–4. Max was once again inserted as a late-inning defensive replacement and was standing in left field as the Bulldogs tried to win it in the ninth. With a runner on second, one out, Ryan Dunn served up a pitch to Austin Wynns that he clubbed into left field for a single. It was a tough play, but Max gave charge and came up firing toward home plate. With the runner off on contact, it would take a perfect throw and a little luck to get Brennan Gowens at the dish. They got neither as the throw flew up the line and late, allowing Gowens to cross the plate easily with the game-winning run.[3] With that, the Beavers left Fresno back at .500, 2–2. Things had not looked good on the diamond for Max so far, but he never doubted whether he deserved to be there, or whether he had what it took to crack it at this level. That sort of thinking was behind him now.

OSU trudged through non-conference play as Max continued to try and provide whatever boost to the club he could. Mostly, he continued to endear himself to teammates with his crazy antics, including impersonations of coaches and pre-game backflips with fellow outfielder Brian Stamps, before the team took the field. Crowding the plate and working deep counts, Max had more walks and hit by pitch (10) than he did hits (4) in non-conference play. His batting average peaked at .176 after he put together a nice little four-game hit streak, which included the first hit of his collegiate career against the University of Hartford. Regardless of the lackluster average, he was getting on base and scoring runs. During one six-game stretch, he scored seven times without regularly being in the starting lineup.

The team rode a 12-game winning streak through most of conference play, pushing them to 14–2 on the season before Long Beach State snapped the streak by handing the Beavers a 2–1 defeat. That sent OSU into a short slump, losing three of their final five non-conference games. That stretch also saw Sam Gaviglio's incredible streak of innings without allowing an earned run come to an end in the Beavers' 11–5 win over UC-Santa Barbara. Astoundingly, he had run that total to 41 consecutive frames without allowing an earned run up to that point. It was the rebound season he was looking for and it put him on the radar of professional scouts.

Max was pumped to finally get into conference play and face off against teams like Stanford, Arizona State, and USC, against whom he had dreamed of playing his whole life. Then he got called into Coach Bailey's office. "You're ineligible," his coach, whom he now knew as "Bails," told him. The words came down on him like a ton of cement. *What now?* he thought.

He was sent to the school's NCAA compliance office to sort things out. In order to have NCAA eligibility, one must have a certain percentage of their degree completed based on what academic year one has entered into. Thanks to Max's complicated academic past, having left Sierra College early, but having gained some junior college academic credits in the meantime, Max's transcript gave compliance some trouble before conference play began. Since conference play opens in a different term than non-conference play, its degree percentage requirements are higher. During non-conference play, Max was far enough along in his degree, but now, with the requirements raised, he no longer was. He practically sprinted over to compliance as the team left for Tucson, the University of Arizona, and the conference opener later that day.

"What can we do?" Max asked one of the compliance office workers.

He was getting an Exercise and Sports Science degree, because that's what he wanted to do after baseball. That wouldn't work, he was told.

"You can't get it with this major," the officer explained.

"Well, can I change my major?" Max asked, desperately trying to find a way back on the field.

"No, you can't. No matter what we switch it to, it's not going to get you to the 40 percent you need," the worker answered. Max was sitting at 38 percent degree completion. Frustrated and scared, he called his mom to see how to fix this dire issue.

"How about that economics class you took in high school that has credits toward Rogue Community College?" she asked.

"I don't know," Max responded, sounding defeated.

"Well, tell them to add those credits," she suggested. "Maybe they'll help."

When Max had the officers go back and look for the economics class, they found a few other credits they might be able to apply. "Oh, child development with human development and family science, that's in the human development branch," they eventually pointed out. "That'll work and get you to 40 percent."

"Okay, let's do it," Max said, releasing a huge sigh of relief. He'd almost had his dream put seriously on hold. Now, with the most important thing in his collegiate career—his eligibility—back, he had only one other problem: how to get to the Pac-10 opener? The Beavers' plane had already left, which left Max alone in Corvallis, scrambling for a backup plan. First, he had to run around to several different administrators and get their signatures to switch out his degree and then bring it back to compliance so he could officially be deemed eligible. Then he called the guy who took care of these sorts of things for the baseball team.

"I'm good, I'm eligible," Max told him.

"Okay, go talk to [athletic director] Marianne Vydra and she'll get you a plane ticket," he replied.

Max did exactly that, was given a plane ticket, and had to drive up to Portland to take the only flight going anywhere near Tucson on such short notice. He landed in Phoenix, about an hour away, and hailed a cab to take him to the team's hotel. He arrived just in time to get everything squared away with the team. In hindsight, though, he could have missed the first game of the conference season, and he wouldn't have minded one bit.

The Beavers suffered an embarrassment at the hands of the Wildcats in the conference opener. The onslaught was initiated by a 12-run sixth inning and five defensive errors by Oregon State.

Everyone loaded onto the team bus, just happy to be getting the hell out of Dodge and back to the team hotel after such a demoralizing defeat.

Max looks on intensely as he takes his signs before stepping into the batter's box.

As all the players were settling in, Coach Casey got up at the front of the bus and, his demeanor like a stone, made an announcement:

"The bus doesn't work," he told the team. "We're walking."

Many players still believe he told the bus driver never to start the bus just so the team would have to walk back to the hotel, but to this day Casey will neither confirm nor deny the validity of that theory. The timing did seem pretty convenient, though. In full uniform and carrying all their gear, the Beavers started their voyage through the middle of the University of Arizona campus. Women dressed up for a night at the bars and frat bros on their fifth hour of partying shot them strange looks. Just some student-athletes making their way through a college campus on a Friday night, nothing to see here. Rubbed the wrong way by the experience, a lot of guys decided to sneak out of the team hotel, leaving a sock in the fire escape door so they could get back in without having to walk past coaches in the lobby.

The first group to come back must not have gotten the memo, because they removed the sock, leaving the second group to fend for themselves. They had to sneak through the lobby at 1 a.m., where coaches were still chatting. Bed check was at 10 p.m., so getting caught would mean a death sentence. Somehow, the remaining players managed to go by undetected and made it back to their rooms.

Pat Casey's ploy (or well-timed bus breakdown) clearly had the desired effect as his team came out pissing vinegar the following day, looking to dominate. They did. Oregon State bounced back for wins in the last two games of the series, outscoring the Wildcats, 18–8, and earning a series win.

After a weekday win over the University of Portland, Casey's alma mater, the home conference opener was upon them. Arizona State faced the daunting task of coming into Corvallis, home to one of the most well-established programs in the country, winners of four straight Pac-10 titles. When Max was coaching at Ashland High School during his year off, he would often visualize playing against Arizona State during his downtime. They were, after all, dubbed "MLBU" because of how many players they sent to the majors, including Barry Bonds and Reggie Jackson.

After taking the opener, 5–3, the Beavers faced trouble in Game 2, behind by four runs in the seventh inning. They fought back, scoring three runs in the seventh and another in the eighth to even up the score at 6–6. With the bullpen holding serve, they entered the ninth inning still deadlocked with a chance to walk off. When Ryan Barnes reached base to start the inning, Casey decided that this was the moment to seize to bring this one home. He had made a career out of recognizing these moments. He wasn't going to plan for extras, and he wasn't going to save anyone for later games. He was going to end this game in the ninth inning. Instead of letting his lefty power hitter, Danny Hayes, hit in that situation or even try to get down a bunt, he summoned Max.

"Max, get a helmet on," he told him. Max assumed Casey wanted him to pinch-run and provide more speed on first base. Over to first base Max ran, tagging out with Ryan as he turned around, ready to take his signs.

Big moment, tie game, packed house, Max thought. Those thoughts were quickly interrupted by Casey screaming at him from the dugout. "Get over here!" he yelled, pointing at his feet, "Get over here!" Now Max was confused. He ran over to Coach Casey.

"Hitting," Casey said.

Max's face grew hot to the touch in seconds; he could feel his heart thumping dangerously hard against his ribcage. As he scrambled, he was more confused than anything; Hayes was a good bunter, so it hadn't even crossed his mind that he would be hitting for him. Rattled, Max searched frantically for a bat, any bat, so he could go take his at-bat. The one he grabbed wasn't even his; to this day, he doesn't know whose it was. He didn't even think to put on his batting gloves. He walked straight back to Casey, who wanted to give him instructions about moving the winning run into scoring position. "We're going to have you bunt here, and if they charge, you need to listen," Casey told his pinch-hitter, "We're going to yell 'Spin, spin, spin!' which means pull back and hit it down their throat."

Max heard him loud and clear. It was the ultimate command for a guy who loved to hit but had learned to bunt out of necessity. He didn't want to bunt; he wanted to swing away. Like any competitor would, he desperately hoped to hear his dugout screaming "spin!" as the pitcher came toward the plate. All the fans, the noise, the pressure, everything dripped away as Max honed in on the pitcher, focusing on this moment and how he would win the game that he'd imagined playing in a hundred times over the years.

Everything in Max's head went silent as the pitch was delivered, a perfect pitch to bunt. Not hearing anything around him, he squared and pushed it right down the first-base line, where it was supposed to go. Satisfied with his bunt, he looked up to start running to first base. To his surprise, the first baseman already had the ball in his mitt and was spinning to throw it over to second. The force out was in order, and Max barely beat the throw back to first, narrowly avoiding a double play. Unknown to Max, the entire dugout was yelling, "Spin, spin, spin!" He had blocked all that out and now he was staring back into the dugout, where Pat Casey was throwing things around. Not one minute earlier, he had given Max specific instructions on what to do. It was a mental mistake, the kind which was rare for Max and could prove fatal for someone of his standing on the team.

I am in deep, deep shit, Max thought as he stood on first base, just trying to stay composed as he still had a responsibility as a baserunner.

Jared Norris, already 1-for-4 with two RBI on the day, stepped up next, trying to pick Max up for his mental error. In short order, he knocked a base hit to right field and Max decided to make up for his previous mistake. Just before he reached second base, he picked up third-base coach Marty Lees, who was throwing up a stop sign. Even though Norris' base knock was a one-hopper straight to the right fielder, Max decided to make a break for third. He was already in trouble, so he might as well take any extra base he thought he could. He sprinted with every ounce of energy he could muster, barreling toward third base and ready to trample any fielder in his path if need be. Knowing it would be close, Max slid in, seeing the throw was a little off-line, and he was safe. He stood just 90 feet from home, the winning run in a pivotal Pac-10 clash. He let out a sigh of relief. He couldn't imagine the wrath he would have incurred had be been thrown out trying for third.

With runners on first and third and one out, Parker Berberet was walked intentionally to load the bases for Brian Stamps. The force was now alive at any base, and the Sun Devils hoped they could turn an inning-ending double play to force extras. However, the problem with walking the bases loaded is that it leaves the defense with no margin for error. Stamps was selective at the dish, and Mitchell Lambson couldn't find the strike zone. He watched four pitches go by, all balls, and the packed Goss Stadium house erupted, Max running home with the winning run as the Beavers poured out of the dugout to celebrate the walk-off win.[4] Major mental error aside, Max had been a spark plug on the base paths and had ultimately forced the Sun Devils into loading the bases. They won the game, and he was last to tap home plate, so all was forgiven in the eyes of his team.

This game, which clinched the Beavers' second straight conference series win, came to epitomize Max's role in his sophomore season. He would play in meaningful games late, but he wouldn't help win those games with his bat. It was his ability to bunt, his aggressive, non-destructive baserunning, or his glove in the outfield. That was the way the Beavers needed him to impact games, and he continued to do just that. "I was good enough to be playing in the situations I was," Max said. "I could come in and do that, but as a guy that's going to be in the lineup everyday, I hadn't shown enough to be a part of that conversation."

That made it all the more frustrating when he kept hearing Casey complain about his center fielders' collective inability to win the starting job. Garrett Nash, Mike Miller, and Brian Stamps all got playing time out there, but nobody was consistent enough to take hold of the position. "I'm tired of the carousel we have in center field," Casey would say. "I want somebody to just man up and take this job. Someone do it. I don't care who it is, but I want a lineup that's consistent everyday."

Though Max didn't feel he had shown enough yet to be in that conversation, Casey's message stuck with him. He was someone who wanted that center field job. He resolved then that if it couldn't be this year, then the spot would be his in the years to come.

Following the disastrous conference opener in Tucson and the long walk back to the hotel, the Beavers banged out 11 straight conference wins and 12 out of 13 to pull to 12–2 in conference play before taking on pitching phenom Trevor Bauer and UCLA. The Beavers had a pitching phenom of their own in Josh Osich, who had raced back from his 2010 Tommy John surgery and was making a name for himself among the best hurlers in the conference. The two squared off in a pitcher's duel for the ages, both working scoreless ball through five innings.

OSU knew it was in for a long day when Bauer made Ryan Barnes look silly in his first at-bat. Barnes was the type of guy who, no matter what he did in his leadoff at-bat in the first inning, he would come back to the dugout and pump everybody up. "His fastball is flat, his curveball is nothing," he would say, emphasizing how bad the pitcher who just got him out was. Just the day before, he had faced Gerrit Cole, who was a projected top 10 pick in the MLB Draft. Barnes wasn't at all impressed with what he saw.

"This guy isn't shit," he said. "I don't know why they have him going so high in the draft. He has nothing, we're going to destroy this guy." To his credit, the Beavers did score seven runs that day and win the game. But with Bauer on the mound, it was a different story. Barnes was again leading off the game, and Bauer started him with a laser of a fastball low and away for strike one. He followed that with a fastball up, at which Barnes flailed and missed. Then Bauer dropped the hammer on him with a devastating curveball, and Barnes was turning to walk back to the dugout before it even crossed the plate. His teammates waited eagerly for him to get back to the dugout to hear him dismiss Bauer's talent. "Well, I don't know what the fuck that was," he said, looking blankly around at his teammates. "We're in for a really long day, guys, because that was fucked up."

That being said, when the Beavers scratched across two runs in the sixth inning, it felt like plenty to win the game. After all, Osich had yet to allow a hit.

Max was on chart duty on the bench, an offensive chart sitting on one leg, a defensive chart on the other. Doing these charts is standard procedure for bench players at the college level. Normally, he might pass off one of the charts on someone else, but not today. Unsurprisingly, Max is a superstitious guy; if he handed off one of his charts to a teammate and Osich lost his no-hitter, he would never forgive himself for it. So there he sat, unmoving, laying one chart over either knee and watching as Osich continued to mow down UCLA hitters. The third-ranked Beavers and 24th-ranked Bruins continued to grind, but after those two sixth-inning runs, nobody could do anything. The unspoken tension that comes with a no-hitter started to fill the dugout and the stands. Nobody dared say the words in the dugout, and nobody would even look at Osich when he came in and sat down between innings. This was his game.

At Jackie Robinson Stadium, the Beavers fans in the house rose to their feet for the ninth inning as Osich still had his no-hitter intact. A fourth-inning walk was the only blemish on his otherwise-perfect day. Osich froze the first batter of the frame, pinch hitter Tyler Heineman, with a fastball perfectly placed on the outside corner for his 12th strikeout of the afternoon. He was two outs away. Next stepped in catcher Trevor Brown. Osich started him with a high fastball, which he took for ball one. Then came another perfectly placed heater on the outside corner and the count was evened up at 1–1. Brown fidgeted with his pants, then his bat before stepping back in. He watched as another fastball sailed even further outside, but Osich was given a generous call: strike two. After fouling the next two pitches off, Brown weakly grounded to third base. Carter Bell fielded the ball cleanly and threw over to Jared Norris four the second out. Osich was one out away from history.

Another pinch hitter stepped into the box. Brian Carroll represented the Bruins' last hope. Carroll, of slender build, wearing baby-blue stirrups, assumed his stance and awaited a chance to do what none of his teammates had done to that point: record a base hit off Josh Osich. As quickly as he had a chance to think about that chance, strike one was past him, another borderline call on an outside fastball. Carroll did not take the bat off his shoulder and Osich pumped strike two by him, this time on the inside corner. One strike away.

Osich rocked back once more and unleashed a fastball with a little extra juice. It sailed high and out of the zone, but Carroll chased it, swinging right through it. Osich pumped once with his left hand, displaying confidence and emotion on a day when he was simply the best player on the field. His teammates flew toward the mound in a frenzy and piled onto the day's hero. Josh Osich, making his return from Tommy John surgery, had just turned in one of the greatest performances ever recorded by an Oregon State pitcher. He became the first Beaver pitcher since 1947 to throw a no-hitter on his own (they had two other combined no hitters in the 64 years in between). He also became the first Pac-10 pitcher to throw a no-hitter in a conference game in 16 years. Improving to 13–2 in the Pac-10, the Beavers were now very much in the driver's seat.

Max had his own seat on the bench, where he had gotten comfortable for nearly a month. He didn't get into a game between April 9 and May 8 as conference play heated up. This enabled him to get a closer glimpse at Pat Casey and to observe the type of man and coach he was. Casey puts a major emphasis on mental fortitude and a disciplined, winning attitude, drawing a lot of inspiration from the military. Every now and then, he was known to give a casual pep talk to a few players, and they would have no idea what he was talking about. Before another conference game, with Max, Norris, and Berberet sitting next to each other on the bench, tying their cleats before warm-ups, Casey swung by, all riled up.

"You know what, men? The fire's going to be hot today," he said, which caused his players to look up. "The fire's going to be hot, so you have to jump in the bathtub with this guy, get to know him a little bit, swim around with him."

Berberet and Norris shared a befuddled look with Max, and none of them knew what to say. Berberet couldn't help but laugh, because he had no idea what Casey was even getting at.

Another time in practice, when the team kept screwing up a bunting drill, he launched into a diatribe. "Listen, I don't get it," he said, "I don't understand why you guys can't compete. You can't compete and you don't want to be here and I don't understand it. If it was just me in the jungle with a hand grenade and a machete, I'm going through the jungle and I'm coming out alive every time."

Hand-grenade and a machete? It's 2011, why are those your weapons of choice? Max chuckled to himself.

It was part of what endeared Casey to his players so much. They loved his convoluted sayings, even if they didn't always know what he meant. They knew there was a lifetime of knowledge and winning sentiment swirling around that legendary brain and trying to distill nuggets of wisdom from his proverbs was one of the players' favorite pastimes.

He enjoyed Casey's interesting anecdotes, but the downtick in playing time caused Max to get stir-crazy. In order to get on his feet and feel productive, he started warming up the left fielder between innings. While he threw back and forth, young fans in the left field corner would talk to Max, and to their surprise, he would talk back. There was a decent-sized group which attended nearly every Oregon State home game. The conversations continued every inning he went back out, every game played at Goss Stadium. These young kids couldn't believe that a real-life, Oregon State Beavers baseball player knew their names. He would even occasionally toss them a ball over the fence at the end of warmups.

After a while, he came to be those kids' favorite player on the team, though they hadn't actually seen him play since their over-the-fence friendship began. The parents in that section even made "Max's Maniacs" shirts, which a dozen or so of the children wore. Thus, Max's Maniacs were born. Max Gordon, bench reserve outfielder for the Oregon State Beavers, had himself a cheering section and fan club. When he finally got into a game on May 8, a rare start in left field, Max's Maniacs erupted. They hadn't seen him in a game, and now he was positioned in the outfield practically right next to them. He went 0-for-4 at the plate, but as usual, he wasn't in the lineup for his offense. He made sure that his Maniacs went home happy.

With the Beavers up, 2–1, in the second inning, Marcus Semien, later the starting shortstop for the Oakland Athletics and one of the best hitters in the American League, sliced a ball deep down the left field line. Max was playing in the gap, so he had to sprint toward it, knowing he would likely have to play it off the wall. As usual, though, he got a great first step on it and read it perfectly. As the ball came down, he realized he might have a chance to lay out for the ball, but he didn't know how much room he had before he would slam into the outfield wall. As the ball plummeted toward the warning track dirt, Max laid full-out, extending his right hand over his head, making an impossible grab. He landed and slid across the warning track, rolling up onto the cinder against the outfield wall. The catch was made for out number three, and you'd think, based on the reaction of Max's Maniacs, that they had just witnessed their favorite team win the World Series. It was pandemonium in the section just past the Beavers' home dugout in left field as more than a dozen kids and their parents went wild for their favorite ballplayer. It was also the first real opportunity for the rest of the spectators in the stands to get a glimpse of Max's uncanny ability to flash leather and make highlight-reel plays.

The special fan section devoted to Max, Max's Maniacs, pose for a picture outside Goss Stadium after a Beavers home game.

"Yeah, that catch was probably the start," Max says, looking back. "Some of the guys had seen it in BP and scrimmages, but nobody really knew that I could make plays like that until it started happening in games that counted."

Watching from the dugout, Sam Gaviglio couldn't help but smile. He'd seen plenty of plays like that from Max over the years, and now he was seeing his friend do it for his team on the biggest stage. The two best friends would always cherish the 2011 season, which seemed more and more like it would be their only one together in Corvallis. Sam was shooting up MLB Draft boards and was likely to be selected fairly high, which would tempt the hero of Ashland's 2008 state title run to forego his senior season at Oregon State.

The two were always catch partners when Sam wasn't pitching, and it was like they were back in Ashland Grizzlies uniforms, except this season, they hoped to be dog-piling with each other after winning the last game of the season in Omaha, celebrating a national championship victory. If they could pull that off, their state title run would pale in comparison. Of course, off the field, they would ride around in Max's bike and sidehack for fun. Once, after then-Beavers and future NFL running back Jacquizz Rodgers messed up his knee, he took a ride in the sidehack with Max pedaling on the bike.

Max's sidehack, which he constructed with Josh Scarminach and brought with him to Oregon State in 2011.

Meanwhile, the Beavers were pedaling toward a conference champion-ship and an NCAA Regional hosted in Corvallis. As the pressure mounted and the season drew near its end, players felt as though the coaches were pushing and stressing more than they needed. Players could sense that the coaches were panicking, and tried to do what they could to assuage their concerns. By the time the regular season came to a close, they mostly had it squared away and dialed in for postseason play. This was when Casey tended to take a slight step back and let his players play their game their way. Going into the final series of the season, the infamous "Civil War" against hated rival Oregon, they needed just one win in three games to win the conference.

After dropping Games 1 and 2, each by a score of 4–1, the Beavers had to beat the Ducks in the regular-season finale to win their first conference title since their initial College World Series title year of 2006. Instead, they were blanked, 6–0, and watched the conference title slip slowly from their grasp.[5] UCLA was the champion, knocking Arizona State off its throne for the first time in four seasons. Still, the Beavers earned one of 16 regional host designations as they were still the sixth-ranked team in the country.

They welcomed Arkansas-Little Rock, Creighton, and Georgia to town, with just one of the four teams advancing to the Super Regional.

Behind homers from Danny Hayes and Garrett Nash, along with a three-hit day by Ryan Barnes, the Beavers dispatched Arkansas-Little Rock in their first Regional game, 7–4. Next came Creighton, the No. 2 seed in the Regional. With Sam Gaviglio on the mound, though, the outcome was never really in doubt. He tossed a complete-game five-hitter, recording 11 strikeouts and leading the Beavers to a convincing 5–1 win. They were now just one victory away from returning to a Super Regional series. Against Georgia the next day, the Beavers took a 6–4 lead into the ninth inning. On came closer Tony Bryant, whose consistency and gnarly changeup made him one of college baseball's best relief pitchers in 2011.

He got into trouble, though, after putting a runner on via the walk. The next batter hit a laser off his throwing arm, earning an infield single. There were now two runners on base, and Bryant was in serious pain. Thinking they might have to remove him from the game, the training team and coaching staff came out and asked him a few questions. They had him throw a couple of warmup pitches for good measure. Just as he delivered his first one, the lights at Goss Stadium shut off. For the next 21 minutes, as a maintenance crew was called to fix the faulty bank of lights, Bryant's pain and nerves went away. By the time the lights were back on, he was refocused and ready to shut the door. That's exactly what he did, going 1–2–3 after allowing two runners to reach base.[6] Call it faulty electrical wiring, call it divine intervention, Tony Bryant and the Oregon State squad didn't care. The Beavers were dancing on to a Super Regional for the first time since 2007, the last year they won the College World Series.

Their opponent: Vanderbilt, on the road in Nashville. In order to prepare for their Friday-Saturday-Sunday series against the Commodores, the team arrived in town on Wednesday to get in a few days of practice. Max, now 20 years old, saw fireflies for the first time in his life. Those on the team who were 21 and older saw much more than that. The Country Music Awards were held in Nashville that same weekend, so the city was at capacity. All the bars were packed, and some guys on the team went out to Coyote Ugly bar that Wednesday night. As the story goes, they were at the bar when a woman began with the famous last words of many a bar-goer, "Who wants to do a body shot?"

"Norris does, yeah, Jared does!" his loving teammates shouted.

"Guys, shut the hell up," he shot back, not wanting to become the center of attention.

"Okay, but if you're going to do a body shot off me, there are a couple things you have to do," the woman instructed him, ignoring Jared's pleas. Norris' face turned beet red. He listened for further instruction.

Katie, as they learned her name was, put Norris on a leash and paraded him around the bar. Then she ripped his shirt off and wrote "Katie's Bitch" in Sharpie on his chest. The whole act brought down the house, especially the Beavers baseball section. None of them would ever forget it. None of them would ever want to forget it, aside from Jared Norris.

Max, still not 21, hadn't gone out with the older guys, but pretty much instantly heard the stories from those who had seen the mayhem first-hand. The next day at practice, he decided to ask Norris about it himself. "Dude, what happened?" he asked his teammate. "Did all of that seriously go down?"

Norris didn't say a word, just lifted up his shirt. "Katie's Bitch" was still written in Sharpie across his chest, slightly faded from what had clearly been a concerted effort to scrub it off that morning in the hotel shower.

Having logged a healthy amount of shenanigans, the Beavers turned their attention toward Vanderbilt, one of the best teams in the country and a tough Super Regional draw. Future MLB regulars Sonny Gray and Tony Kemp were on their roster along with Mike Yastrzemski, the grandson of Red Sox legend Carl Yastrzemski, who would make his major-league debut with the San Francisco Giants roughly eight years later. Before Game 1 of the pivotal series, Max sprinted out to center field to take pre-game infield-outfield practice. With that drawing to a close, every outfielder got two throws from their outfield spot to home plate before running in. On Max's first throw, he short-hopped the first baseman, the ball kicking away nowhere near its target. As he prepared for his second try, Bailey and Casey ended his session prematurely, signaling for him to come in before getting a final throw. Pulled in front of more than 3,000 people, Max felt insecure. This moment stuck with him and, down the line, the seemingly mental hurdle of throwing a ball in from the outfield threatened to derail his career.

In Game 1, Sonny Gray imposed his will on the Beavers hitters. He went 6 2/3 innings, allowing just one earned run while getting tons of offensive support. Sam Gaviglio struggled mightily, allowing 10 earned runs across 5 1/3 innings of work. The Beavers had their work cut out for them: win the next two, or the season is over.

Tied 2–2 , it seemed like the second match-up would not be decided until the very end. Instead, Vanderbilt struck for five runs in the middle innings and effectively put the game on ice. Up 9–3, they sealed the deal, dogpiling on the mound, punching their ticket to Omaha.[7] This time on the other end of the dogpile, watching from the dugout as they packed their equipment for the final time that season, the Beavers were utterly dejected. Oregon State had its best season in years but had been easily handled by the Commodores. Max took it all in as his opponents celebrated reaching college baseball's greatest level of competition.

I made sure to sit there and watch it all, I watched their whole team celebrate. I really wanted to feel that loss. I wanted to make sure that hurt, because that's the type of person I am. I'm not going to forget that. So, I sat there and watched while they were all having fun and I'm like, "That needs to be our team. We're supposed to be doing that right now." We found out that year we can go out and play in the Pac-10 and all that, but it doesn't matter if we don't win in the play-offs. That's all good and fun, but it doesn't mean shit until we get to Omaha.

The loss left a bad taste in everyone's mouth as the off-season began and the team started to lay out plans for 2012. An end-of-year meeting was scheduled with Coach Bailey to discuss summer plans and feedback from the past season. Max hadn't gotten a lot of playing time nor had he wielded a big bat, but he was exactly what the coaching staff imagined he could be for them. He was a great clubhouse guy and he grinded out at bats, getting on base in any way he could. His batting average over a small sample size was just .130, but his on-base percentage was more than double that, at .300. That's because he worked walks and never minded getting hit by pitches. He either walked, was hit by a pitch, or recorded a sacrifice fly or bunt in 26 percent of his plate appearances. It was clear that he would have to improve in other areas to get more playing time, but he had fulfilled his role as a bench player in his first season as a D1 ballplayer.

When Bailey met with him, Max came away thinking perhaps he had further to go than previously thought. It started with Max asking about scholarship money. "Hey, I'm paying for all of this out of pocket. Is there any way I can get a little piece of scholarship money, something like that?" Max asked. "I made the team and I'll be a returning player."

"No, sorry, Max," the Beavers' bench player remembers Bailey telling him. "You need to stay in school, though, and get your education. I'm going to warn you, we have a talented class coming in and I can't make any guarantees, but if you want to try out again, you can."

Coach Bailey doesn't recall thinking Max wouldn't be back with them in 2012, but that was the impression Max walked away with, and that left him rattled; in his mind, the hard part was over. He was a member of the team and just had to worry about how to make a more significant contribution. As he was coming to realize, however, his status on the team was very much up in the air. "Okay, I'll be here. I will try out again," Max shot back angrily. This conversation lit a fire in him that would burn for the entire off-season.

He had worked as hard as he possibly could and had given his coaches everything he had, but now he had to come back out and do it all over again. With a new crop of blue-chip talent, he would have to make a Division 1 roster for a second time and with almost zero chance at earning a scholarship. It left him feeling bitter as the summer got underway. Once again, baseball didn't seem as much fun to him now that it wasn't showing him the same love he had always shown it. It was like he was still climbing this mountain, the peak of which only seemed to get further away the harder he climbed.

Regardless of the outcome, he was certain at least that the summer in Swift Current, Canada, with his new team would be an adventure. He had been through the ebbs and flows of many baseball seasons by now, and even after playing on one of the sport's highest stages, he needed a way to make baseball fun again. He needed something to bring the romantic notions of baseball back into the fold. If he could do that, then maybe he could not only secure a spot on the 2012 team, but maybe also stake a claim as a real contributor to a top-tier program.

What Max didn't know was that while he was north of the border, rumors started swirling back home in Corvallis. Just as he thought he was getting to know one of the best coaches he'd ever had, Max learned that Pat Casey was thinking about stepping down.

CHAPTER 15

Junior

If he couldn't give 100 percent, he wasn't going to do it at all. After 17 seasons in charge of the Oregon State baseball program, head coach Pat Casey wasn't sure he could live up to the expectations he had established. He wasn't worried about records or pressure from the outside, but he was concerned that he could no longer compete at the level he had learned to expect from himself.[1] Word of his potential departure hit that offeason as Beavers players were scattered throughout the country, playing at various levels of summer ball.

"There have been conversations," Casey told the press one afternoon. "I can't tell you that's something that I haven't been thinking about."

Casey was the one who had stuck his neck out for Max. He had made the unilateral decision to keep him on the team, one of only a few times he made a call on a roster spot without the direct input of other coaches. If he left, that presented a serious concern to Max, who figured he might only have a spot waiting for him in 2012 if Casey was the one extending it to him. He already had to earn a spot again by trying out, but if Casey was gone, what were his chances of actually making the team a second time? As these questions swirled, Max was busy playing ball in Canada, trying to remember what playing baseball purely for fun was like.

He arrived in Regina, Saskatchewan, at two in the morning and was picked up by a couple of teammates from Nebraska who had been given gas money to drive out, scoop him up, and take him to their home city of Swift Current. It was a not-so-swift, two-and-a-half-hour drive. Swift Current is basically in the middle of nowhere, and Canada was a land completely unknown to Max to begin with. His teammates came from all over the United States and Canada, and it was a diverse group. Their budget was low, but their talent level was fairly high. Max met his head coach, Joe Carnahan, and aptly judged him as an intense but lovable coach who wanted his high-level college players to enjoy the summer.

"I was really stressing myself out and I didn't have a lot to show for all the work I put in," Max remembers of his time in Corvallis leading into his summer season. The endless climb toward that mountaintop seemed steeper and steeper, and he needed a guide who would remind him that it was okay to take a little break. Coach Carnahan did just that, keeping the team loose at all times. The governing rules of the league provided some comic relief to guys like Max and his teammates; although most of them were collegiate athletes with serious careers to train for; the Western Canadian Baseball League, the league in which they played, allowed non-collegiate players to compete as well.

Coach Carnahan would throw BP to everyone, and then he would hit with the last group. He had to prepare for his own at-bats in the game, after all. "He was in his 30's, but he would hit nukes," Max remembers of his summertime player-coach. "He would hit bombs."

That season was also the swan song for a Swift Current legend, Conrad Funk. He first played for the Swift Current Indians when he was just 16 years old and played at Winthrop University in South Carolina, and eventually for the Canadian National Team.[2] When he returned to the area with a job as a CPA, he returned to the Indians as well. Funk would be turning 30 soon, but he was still the best player on the team and a guy the fans came to see patrolling right field and clubbing home runs. He would show up at the field after a long day at work, wearing slacks and a dress shirt. He would change into baseball pants and run onto the field as if he hadn't just spent eight long hours staring at a computer monitor, balancing spreadsheets. While he may have been the team's main attraction, he was rather quiet, kept to himself, and let his bat do the talking. He and Joe Carnahan were great friends and symbolized the old guard who enjoyed watching the next generation of ballplayers develop.

It was easy for the atmosphere to be laid-back in the Western Canadian Baseball League, and it was exactly the sort of environment which Max needed at this time in his career. Once, years earlier, with Swift Current playing in the championship series, the umpires had to call time-out in the middle of a count. Everyone looked up, and there were streakers sprinting onto the field; having first hopped the fence near the first base line, they made a break for it near the left-center field fence. As naked as the day they were born, they hopped the fence and continued on down the street as if nothing had happened. Onlookers hooted and hollered for a few minutes, and then the umpires called time-in, and the game continued in relative peace. That sort of thing was not entirely uncommon, so it was a league where it was difficult to take anything too seriously.

Max started buying into that laid-back style of ball in the summer. Every now and then, Coach Carnahan would be perched near the dugout steps and hear AC/DC from off in the distance.

"What the heck is going on here?" he wondered.

Sure enough, there would be Max standing in centerfield, singing, belting really, AC/DC's greatest hits in between pitches during a live game. Suddenly, his singing would stop, the pitch would be thrown, and Max would make one of his vintage diving grabs in the gap, after which he could continue his rendition of "Hell's Bells." That turned out to be merely the prelude to his first live concert performance.

Swift Current was in the midst of a long rain delay as storms pummeled its field. Bored and restless, Max decided the team would put on a rock show. He and some teammates grabbed rakes, climbed on top of the dugout, and started pretending they were putting on a concert; they really got into it, headbanging and sticking out their tongues. Coach Carnahan couldn't believe what he was seeing, but he couldn't help but laugh. Once they played their encore, Max did a stage dive off the dugout and onto the field, where his teammates caught him.

Holy crap, Carnahan thought. When he was having fun, everyone could see that there was something special about Max Gordon.

Shortstop Collin Hetzler and Max became quick friends, and once that happened, the in-game antics grew more and more ridiculous. They would almost always bat 1–2 in the lineup, and if one attempted a bunt and got on base successfully, the other guy had to try to follow that up with a bunt single of his own. Several times, both reached base safely, frustrating opposing teams.

For all the fun they were having, Max did also glean important baseball wisdom from Coach Carnahan. In practice, Canrahan would use a level with a bubble in the middle and tape it onto his helmet. "Boys, all you have to do is just stay level," he would say. "Get off the roller coaster. Don't get too high, don't get too low. Stay level, have fun, and play hard."

That message resonated with Max, who had been on a roller coaster ride of a baseball career for several years. Carnahan thought it was important to take these kids, most of whom were playing at high-level, high-stress programs, and let them decompress over the summer. If they were getting to know each other and having fun, their baseball skills would not drop off during the summer he had them. They might even be more receptive to what he had to teach than they were to their coaches who piled pressure and discipline onto their heads day after day during the college season.

The players carried his message with them off the field as well, especially when they were all hired to umpire a 12-year-old baseball tournament that summer. Of course, they all turned the event into a carnival-like spectacle. It became a pageant of emphatic punch-out calls, engaging with unruly parents, and sporting $5 drugstore sunglasses a la "Reno 9–11." One of Max's favorite performances came when he threw his clicker in the air and pretended to shoot it out of the sky to ring up a seventh-grader. They knew that the parents would probably not be happy with their antics, but they were out there to have fun. Sure enough, right after the game was over, a trove of parents headed toward the crew. Kids by their sides, they came up to the ballplayers-turned-umpires. Max and his teammates braced themselves for the chewing-out that they knew they had earned. "Hey, are you going to umpire later this afternoon?" they asked, taking the group by surprise. "Because that's the greatest thing I've ever seen. These games are so boring and you guys made it fun."

The unexpected response was a signal to Max that coming up to the Great White North to play his summer ball had been a good decision. He was having fun again, and people were responding to it in a way that he had never expected. As outrageous as their behavior off the field got as the summer wore on, the team's performance on the field stayed solid and consistent. They made the playoffs. In Max's mind, the playoffs might as well be the championship as far as competitive juices are concerned. Yes, the team had been loose and having fun all summer long, but everything was more fun when they were winning.

Max was on first base in the team's first playoff game when the ball was hit right at the shortstop, a seemingly easy double-play ball. Max barreled toward second base, intent on forcing an errant throw to first by using a takeout slide, which was legal in 2011. He tried to make it look as legit as possible, but he had only one goal: take out the second baseman's legs. As he slid, he did just that, throwing his arms out toward second base to sell the slide to the umpire. The infielder's throw sailed into the stands, so Max's job was complete. However, in flipping him, Max's hand had snagged on second base, and as his body kept sliding past it, he felt a rip in his shoulder.

The next day, Max tried to take BP, but he couldn't follow through with his swing. He had to sit out what turned out to be the team's final game of the season anyway as they were eliminated from the playoffs. The pain in his shoulder was tremendous. He had dislocated it, and before the doctor even told him, Max knew he had a fairly long rehab process ahead of him. With fall camp right around the corner, though, he couldn't afford to take much time off. He would have to compensate somehow and make sure the coaches weren't aware of the injury through which he would have to play.

After finishing his annual self-evaluation period, Pat Casey put everyone at ease by deciding to return as Oregon State head baseball coach. With that public ordeal behind them, it was full steam ahead going into the 2012 season, one that was once again filled with high hopes for the Beavers. When Max returned home from Swift Current, he was ready to celebrate his 21st birthday. He had a late birthday for his graduating class and, ahead of his redshirt junior season, he was finally of legal drinking age. Gone forever were the days of pretending to be wasted with his friends. Now he could have the real thing without worrying about getting in trouble or ruining his athletic future.

The day he got back on American soil, he officially became legal, and he partied with a handful of friends which included Sam, who had been drafted by the St. Louis Cardinals in the fifth round of the 2011 MLB Draft.[3] He would sign with St. Louis four days later and had to say his goodbyes at Max's party, because he was shipping out to Batavia, New York, for his first stretch with the Cardinals' Low-A affiliate. It was just like old times: Sam soft-spoken, Max not so much. After so many years of knowing each other, it was as if Sam was passing the baton to Max to represent Ashland on the Beavers' roster. Max, in turn, was proud of his good friend, who was about to chase the biggest dream there was.

Though hampered by his shoulder injury, Max returned to Oregon State for fall camp feeling rejuvenated. He had just finished one of his hottest seasons at the plate in Swift Current and was ready to carry that over into his second season with the Beavers. Sam wasn't the only player leaving from the 2011 team; outfielders Brian Stamps and Mike Miller had graduated, clearing the way for two hot recruits in Dylan Davis and Michael Conforto. The two were high school teammates out of Redmond, Washington. Davis was a 6-foot, 215-pound freshman power hitter and Conforto a 6'2", 217-pound lefty offensive phenom who would go on to star for the New York Mets. Luckily for Max, they were both corner outfielders. They could hit, but they didn't have the speed for his position in center field.

That left Casey's words echoing in Max's head: "I don't care who it is, I just want someone to take that center field job." It may have been out of reach last year, but with newfound confidence at the plate and a year of collegiate experience under his belt, Max believed this could be the year he made good on his promise to himself that he'd take that job for good.

He knew a lot of his success would have to come from his mindset. He took some words from Casey to heart: "Walk around like a champion. Start your car like a champion. Get dressed like a champion, brush your teeth like a champion. Do everything like a champion," Casey would tell his team.

"I'm going to be the starting center fielder," Max would say with conviction. "I'm making that decision right now. I'm going to be that person."

After a while of settling into that attitude, his persona around the house and campus began to change. He walked with more confidence, his chest puffed out and chin pointed up. He was getting his swagger back. For the first time in a long time, he began feeling like his whole, genuine self again.

Clearly, he had shed the timidness with which he had played during sophomore year. No longer did he regard coaches' words as gospel, but merely as guidelines in his process of deciding what would be his dominant strategy. Upperclassmen had started to teach him not to take everything the coaches said to heart or worry 24/7 about what they thought. It was hurting his game, they told him. Hear them, but don't blindly listen. With this selective listening approach, he felt his batting improve that fall, further building on his newfound swagger.

"I went back saying, 'I'm not going to get pounded anymore, I'm not going to be the human punching bag you guys might think I am,'" Max remembers. "'I'm going to take this or you're going to have to fight me.' That was my attitude. I basically had the mentality where I'm going to show up and take this job or you're going to have to fight me for it.'"

His attitude extended to just about everything, including his facial hair. Max grew it out, letting his hair get shaggy as a small beard came into full bloom. His coaches were having none of it. The Beavers had a rule similar to the New York Yankees, which didn't allow facial hair below the lip.

"Hey, you need to clean that up, before the season starts," the command was handed down by the coaching staff.

Well, Max abided by the rules, all right. He shaved below his lip, leaving only thick mutton chops on the sides as well as a mustache. Then he dyed the whole thing black to make it pop. As for the hair on top of his head, he let it grow into a mullet. There wasn't much the coaches could do. There was never much that anybody could do when Max felt defiant.

There were a few times when his newly-adopted attitude threatened to get Max into trouble. That fall during a bunting drill, he struggled to get one down facing teammate Cole Brocker, who was pitching live. He fouled off a 90-mile-an-hour Brocker sinker, the ball hitting the plate and bouncing straight back. Ever the preacher for successfully placing a bunt, Coach Bailey lost it.

"Get your stinking bunt down!" he yelled.

"Oh, well, *excuse* me!" Max replied sarcastically as he stepped out of the box and looked over at his position coach.

"That's it, come over here," Bailey said, signaling him. Then, getting in Max's face, as the Beavers center fielder recalls, he was more stern than usual. "Don't ever talk to me again like that in front of your teammates," he told Max. "That's the last thing you're going to do on this team. Now, go get your bunt down."

With his parting words, Max remembers getting a shove back toward home plate. With that, something in him snapped. He had been going about his life as if he were the sole authority in it, and now a coach was challenging that and trying to put him in his place. He decided not to back down, and a rage filled him for having been shown up in front of his teammates.

Max growled a few obscenities as he turned back around and got closer to his coach. He started to follow Bailey, who was trying to mitigate an escalating situation by walking away. Max dared his coach to turn around, but Bailey could feel the tension rising and relented.

Max had used fighting words. If Bailey had taken the bait and turned around to face him, the Beavers outfielder is convinced he would have been ready to throw down; however, his coach kept walking away as a few of Max's teammates came and restrained him, making sure it didn't go any further. Even though on its face Max's actions may have represented a blatant disrespect of authority, he understood that showing his unwillingness to cow to intimidation earned him a note of respect from his coaching staff. He had struggled to be seen and to stake a place for himself in his first year on the team, and he was making sure that that would not be his problem again this season.

"I know there are times he got mad at me and I was good with that," Bailey says, looking back at Max's conduct. "Wouldn't you rather have that than have him be timid? I thought that was great. If he had questioned what we were doing coaching wise, that would have been an issue, but that was never the case. It's a respect thing and he'd earned our respect, so he had the right to do that. That's what leaders do."

Max had pushed back a bit, which wasn't something the coaching staff had seen from him before. They knew the work ethic was there, but perhaps the competitive fire would enable him to get more playing time in his junior season. Coach Casey could see Max's progression that fall as the regular season loomed.

"His confidence level went up that he could play the game," Casey says. "Once he started believing he could play, I think that helped him become a much better player."

An improving social life also contributed to Max's fiery, carefree attitude. Now that he was finally 21, he was living what he viewed as a more conventional college life. He was out of the family trailer and into an apartment with teammate Ryan Gorton, with whom he had played the previous season in Corvallis. Gorton was a catcher, and 2012 was his senior year, his last shot to win the big one. The duo didn't talk much in their first year as teammates, but once they were living together, they found themselves among each other's best friends on the team. "Max is just so funny," Ryan says. "He had me in stitches when we'd get home from practice, talking about practice or whatever. I mean, who doesn't like a guy that can make them laugh?"

The two have frustratingly similar last names, which made things interesting whenever one had friends over. Max's whole life, he had been called "Gordo," while Ryan had always been called "Gorto." Well, Ryan was older, so he laid claim to that nickname with teammates by default. However, when Max's buddies from Ashland came by, Max would become

Max, draped by teammates, reaches for a high-five from roommate Andy Peterson.

Max pumps his fist after avoiding the tag and scoring a run against Portland State early in the 2013 season.

"Gordo" again and Ryan would have to bite his tongue to keep from responding when he heard his nickname being used on someone else. With teammates, it was always Gorto and Max.

They began to call themselves the "Gordo Conspiracies," because they would watch conspiracy theory Netflix series all the time. That nickname progressed to the "Rooftop Conspiracies." Gorto played guitar, so Max went out and bought a cheap harmonica and taught himself how to play. They would go onto their roof and play music at two in the morning, much to the chagrin of their neighbors. On the frequent occasions when a neighbor would come out to yell at them, they couldn't see them, because their house was lit poorly enough to help them avoid detection.

Sometimes, these shows would take to the streets, with Max playing harmonica and steering his bike and Gorto standing up in the side hack, strumming his guitar, playing loud for everyone to hear. The pair were truly a sight to behold. Before they could translate this newfound chemistry into an on-field one, however, they dealt with a bit of trouble.

During that fall, the pair walked to a football game at Reser Stadium, which was down the street from their place. For student athletes to get into other sporting events, all they had to do was walk up to the window, present a student ID, and they would be given tickets to the game. Max pulled out his student ID first and gave it to the woman at the counter, who was a fellow Oregon State student. In fact, she was in many of the same classes as Gorto.

"Oh, I don't have my student ID, here's my driver's license," Gorto said, handing her an alternate form of identification.

"No, sorry, I need your student ID," she responded.

"Come on, you know who I am," Gorto said. "My name is right there on the list. You just marked off Max Gordon and I'm Ryan Gorton, that's me. I have my driver's license, so let's go."

She would not accommodate them, so Max and Gorto walked back to the house and watched the game on TV, still able to hear the crowd just a block away. A couple of weeks later, it was "Dad's Weekend," with rival Washington in town on Saturday. Zach Reser, whose dad, Marty Reser, had the stadium named after his Reser's Fine Foods empire, was on the baseball team, so for Dad's Weekend, all the sons and fathers got passes up to Marty's box for the game.

After a large group of dads and sons pre-gamed the Beavers football game with beer pong at Max's and Gorto's place, they made their way to the stadium. As Max remembers, everyone had a good buzz going, while Gorto had maybe gotten a little more than that. Walking through a few tailgates, they caught sight of the woman who wouldn't let Gorto into the stadium the previous week. With a bit of liquid courage and very little self-awareness,

Gorto blurted out to her: "Hey, I don't need my student ID this weekend." He flashed his box credential. "I have a pass."

Thinking nothing of it, the group continued into Marty Reser's box, where Reser was, as always, the life of the party.

"Every time Oregon State scores," he suggested, "we're going to get in a line and do a shotgun race, dads versus kids."

Oregon State was lousy at football and, had they stuck to those rules, everyone would have been sober by the middle of the second quarter. Realizing this, Reser instituted a new rule: every time Oregon State got a first down, they would have a shotgun race. It turned out that even that was too lofty for a struggling Beavers football program, so finally they decided that any time anything good happened, there would be a shotgun race. Everyone was having a great time, and Max got up to walk toward the bathroom. He was waiting outside the bathroom door, which was in front of him, when a knock came from the door to the box, directly to his left. Wondering what was up, he opened the door.

"What's up, Alex?" Max said, seeing it was Oregon State's NCAA compliance officer.

"I'm just looking for Ryan," Alex Parker responded. "Is he here?"

"Yeah," Max said, sobering up quickly, not knowing what was going on. "He's in here somewhere. You want me to get him?"

"No, I just wanted to check and see," he responded.

"Okay, have a good one," Max said before shutting the door.

Somehow, the Beavers recovered that day and ended up upsetting Washington, 38–21. The ensuing shotgun races ensured that the next morning would bring mighty hangovers to the boys, who both had early practice. They woke up and went to practice with searing headaches and feeling nauseous. That was before they were called into Casey's office, not entirely sure what the meeting was about but knowing it wasn't likely that they'd won any awards for which they hadn't known they'd been nominated. They were both nervous as they sat down.

"Did you go into a box Saturday night?" Coach Casey asked each of them point-blank.

"Yeah, so did everybody else," they told him.

"Well, Alex from compliance saw you guys and you're going to have to miss some games," Casey explained.

They couldn't believe it. Most of the baseball team had been up there, but since Gorto had been told on, likely thanks to his confrontation with his classmate from the ticket office, and Max had answered the door, they were the two who got popped. Soon after, they learned that they had been suspended for five games, a large chunk of the non-conference schedule. Several months later, as the regular season began at UC Santa Barbara, a series in which the Beavers took three out of four games, Max and Gorto were forced to listen to the games on the radio back in Corvallis.

Finally, they could make the trip with the team to San Diego, where they would play a few different teams in some refreshingly warm weather. They still had one more game to serve on their suspensions, so for the first game against Pacific, they had to sit in the stands on opposite sides like two kids placed in time-out for fighting. Gorto sat on the first-base side, Max on the third-base side, and they twiddled their thumbs, impatient to be eligible again. After a 10–7 win over Pacific on Thursday, the stage was set for the "Gordo Conspiracies" to return on Friday night against San Diego State. Pitching coach Nate Yeskie knew they were hungry and pissed. When they climbed out of the bus, Yeskie chided them. "We've got some new blood," he said. "They better be ready to keep up."

Oh, they were ready. The rest of the team was not. Max went 2-for-4 at the dish in his first action as a junior. It was clear that all of his worry over having to make the team again had been for nothing. As long as he continued to show his coaches he would be a growing presence in the locker room and on the field, there would be a spot for him. Gorto also went 1-for-3 with an RBI, but those two were lone bright spots in an otherwise pitiful game, which the Beavers lost, 18–2.[4] They followed that with an equally uninspiring 13–2 loss to the University of San Diego and its emerging power hitter, Kris Bryant.

OSU bounced back from those rough losses and won six of their next eight non-conference games, despite Max struggling to a 3-for-18 mark at the plate. Still, he felt he was on the verge of a breakthrough. By nature, he was very aggressive, but he was working deep counts at the direction of his coaches. They couldn't have him consistently recording outs on the first or second pitch of an at-bat. Ahead of their game against Oklahoma, the last before conference play began, Pat Casey decided to give him a stroke of motivation. Max had been competing for the starting center field job with Joey Matthews, a former junior college foe at Sacramento City. Third in the race was Ryan Dettman, who hadn't gotten much playing time. Before the Oklahoma game, Max saw Dettman's name penciled into the starting lineup in center field.

Deeply disappointed, but wanting to be a good teammate, Max went over, gave Dettman a pat on the butt, and wished him good luck. Then he went over and started joking around with the guys, trying to stay loose, so that his disappointment wouldn't show.

"I want to talk to you," Casey said to Max 15 minutes before the first pitch. The two walked back into the coach's office in the stadium, and Casey told Max to shut the door.

"You're not playing today," he said, which Max already knew. "I'm playing Dettman, because you just decided you can't do the things that we ask you to do. You're up there trying to hit home runs."

Max was immediately confused and defensive. He did not feel that Casey was being fair.

"Now, we have to play Dettman, because you and Joey Matthews can't figure it out," he continued. "We're giving this kid a shot. If you wouldn't be on the bench screwing around with your friends and actually cared a little bit more, maybe you'd be playing."

Now Max began to feel rather petulant; the way he saw it, he had only been screwing around with teammates to keep morale up while he was processing his emotions over being benched. A small argument ensued. "I'm just trying to do my job and I am doing all the little things," Max pleaded.

No matter what he said, he wasn't getting into the starting lineup that day. He left the office even more bitter than when he entered it and went back to the bench from which he would watch the whole contest. It was drizzling that day, and with the bases loaded and one out in the second inning, a lazy fly ball was sent out to Dettman in center. It was shallow enough that the runner from third would not be able to tag up and score. Dettman sprinted in on the ball way too hard, realized he had overrun it, and threw on the brakes, which on the wet grass forced him to wipe out. As a result, the ball fell not into his mitt, but onto that wet outfield grass behind him for a triple which cleared the bases. Casey and Bailey were beside themselves. Even in the weather, it had been a routine play for a D1 center fielder playing for one of the most competitive programs in the country.

By the time the inning ended, the Beavers trailed, 7–0, and Dettman's day was done. It was his first start, and now it looked like it might also be his last. "Max, get a bat," Casey told him.

He knew this was his chance to own the position. He thought back to his conversation with Casey before the game. He realized that the coach could easily have called Matthews' name when he decided to replace Dettman, but he hadn't. He had called on Max. It was now or never.

In the third inning, Max pinch-hit and rocketed a double to the gap, marking only the second extra-base hit of his collegiate career. That set the tone for what turned into a game-long comeback, ending in an impressive 11–7 Beavers win.[5]

"The Oklahoma game is what got me started," Max realizes, looking back. "That kept the momentum going."

In the days and weeks to come, Max realized that Coach Casey had a purpose behind what he had done, and there was a reason he said what he said. Throughout fall and the non-conference slate, Casey could see that Max had progressed to the point where he was ready to take over the center field job. Now he just had to get him riled up and push him to actually take it. It was his way of saying to Max, "You can do this, so why don't you just do it already? I've been waiting for you to do it." Following the Oklahoma game, Max finally heard his coach loud and clear.

He and Joey Matthews continued to share time in centerfield throughout the season, though. Max started 29 games while Matthews started 24, with the pair putting up nearly identical numbers at the dish—Max was hitting .250 with a .400 on-base percentage while Matthews was hitting .254 with a .388 on-base percentage. Notably, Max was creating value by getting on base by any means necessary rather than by hitting for extra bases. At this juncture of the season, he had clubbed just four extra-base hits and was slugging .316. However, he had reached base 19 times by walk or hit by pitch. Flanked by two star hitters in Dylan Davis and Michael Conforto, all they had to do was play solid defense and hover around a .250 batting average while doing all of the little things right. Do that, and their coaches would be pleased.

Somehow, Max made a living that season teeing off against Stanford's Mark Appel, who became the No. 8 overall pick in the 2012 MLB Draft, returned to Stanford, and was taken No. 1 overall the following year. Max went 5-for-6 in his career off the future No. 1 overall pick. He couldn't explain it, but he just had Appel's number.

By the time Oregon State got to its series against Stanford, it was clear they weren't the same team as a year before. Their lineup had gotten a boost with Davis and Conforto, but the starting rotation had taken a major hit by losing both Gaviglio and Osich. They were just 9–9 with no chance of taking home a conference crown. After a solid non-conference campaign, though, they still expected to play in the postseason. The Beavers may have taken a small step back as a team, but Max had taken a considerable step forward as an individual. Part of that growth was thanks to playing with a more loose, confident style. Another part was the result of finally being given the opportunity to start consistently.

Max's Maniacs were as maniacal as ever, having to cheer even more loudly for him to hear now that he was all the way out in center field. Now, he had another mini-cheering section behind him: a group of older men would climb up onto scaffolding beyond the left-center field wall at Goss Stadium and heckle opposing outfielders. Of course, they were more friendly with Max. They would tell him what they had said to the opposing center fielder, and he found them hilarious. Although they were already clearly inebriated at the games, they were the same men who would greet Max as he left the stadium, beers in hand.

"You want a beer?" they'd ask Max, who could get in a lot of trouble for accepting.

He would politely decline before moving quickly through the parking lot, away from any more trouble since he had already been suspended once this season.

One time, when the Beavers were hitting and Max was sitting in the dugout, he heard that group start yelling. It was in the middle of an at-bat, and suddenly everyone's attention was pointed toward the left-center field wall. A wrestling match had broken out between some of them, who were drunkenly fighting on top of scaffolding just beyond the fence. It was like something out of a cartoon. With seemingly the entire stadium watching, they continued to punch each other until they fell off the scaffolding and disappeared behind the outfield fence.

"It was one of the funniest things I ever saw," Max remembers.

While on the outside, Max was a more confident hitter and leader in the clubhouse, on the inside he was hurting. His errant throw in infield-outfield practice before the 2010 Super Regional had not been a fluke. He was having real difficulty throwing the ball accurately from the outfield. Minutes before a conference game, it was the worst it had ever been.

Max had gotten into the routine of warming up with Michael Conforto, softly tossing it back to the team's star so as not to reveal how inaccurate his own throws were. It helped get Conforto loose and didn't require him to go chasing Max's wild throws. As Max began his motion backward to return the ball to Conforto, his mind so warped by his inability to throw accurately, his entire body seized up and his arm was stuck in place. For five seconds and what felt like a minute, he stood there as still as a statue. It was clear that his problem was more than physical. He had been throwing balls in from the outfield his whole life and, although he never had a cannon of an arm, he had always been proficient and accurate. Now, no matter what he did, he just couldn't get his limbs to obey him.

Throw the ball, he told himself. *Throw the damn ball.*

But he couldn't. He got sick to his stomach and felt deathly afraid that he had simply forgotten how to throw a baseball. It was clear to him that he had a serious case of "the yips," a sudden, all-encompassing inability to throw a baseball accurately. The name alone is enough to send uneasiness down the spine of any ballplayer. There is no telling when the yips might come on, and it's even more difficult to say when they'll go away.

I might not be able to throw anymore, he thought. *Something might have just gone so wrong that it could be over. My career may have just ended.*

Quickly snapping out of his frenzy of thoughts, he tossed the ball back to Conforto underhand and without a word, walked back toward the dugout. His throwing partner followed him into the dugout with reasonable concern.

"Hey, don't tell the coaches that just happened," Max pleaded.

"What just happened?" Conforto asked, confused.

"I can't throw the ball," Max replied. "I don't know what happened. I don't know if I can throw the ball."

"Dude, just relax. You're fine, you can throw a ball," his teammate replied. "It's not a big deal."

Conforto was trying to comfort his teammate, but he didn't know how serious the issue brewing inside Max's head really was. Minutes later, Max told Bailey he wouldn't be taking infield-outfield that day and provided no explanation. From that point forward, he never took infield-outfield before a game again. He figured it would only give opposing teams an advantage to see his unpredictable arm before a game. If they saw him throwing it weakly and/or inaccurately, they would know they could take an extra base if the opportunity presented itself. Max recognized with terror that he was becoming a liability to his team. He couldn't put himself in a position to be embarrassed or put the Beavers in a vulnerable spot.

He tried everything, from visualizing to reading books on the subject to going to the batting cages at midnight to throw hundreds of balls at the screen, trying to get his throwing motion just right. "I was doing everything in my power that I thought I could do to get rid of this demon, and nothing I did worked," Max said. "It honestly made it worse."

"Yeah, it was no secret," Gorto remembers. "Everybody would give him crap, which he probably didn't like. Still, he willed it to happen. It ended up being good enough."

Miraculously, his yips never played a significant role in a game. When the lights were on and the game was at full speed, he could instinctively field a base hit or fly ball and throw it in when it mattered. However, if it was a single with the bases empty and he had time to think about his throw to second base, he was liable to airmail his cutoff man and look silly in the process. The key, though, was that the scary arm issue was not hurting the Beavers, so it wasn't costing him playing time.

Entering the team's final series of the year, they saw that the script had flipped from 2011. It was now Oregon vying for a conference title, needing just one win to lock it up in the final three-game series against the Beavers. Just as the Ducks had done to them the previous year, Oregon State swept their rivals to end the regular season, denying them a conference crown.[6] UCLA got lucky for the second straight year, as the sweep once again gave them a conference title, this time shared with Arizona. At 38–18, the Beavers had done plenty to earn a trip to a Regional, but they hadn't done enough to host one.

They traveled to Baton Rouge and iconic Alex Box Stadium, perhaps the most renowned venue in all of college baseball, to compete in a Regional hosted by perennial power LSU. The Tigers' roster boasted infielder Alex Bregman and pitcher Aaron Nola, both surefire future MLB stars. After beating Belmont in their first game of the Regional, Beavers players littered the stands, watching LSU take on Louisiana-Monroe, knowing they'd play the winner the following day. Max's hair, both on his head and his face, was out of control by this point in the season. His mullet was in prime shape, and there were now racing stripes cut into it. A handful of LSU fans walked past him, letting him know how much they liked his do. "Good for you man, bring back the mullet," they shouted out to him.

With LSU pounding Louisiana-Monroe into submission in the later innings, the Beavers, many proudly wearing their black and orange gear in the stands, made their way to the exits. The entire section around them started chanting, "Tiger bait! Tiger bait!" as they walked away. Soon the entire stadium was looking over and chanting, realizing it was LSU's next opponent leaving the stadium.

For Max and Gorto, the vitriol hurled their way by the Tigers faithful was all the motivation they needed to come out with a vengeance the following day on the diamond. "We'll see you guys tomorrow!" they shouted in the raucous fans' direction as they finally walked out.

They returned the following night to take on LSU in a prime-time matchup that would leave the winner one victory away from a Super Regional berth. As the national anthem played and Max went through his usual routine, he looked up at the Tigers' massive scoreboard, which was the largest in the country at the time. On the board was a camera view of every player as it panned slowly down the line. Suddenly, all that was in the shot was Max's face, tight and in focus. His hat was off, mullet, mustache and mutton chops making him look like a mangy greaseball. All you could see in the frame other than Max's ridiculous style were two pairs of shoulders, one on each of his sides, bouncing up and down, each a teammate laughing at his larger-than-life depiction.

By this point, Max was also trying not to laugh, stone-faced with his vintage game face already painted on. He stared into the camera, embracing the challenge. They held the shot on him for more than 10 seconds as fans in the crowd started to laugh. Just before they cut to a different shot, Max flashed a small smile.

Finally, after all the pregame antics, the two teams were ready to do battle. Max did not even play in the game despite his popular appearance on the big screen beforehand. LSU had the game in hand relatively quickly, beating the Beavers in business-like fashion in the first game. Max and his squad now found themselves on the brink of elimination. Now, they would have to beat Louisiana-Monroe to get another crack at the Tigers.

Getting the start in that game, Max went 1-for-4 with two walks and scored three runs, helping the Beavers to an 11–2 win, and keeping their season alive for at least one more day. It would be them and LSU fighting for a spot in the Super Regional, with the Beavers having to win two straight to advance.

Amped up to be playing at Alex Box Stadium, the nicest college venue he had ever seen, Max sprinted out as his name was announced. After all, he hadn't been in the lineup to get a shot to take out the Tigers the first time around. In front of more than 10,000 fans, he tripped on the lip between the grass and dugout turf and went flying face-first, launching his sunglasses into foul territory several feet away. *Good start*, he thought.

Taylor Starr, a redshirt senior, started on the mound for Oregon State, a decision with which not every player on the team agreed. Max thought Starr was a very talented pitcher, but he and others thought he was a little soft and might not have the mental toughness to show up for a big game. Unfortunately for them, in this case, they were right. After allowing three runs and recording just one out, Starr was yanked in desperation for freshman Scotty Schultz. He had just a handful of innings under his belt so far that year, but it would be up to him to keep the Beavers' season alive. At the mound before Schultz took over, Coach Yeskie gave an unusual order. "I don't know what to call, you guys figure it out," he said. "Whatever I call, they're hitting it a country mile, so you guys got it."

It was extremely unusual. With Ryan Gorton or anyone else behind the plate, Yeskie would call pitches from the bench and relay them to his catcher. Almost never did he rely on the catcher to call his own game. With the season on the line, though, that's exactly what he did. It was unconventional, but it worked. By the sixth inning, the Beavers had turned a 3–0 deficit into a 5–3 lead. Schultz and Gorto had natural chemistry and were calling a very effective game. Slowly but surely, however, LSU clawed back into it, scoring once in the seventh to cut the lead to one entering the ninth inning. The leadoff man clubbed a gap shot into left-center in the ninth as Max gave chase. He sprinted toward the gap, thinking at the last second that he might actually have a play on the ball. Perfect route, perfect jump, and a dive … and the ball grazed off his mitt, dribbling onto the outfield grass. The Tigers had a leadoff double. Max wasn't sure how much more he could've done to make the catch, but his inability to make the snag ate away at him. It hurt even more when another hit tied the game and sent it to extra innings.

Schultz had given his team a chance to win, allowing just two runs, one earned, over 8 2/3 innings of work. Into extra innings the teams went, and it would come down to Dylan Davis, who, on top of being one of the team's best hitters, was also a relief pitcher for the Beavers. With a runner on third base, he delivered a wild pitch, giving the Tigers a 6–5 lead. Oregon State was actually considered the home team based on Regional rules, so they got one last shot to salvage their season. LSU reliever Nick Goody, however, made sure to squelch any thoughts of a comeback. He tossed a scoreless 10th, sending LSU to a Super Regional and Oregon State home short of a College World Series berth once again.[7]

Now, Max had images of Vanderbilt dogpiling for their trip to Omaha and the image of his diving attempt, the ball barely grazing off his glove. Both continued to play in his head throughout the summer, symbols of how close his team had been to Omaha, and how far he still had to come to help get them over that hump. When the team gathered back in Corvallis the following fall, months after the LSU game and months still until the 2013 season would get underway, Coach Casey switched on the projector screen and played the final frames of the LSU game again. As he saw himself dive unsuccessfully for the ball in the gap, Max slammed his hand on the desk in front of him, the emotional wound still fresh months later.

Unlike many of his teammates who were destined for professional baseball careers, Max knew 2013 would be the last time he would play competitive baseball. He had one more year of eligibility, and one more year to reach the mountaintop at which he'd been grasping for most of his life. For the past four years, he had given his entire soul to baseball. In his final season, he just wanted to get something back.

Head coach Pat Casey was confident that Max's immense investment would pay further dividends. Though it was a loss, Casey knew the final game against LSU in 2012 would power his program back to heights it hadn't reached in half a decade.

"I was never more confident coming off a loss than that," Casey remembers. "That game convinced me we were in good shape for 2013."

CHAPTER 16

Senior

Sitting still in the cold pond on New Year's Eve morning, Max was deathly quiet. He squinted through one eye, with the other one totally shut. He found his target. Two big splashes sounded from the water as he and his pal, Miles, jumped in and took aim, firing into the morning fog. Two hits: a goose, and a duck. Max had winged his goose, so he had to walk up and finish it off. Miles had killed the duck with one clean shot. They trudged up through the murky water and collected their kills, knowing that the noise and commotion of their first kills had probably scared off the rest of the day's game. They packed up and headed home. It was just as well; Max had to get back for a New Year's party with some Oregon State teammates.

On the ride home, Max turned to Miles and said, "I'm going to Corvallis and I really want a duck. Wanna trade?"

"For sure, I'll take a goose over this shit duck," Miles replied, looking at the size of the two birds and wondering why he had been offered such a lopsided trade.

From his hunting trip, Max drove to Bend, where he had once gone snowboarding with Nick at Mount Bachelor. That's where his New Year's party was, nearly three hours east of Corvallis. As he ventured toward the party, duck fastened in a Safeway bag, bouncing on the passenger seat, he wondered how he would keep it from spoiling while he partied that night. Luckily, Bend was a ski town; when he arrived at the party, he banked his car against a curb and put the bag in the nearby snow. He figured that should keep it cold enough. After ringing in 2013, which would be his final year as a member of the Oregon State baseball team, he walked back to his car, retrieved the duck, tossed it back in the truck, and was on his way to Corvallis.

Once there, he put the duck into a freezer he shared with Ryan Gorton, who had graduated the previous year, Jerad Casper, and Andy Peterson. Petey was a junior college transfer and had met Max through Coach Casey, who had connected the two, since Max needed another roommate for his senior year. After sending Max a text asking what he needed for the house, Petey Googled him to see what was up.

"The first thing I did was look him up online to see what he looked like, and I saw his big old mullet, mustache and sideburns almost connecting to his mustache," Petey remembers with a laugh. "I was like, 'Oh jeez, this is the guy I'm moving in with? We'll see how this goes.'"

Already having lived with Max for months now, seeing a duck in the freezer wasn't a shock to him. In fact, it tracked perfectly with the Max he had come to know. The duck was placed in the freezer without anything covering it, so there sat a dead duck for months on end in the four guys' fridge. "You're taking chicken nuggets out and you have to move the duck over a little bit to get food out," Petey says.

Max let his roommates in on why he was keeping the duck in the freezer for so long, and they were on board. He had a plan for it, but the duck was going to be there throughout the baseball season. He asked the guys to keep the duck's purpose under lock and key.

"I usually don't care so much about secrets," Max told them. "But I really want you guys to hold on. Do not tell anybody that I have this. It's really important to me, so don't say anything about it."

They agreed, and thus began the duck's months-long stay in the Corvallis freezer. Although the guys didn't mind it much, Max could think of a group of kids who would have freaked out at the sight of that dead duck. Having not found a summer team to play with through Oregon State, Max spent the summer at a baseball camp for kids; specifically, it was a camp for kids with very wealthy parents. Most of them had parents who were moguls, MTV or VH1 executives, etc.... When he told other camp counselors that he played for Oregon State, they thought he meant the club team. Only at the end of the two months did they find out he had played in an NCAA Regional at Alex Box Stadium just months before.

Coaching kids who were born with silver spoons in their mouths had made Max realize his journey in baseball was one to be thankful for rather than one to complain about. "I saw how easy all these kids have it," Max explains. "I'm going to work my ass off my entire life and I'm never going to live the kind of life these guys are living. It didn't make me mad, it made me feel really grateful for what I'd been through and accomplished."

It had rendered him grateful, but he was nowhere near satisfied; if anything, his dynamite work ethic was reinforced by his experiences that summer. Upon returning to Corvallis for his senior season, Max felt rejuvenated and ready to make a championship run with Pat Casey and his teammates. That mountaintop still seemed pretty far away, but with one last chance to climb it, he wasn't about to look down now.

As Andy Peterson got to know Max, he was inspired, as many other teammates were, by his work ethic. "He was a role model," Petey says. "He never took one second off from life. He had no business being at Oregon State, but he was there, because of his competitiveness and drive."

When it was time to get up for 6 a.m. weights, Max would be full of energy, shouting up and down the halls to wake Petey and Casper up, "Let's go! It's a beautiful morning!" It might have been a miserable day, but not on Max's watch.

"We were exhausted, but just because Max is our roommate, we have to pretend we aren't tired," Petey recalls. "If we showed that we were tired, then we were never going to hear the end of it." Max pushed them to their limits, and ultimately, they were thankful to him for it.

Occasionally, Max would get bored before the three piled into the car, and with Casper and Petey waiting for him, he'd just bolt out the door. "Screw it! I'm running there!" he'd yell as he took off down the street, sprinting into the pitch-black Corvallis morning. His high-octane nature had ebbed and flowed over these difficult college years, but it was back like no one had ever seen it, in pursuit of the perfect senior season.

Petey talks mostly about how much Max made him laugh, which is a common theme among people who knew Max around this time; however, Max and Petey shared more than just laughs: they had both lost someone close to them. In quick succession, Max had lost Coach K, Grampy Norman, and Nick. The previous fall, Petey had lost his dad.

As Petey got ready to graduate from high school, he still had to decide whether to play baseball or football in college. He had his mind made up to play football, but when his high school baseball coach implored him to go the junior college baseball route, he reconsidered. Eventually, his coach convinced him. He returned home to tell his parents that instead of going to Missouri Tech or Northern Arizona for football, he was going to play baseball at a junior college. While he was sharing that news with his parents, his dad cut in with more pressing news of his own. He had brain cancer. Doctors had given him just a few months to live. Later that year, he was gone. Max was one of the few people Petey could relate to and with whom he could discuss ways to cope.

"Especially at that age, most of my friends growing up hadn't gone through something like that," Petey says. "I grew up in Southern California where everyone lived pretty good, easy lives. Just hearing Max's entire story, it was definitely an eye opener."

And so, one of Max's favorite sayings was used a lot to motivate the two roommates and teammates throughout fall camp. "Compared to what?" Max would ask any time Petey complained. He would hear the same back from his roommate if he got down.

"Why? Compared to what? I have the same thing going on. We all do. Oh well, suck it up."

Max's "compared to what" philosophy was partly forged by a *Beavers without Borders* trip he made with other Oregon State athletes to Guatemala, where he witnessed first-hand just how good a life he had. He helped build houses for families there, and he watched as they grinded for everything they had. It reminded him of how he had grinded on the baseball field to get to where he was, but he knew that unlike his work on the baseball field, the work he saw the locals doing dictated their livelihood.

Petey looked up to him as a tough older brother. He needed someone like that while his mom went through chemotherapy for her own cancer battle, which was well underway. Petey's first year at Oregon State was an emotional roller coaster, but using Joe Carnahan's lessons about level-headedness, Max tried to calm the ride for his teammate. He had to keep his whole squad level if they were going to get where he needed them to go.

Entering 2013, Max was still competing with Joey Matthews, Joe Bags to his teammates, for playing time in center field. Possibly a greater threat was the talented freshman, Jeff Hendrix. It was clear to Max that he was the heir apparent; Hendrix would be the next everyday center fielder for the Beavers. The only question was who would be Hendrix's true predecessor. Knowing he couldn't keep up with him talent-wise, Max started playing mind games with the shy freshman.

"Hey Jeff, I'm going to be better than you today, and you're not going to play anymore," he would say, looking unflinchingly at his teammate. He was equal parts protective of his job and cognizant of the fact that if he pushed Hendrix now, the Beavers would be better for it once he left. "I would try to get in his head and make him think he wasn't good enough to play over me," Max explains. "Because he definitely was good enough and if he had any confidence or killer instinct to him as a freshman, I wouldn't have seen the light of day."

As much as he tried to keep his own position safe, Max taught Hendrix where he needed to play in the outfield and how to handle the coaches, and he tried to improve his baseball IQ. Hendrix came from a small school and wasn't as baseball savvy as many of his teammates. Max made it a point to get him ready to take over. "Thank you, man. I needed that," Hendrix, referencing the tough-love approach, would tell Max after the season.

After a little bit of fall practice, it was clear that for that season, the center field job was down to Max and Joey Matthews. The day after returning to Oregon State practice for the first time since surgery to repair a broken hamate bone, Joey wanted to get right back into the mix. He was antsy. It had been nearly two months since he had practiced fully with the team, and he just wanted to do something before fall turned to winter.

"Just wait for the weekend," Coach Casey told him. "There's no need to rush this. We'll wait for the weekend and be good to go."

"Man, I really want to do something," Joe Bags replied. "Just let me get back in the cage."

"Just go over to the bunt machine and track some pitches," Casey said. "You haven't seen a pitch in a couple months, so just hang out over there."

The wrong type of ball popped into the pitch machine as Joey walked up to the bunting station. With no warning, the ball took off on its own and shattered his face. He had 14 broken bones and required reconstructive surgery, including plates being put in. His face was destroyed. He found himself plagued with the most bizarre injuries, but it shed fortune on Max's senior season in the Beavers outfield.

That series of injuries changed the way Joe Bags played in 2013. After rehabbing his facial injuries all fall, he was back in time for the season, but he hadn't taken live at-bats in nearly half a year. Every time out, he was skittish, because in the back of his mind he feared he would injure himself again; he didn't attack the game with the style he used to.

"Once you start playing like that, your game changes a little bit," Joe Bags explains. "You can't really compete at the level you want to, because you don't want to get hurt."

As the team moved into 2013 conference play, Max was essentially the team's everyday center fielder. Joe Bags grabbed a handful of starts, but he just wasn't the same. After a near-school record of 15 straight wins to start the season, and 20 wins in the team's first 21 games, the Beavers clearly were among the top teams in the country. Max found himself playing a key role on a championship-contending squad, thanks in part to Joey Matthews' poor luck. Just as his luck was seemingly turning a corner, Joe Bags' fortune sank even lower on a team trip to Utah.

Playing at a Triple-A stadium with a pro surface on the warning track, it was Joey Matthews in center, Max in right, and Michael Conforto in left. The crack of a bat sent a fly ball toward the left-center gap, forcing both Joey and Mike to gun it into the alley. Max watched the play develop from right field, slowly drifting in the direction of center. He watched in horror as Joey and Mike dove for the ball in the same spot, causing a gruesome mid-air collision. Joe Bags spun around backwards from the force of the blow, which sent his head slamming against the hard surface of the warning track. Seeing what had just happened, with the ball falling into neither fielder's mitt, Max sprinted in their direction.

"Joey, Joey!" Conforto yelled, standing over his unconscious teammate. Max screamed at him to get the ball. It was still a close game, and an inside-the-park home run, by now, seemed inevitable. Conforto did eventually throw the ball in, but the Utah hitter had already scored. Once they took his glove and hat off him, and the training staff checked him out, Max and Mike carried their teammate off the field. The dugout was rendered

silent. Everybody loved Joe Bags, and here he was with yet another gruesome, freak injury. He didn't play another game during the regular season.
If Max hadn't already been securely in an everyday starting role, he was
now.

"We literally couldn't keep him off the field," Coach Bailey said of Max,
citing a major difference between the way the team performed with him in
the lineup as opposed to on the bench. Max was not a team captain—Oregon State did not formally name captains—but he might as well have been.
When he was in the lineup for the Beavers, things just felt *different.*

In games Max started during the 2013 season, his team was 33–6, as
opposed to 19–9 when he didn't start. His team won 17 percent more often
when he was in the lineup, which indicates a significant change.[1] As his
mother, Michelle, already knew, he was a guy who changed the energy in
the dugout simply by being on the field. There was something about him
being out there that made the team more confident. Nearly everyone else
on the field had more natural ability, but he may have moved the needle
more than any single one of them.

"There are some guys on a team who you really pull for," Max explains.
"They work their asses off and might not be the best guy on the team, but
they work so hard to help the team win in any way they can. When I would
come up in a situation, the whole dugout, everybody wanted me to do well.
It makes it a lot easier to root for those types of guys, so when I'd go up
and play well or do something that helped us win, everybody got a little bit
more excited about that than they would for other people."

Regardless of his extreme aptitude for leadership, the team would not
have followed him the way they did that season had his play not spoken
for itself. He had made great strides on the field since his days as a redshirt
sophomore, struggling to find his place on a supremely talented squad. He
was now a senior who led by example on and off of the field.

"He became a better individual player, because he worked on it,"
Coach Casey remembers. "Since he became a better individual player, we
became a better team. I don't want it to be overlooked that not only did
he have such an impact on us, because he was such a team guy, but also
because he became a good player."

"When you think about those Oregon State teams, you always think
about guys like Michael Conforto, Dylan Davis or our ridiculous pitching
staff," Coach Bailey adds, "But if you built the foundation of a house for that
team, I thought Max was the foundation of our house. He did that not so
much by his words, but by his actions. His teammates loved him."

This was most evident in the outfield, where Max came into his
own as a defensive wizard. Fans already knew what he could do defen-
sively, but given the chance to start most days, he took it to another level

A ritual he did in every at-bat for the rest of his career, Max looks up to the sky to remind himself whom he is playing for.

in 2013. Against Stanford with Matt Boyd pitching, a ball was rocketed to the left-center gap, causing Stanford fans immediately to cheer what they thought was a sure double. Max turned and started sprinting, thinking he would likely have to play the ball off the wall. However, the ball hung up a little longer than Max expected, and the more he ran, the better chance he thought he had at making the grab.

As he approached the wall, he leapt as far as he could onto the warning track, where somehow, the ball landed in his glove, completing an unbelievable run and turning it into a spectacular play. When Max realized he had caught it, he let out an emphatic scream as Conforto came over and gave him a chest bump in celebration. Max whipped the ball in with ease. He knew he was playing defense at a whole new level, and there was nothing getting in his way now. The Beavers turned that weekend into a three-game sweep of Stanford. On Monday, when the team returned home, it was an off-day, so Max could sleep in. For Max, sleeping in meant waking up around 8 a.m. When he rubbed the sleep out of his eyes around 8:15, he looked at his phone and saw that he had more than 50 texts from his closest friends, family, and teammates. He was worried that something horrible must have happened until he read the first couple of texts.

"Have you seen SportsCenter this morning??"

He flicked on the TV.

Max makes a sprawling, backward catch, one of the finest of his career.

The SportsCenter top plays didn't come on until the end of the show, so there he sat for nearly an hour watching highlights and news pieces, waiting to see how any of it pertained to him. Finally, SportsCenter's top 10 plays segment came on, and as they went through No. 6 and No. 5 and having not seen his play, Max was dejected.

Oh man, they must have taken it off or something, he thought.

The countdown got to No. 2, and he saw an opening shot at Stanford. At that moment, he knew what was coming next. He had lived it, and now he was watching it on his TV. He watched himself tracing the ball, surprising even himself with the sheer closing speed he employed to get to the ball. Goosebumps trickled across his every nerve as he watched, paused, rewound, and watched again. His diving catch was among the best plays in sports that weekend.

"That was one of those childhood dreams that I never ever thought would come true," Max says with a smile. "I always wanted to be one of those people on that top 10 highlight video, and when I finally did it, that was a really cool experience."

From robbing Nick of three straight Wiffle ball hits with diving plays to being featured on national TV for a catch he had made, his baseball career had come a long way. He was on SportsCenter several other times that season, solidifying his outstanding defense as his trademark skill. At one point, he claimed the No. 1 and 3 spots in the same week. Since those plays would come just a week after he had recorded another top play, SportsCenter put together a piece highlighting all three plays in one segment. He was becoming a defensive phenom in the college baseball world. "Max has average speed, but he's not a burner," Coach Bailey says. "He got great jumps, took great routes, and was absolutely fearless. I mean, that guy just has no fear."

What he lacked in speed, he made up for with tenacity. Those putting together the "Catch of the Game" videos, which played on the Goss Stadium big boards during home games, had an easy job. All they had to do was choose which Max Gordon catch to show that evening. Back home, his mom, dad, and Granny Dorothy, who was still living in her adult foster care community, couldn't believe what a sensation Max was becoming. They saw his plays on a national sports TV show, and they couldn't believe it. He had put himself and his family on the map.

Behind Max's diving catches as well as the emerging bats of Conforto and Davis, the Beavers were humming like a well-oiled machine. Their starting rotation could hang with the best in the country as well. At 20–4 in conference play heading into the Civil War against Oregon, the Beavers, just as they had in 2011, needed a series win to clinch the conference crown one week early. The day before the Oregon series started in Eugene, the team had just been dismissed for the day by the coaching staff. However, Max didn't want anyone going anywhere just yet. "I'm holding a team meeting in the locker room right now," Max told his teammates as the coaches started walking away. "No coaches allowed."

He didn't want any coaches there, because he knew if any staff saw what he was about to do, there was a good chance they'd lose their job. "I would've loved for all of them to be there," Max said. "I especially would've loved Case to be there. He would've been so fired up. But I knew that probably wasn't a good idea."

As players filed into the players-only meeting in the locker room, Max had already put on his Camelback backpack, with the zipper slightly open. What was that hanging out of it? Max surveyed the room, walking around with a hunting knife on his hip as he paced.

"All right, listen up, boys. My first year here, 2011, all we had to do was win one game against these assholes and we'd win the conference championship, and we lost every goddamn game when we went down there," he began. "We folded. Last year, all they had to do was beat us once, same situation. Mike makes a great play, Gorto tags their dude out at the plate, and we beat their ass."

The vibe in the room was a mixture of anticipation and confusion. Clearly, Max was working toward something, but few on the team had any notion of what it would be. The passion in his voice was palpable. "The Pac-12 runs through the Civil War every fucking year and you better believe it," Max said. "They don't want us to win this shit. Last time we went down there, we got our faces shoved in the dirt. It ain't going to happen again."

Just as he said those words, he reached back and grabbed what now appeared to be a small head with a bill on it hanging out of his backpack, and in one motion, he slammed it on the table in front of him. It was the duck he had been keeping in his freezer for months, only to let thaw that morning in preparation for this very speech. He'd had this speech planned for nearly a year.

"This year, we're going to kill the fucking Ducks!" Max shouted.

Everyone looked around the room at each other. Some of the guys were really into it, while others were totally confused. Petey thought straight-laced Boyd might call PETA.

"First game, we're going to stab them in the chest and open them up," Max said, slinging his hunting knife from his hip and cutting the duck down the middle. As teammates watched in shock, disbelief, even horror, he continued.

"Game 1 is done. We're not fucking finished," he said. "We're going to take this goddamn series and we're going to rip their fucking hearts out."

Max reached into the duck, which at this point had been dead for nearly half a year, and pulled its heart out of its chest. Duck fat and guts dripping out of his hand and down his arm, he forged on.

"These motherfuckers don't know what they're getting themselves into," he screamed. "So now, we've won the series, that's over. Just for good measure, we're going to sweep these assholes and rip their fucking heads off."

He went to cut the duck's head off, but it was too stringy and rubbery from being frozen for so long, so he couldn't get it off. Finally, he ad libbed and simply ripped the duck's head free from its body. He held the duck's head on display. "There were a few guys who were like, 'Fuck yeah!'" Max remembers. "And everybody else was like, 'This guy's insane.'"

Before heading home, Max lifted up a grate that ran underneath Goss Stadium and threw the duck carcass inside. Still somewhere underneath Goss Stadium, the duck finally rests in peace. He put the long-dead duck's head into his game bag and went home. The next day, the team made the short trip down to Eugene for the start of the Civil War, a game that could see the Beavers win a conference title.

Max, Ben Wetzler, and Nate Esposito crouched down in the team's huddle before the game, pumping up the rest of the Beavers, who crowded around. Just before getting their break, but before taking the field, Max took the duck head out of his back pocket and slapped it in the middle of the group. "Let's fucking kill them!" he shouted as everyone on the team went insane. As everyone dispersed, he tucked the duck head back into the back pocket of his baseball pants and sprinted out to center field. When he came back in from the field, a clear stain starting to form in the back of his pants, teammates chuckling, Coach Casey took notice. His center fielder was really playing with a duck head in his back pocket?

This guy's a beauty, man, Casey thought.

Despite Max's theatrical ritual, the Ducks were very much alive, knocking off Oregon State in Game 1, 3–0. Now they had to win the final two games of the series to guarantee a conference crown. They won Game 2, 9–0, setting the stage for a potential clinching game in the series finale. In a battle of top 10 teams (No. 10 Oregon and No. 6 Oregon State), the Beavers prevailed. With the bases loaded in the second inning, Max standing on third base, Conforto crushed a ball into the stratosphere. "I've never seen a ball hit so pure in my life," Max recalls.

Conforto's grand slam started the scoring, and OSU did not let up. They won the game, 12–2, the series, and their first conference title in six seasons.[2] The Beavers were headed to the postseason, and if they played their cards right, the road to Omaha would run through Corvallis. First, they would have to take care of business in their Regional, which saw them hosting once again. This time they would take on UC-Santa Barbara, Texas-San Antonio, and Texas A&M in Corvallis.

Surprisingly, the team found itself on the ropes in its opening game against Texas-San Antonio. Trailing 4–3 going into the ninth inning, they needed a rally or their season would be one loss away from ending. Tyler Smith worked a leadoff walk, putting the tying run on base. Petey bunted him successfully over to second, meaning a base hit could tie the game and force extra innings. Down in the count 1–2, Conforto was hit by reliever Matt Sims, placing the winning run on first. Up walked Dylan Davis, Conforto's high school teammate, who rounded out the heart of the Beavers' order. Coming through in the clutch, Davis took a hack and clobbered the ball to the right-center gap, sending the ball rolling all the way to the wall. Smith scored the tying run, and Conforto was intent on winning it right then and there. His long strides pushing him, his arms pumping at his sides, he rounded third and made his break for home. The umpire loaded up to make his call: safe at the plate. The Beavers had won it in walk-off fashion. It was harder than they had expected it to be, but they were now just a couple of wins from a Super Regional appearance.

Next up was UC-Santa Barbara, which had Cameron Newell, an outfielder who had failed to make Oregon State's roster in Max's first two seasons with the team. Newell was having a breakout year for UCSB, and as a Roseburg, Oregon, kid, and someone Max had faced in high school, it was a stellar opportunity to show up the squad which had denied him. He went 1-for-4 with an RBI, helping score one of just two runs the Gauchos scratched across. Tied 2–2 in the ninth inning, the Beavers, as the visiting team, once again had to muster some ninth-inning magic.

The script went nearly exactly the same as it had the day before. Petey pushed a perfect bunt single slowly across the infield with one out, bringing up Conforto. Once again, the lefty power hitter was hit by a pitch, putting

Max embraces Pat Casey on 2013 Senior Day at Oregon State, nearly three years after their improbable journey began.

Max (front, center) and his Beavers teammates celebrate winning the 2013 Pac-12 baseball title.

the go-ahead run in scoring position. After a groundout, Ryan Barnes drew a walk to load the bases with two outs. Danny Hayes strolled up.

Just as Barnes had, Hayes worked a bases-loaded walk after starting the at-bat 0–2, which gave the Beavers a 3–2 lead. They held on in the bottom half, and victory was theirs. Into the Regional championship game they went, where they would soon play Texas A&M. The Aggies needed two straight wins over the Beavers to advance. Max and friends would not let that happen. OSU cruised over Texas A&M, 6–1, not allowing nearly as much drama to unfold as in the previous two games. For the first time since Max's redshirt sophomore season, the Beavers were headed to a Super Regional, and unlike the first time Max had experienced it, this time they would be hosting.

Kansas State came to town, with each team needing two wins to advance to the College World Series. As he often did, Conforto opened the scoring in Game 1, hitting a towering two-run homer in the fourth inning. Matt Boyd pitched a fantastic game, allowing the Wildcats just a solitary run. The Beavers entered the ninth inning with a 2–1 lead. With a runner on second and one strike from losing, Kansas State's Tanner Witt shot a base hit up the middle to knot things up at 2–2. OSU had been one strike from victory, but now they would have to battle for their playoff lives.

To extra innings the two teams went, and the Wildcats poured it on, using the momentum from the ninth inning. A bases-loaded triple and subsequent single later, the Beavers were dumbfounded to find themselves down, 6–2. They couldn't muster anything in the bottom of the 10th and the Wildcats took Game 1. It was the third Super Regional game in which Max had played, and after going 0-for-2 with a walk in this one, the Beavers were now 0–3 in his Super Regional games. If he added another to that margin, he would fall just short of the mountaintop he'd been climbing toward for the past three years. He and his teammates, including Michael Conforto, who had bloomed into a full-on superstar, were still confident after the crushing loss.

"We take it like we always have," Conforto said to the media after the game. "We've done this before. We did this against Oregon. We did this

Max's intensity shows as he takes a healthy lead off first base.

against Washington State. We did this against UCLA. We've been in this position before. Maybe the stakes are higher, but I really think this team, in front of our fans, I think we can respond the way we know we can."

Max truly hoped that his teammate was correct; Game 2 now had the chance to be his final baseball game. He wasn't the only one. Calmly and emphatically, Coach Casey made that fact clear to the young men sitting in front of him in the locker room before the game that threatened to end their season. "You guys need to look around and understand that some people aren't going to ever play this game again when this thing's done," he started. "I hope you understand that, and I hope you're playing for those people, because we all know who they are."

With intensity showing on their faces, everyone thought about the handful of seniors in their group, even the ones they knew would end up playing pro ball. There was a lot of potential left untapped in this group, and none of them wanted this to be the last time they played together. "It's really hard to have the jersey taken off your back," Casey said, recalling his experience in professional baseball. "Don't let anyone take the jerseys off your backs."

He kept his closing short and simple: "You have to go out there and win, go out there and compete." He looked out at them all, feeling the love in the room. "You have to believe in each other, believe in the guy next to you."

With that, the team headed out to the dugout. In the stands, Stan and Michelle could hardly look. It seemed like everything for which they had worked and endured hung on every single pitch.

As the teams were introduced, Oregon State lined up on the visitor's side and stared vigilantly into the Kansas State dugout. Everyone had their hands on their hips or arms crossed in front of their chest. Coach Casey's speech had gotten to them, and now they were locked in. It was not good news for Kansas State that the Beavers got to bat first.

Before fans even had a chance to get concessions, the Beavers grabbed a 5–0 lead. By the end of three innings, they extended the lead to 9–1. The usual suspects, Michael Conforto and Dylan Davis, homered as the Beavers rolled through the Wildcats. With that drubbing, they set the stage for an epic Game 3, one which guaranteed to send one team to Omaha and the other home. Stan and Michelle let out a sigh of relief, knowing Max would get at least one more game in a Beavers uniform.

Since the Beavers were in the visiting dugout, they had to walk out onto the concourse past fans to get to their home clubhouse in order to change back into street clothes. Every remaining Oregon State fan at the stadium created a human tunnel as they walked out, which stretched along the entire back of Goss Stadium. The players were still amped up from the game that had just saved their season. Michelle was out there getting

Before Game 2 of the 2013 Super Regional vs. Kansas State, the entire Oregon State team decided to go with stone-cold looks on their faces. Here, that included Dan Childs, Zack Reser, and Max (left to right).

hugs from nearly every player on Oregon State, including the towering, 6'4" Danny Hayes, who shouted, "Oh yeah, Mrs. Gordon!" as he embraced Max's mom, who was more than a foot shorter than he was.

"Who the heck are you?" a woman asked Michelle as she passed by, wondering why she was getting so much attention from the players on the team.

"These are my kids; these are my boys," she responded, smiling.

They were the boys that had been there for Max and for whom Max had been there over the past several years.

"My biggest fear was that Max would be left alone after Nick died," Michelle explains. "But he has a lot of brothers. I don't worry much about that anymore. He has a home any time he wants."

With a momentous, winner-take-all Game 3 looming, Michelle hoped Max would get to take one more trip with those boys in pursuit of college baseball's ultimate prize. Before Game 3, knowing it would be his last game at Goss Stadium no matter what, Max broke out his old BESR aluminum bat. That style of bat was outlawed years prior in favor of BBCOR bats, which had less pop in them and thus posed less risk of harm to fielders. He still had it from high school and decided to bring it up to the plate with him for pre-game batting practice, because why not? "It's my last day, I'm not going to get up here and bunt for all my rounds," Max laughs. "I'm just going to hit bombs."

He had never hit a home run at Goss Stadium, and on his final night there he decided he would do just that, even if it was just in batting practice. Instantly, guys on the team could tell by the sound of the ball bouncing off his bat that he was not using a normal BBCOR bat. Some gave him weird looks, wondering what exactly he was doing.

They soon saw what he was doing. He jacked several home runs, one hitting off the scoreboard far past the outfield fence. He was having fun and staying loose before the biggest game of his career. Coach Casey couldn't help but laugh at his one-of-a-kind center fielder as he continued to crank balls beyond the wall. Once his first round was over, that was it for the BESR bat. He was ready to play.

He grabbed his glove, ran to the outfield, and didn't take another batting practice swing. Prior to the game getting underway, though, there was an argument as to whether the team should celebrate should they win that night. "Boys, we're not going to dogpile," Matt Boyd said. "We need to act like we've been there before. We have more business to do. We don't want to celebrate this."

"Fuck that," assistant coach Andy Jenkins, a member of the 2005 team that reached the College World Series, shot back. "You haven't been there before. You guys are dogpiling tonight after we win."

Before the first pitch was thrown, the team had decided on the dogpile. One of its most vociferous supporters was big, bad Danny Hayes. Hayes was becoming something of a clutch performer for the Beavers that postseason, and he continued his heroics with a towering two-run shot that gave OSU a 2–0 lead in the second inning. Ben Wetzler pitched a great game, leaving with two outs in the eighth inning, his team up, 4–3. In came Matt Boyd to try and strand the potential tying runner on second base. R. J. Santigate sliced a single to left field, almost sure to score Blake DeBord from second. The ball bounced into the outfield with Conforto charging hard toward it. He scooped it up on the run and fired a bullet toward catcher Jake Rodriguez, waiting in front of the plate. It was an absolute missile, the only throw giving the Beavers any chance to make the play. It landed in Rodriguez's glove with a pop as he applied the tag to DeBord a split-second before he crossed the plate. Goss Stadium erupted as the home team escaped sure disaster in the eighth inning. For all his hitting heroics, Conforto delivered his signature Oregon State moment in the field, and the Beavers were now three outs away from returning to Omaha.

Boyd came back out for the ninth inning in search of completing the four-out save. After putting a runner on first with two outs, he coaxed a high fly ball, heading toward foul territory down the first base line, out into no man's land. Often, similar foul balls at Goss Stadium would be pushed back into fair territory because of a little jet stream that tends to blow them back toward the field. Max had watched this play dozens of times before, and he knew it was a tough one for the first or second baseman to make. Hayes ranged over from first base, but Max was screaming from center field for Petey to make the grab from his position at second base. He felt Petey had the better shot at it. Petey didn't give much chase, leaving it to Hayes to make a play. After what felt like an eternity, the ball started plummeting back toward the earth. Max was afraid it would push back into fair territory, which could tie the game.

As it got closer and closer to field level, it was clear it wasn't going to be a fair ball. The only question was, would it stay in play? Hayes positioned himself near the barrier down the first base line, and that jet stream ever so gently nudged the ball just within his grasp. With his arm outstretched, Hayes caught the ball, and Goss Stadium erupted. Conforto turned and ran toward Max as the two hugged, grabbed each other's jerseys, and ran full speed toward the dogpile that was forming near the mound. In tandem, they jumped on top of the mass of humanity, celebrating the tickets they had just punched to the College World Series.[3]

Fans stayed standing, the cool air of a June night brushing gently over those in attendance who had just seen the Beavers get back to Omaha for the fifth time in school history. After six years away, Pat Casey's squad had gotten back. Stan and Michelle celebrated in the stands with the other parents who had endured the season's ups and downs together all year long. As the celebration continued into the locker room, Pat Casey was fired up, telling his young men just how impressive that two-game stretch was. "That's how you stand up to adversity, that's how you be a man," he told them. "When bad things come your way, you have to stiffen your spine."

Max had been doing just that for the last four-plus years of his life, and now all of it was validated. The team he had watched win back-to-back national titles when he was in high school was now heading back to the promised land with him as its starting center fielder. He thought about that as the locker room started to empty out, players finding their friends and families and leaving the locker room to go celebrate in downtown Corvallis. As he often did, Max did a good job keeping his emotions in check during the celebration and Casey's subsequent locker room speech. Now that it was over, though, he was left to process everything that had happened. He didn't know which emotion he was feeling the strongest: pride, shock, appreciation, or melancholy that not everyone could be here to enjoy this moment with him. "We love and care for each other," echoed through his head as he sat in the empty locker room, fiddling with the toe tag around his neck.

Everyone else had cleared out of Goss Stadium for the final time that season, ending in the best way imaginable, with a trip to the College World Series. But there Max sat, looking around, taking mental snapshots of what he had just experienced. The mountaintop, which had been getting further and further away, was now within sight. The steepest climb yet, however, now lay before him.

"All the time and everything that I had put into what I had done for myself at that field, it made me emotional," Max remembers. "That field really helped me heal and really helped make me a better person. It also made me more competitive, which has a lot to do with Case, honestly. I was able to accomplish a lot of things on that field, so I was the last guy sitting in the locker room." It had become a spiritual healing-ground for Max, and he would carry its blessings with him to Omaha and beyond.

"I didn't quite want to leave yet, because I knew I wasn't coming back."

CHAPTER 17

Omaha

Oregon State baseball parents scrambled to get tickets to Omaha, knowing that they wouldn't be cheap. After hemming and hawing over airline prices, the Gordons finally pulled the trigger and were en route. There were a few players on the 2013 Beavers baseball team who wouldn't have parents to watch them compete on college baseball's biggest stage. Catcher Jake Rodriguez's dad had died the year before after complications arose during routine surgery. Petey's dad had passed, and his mom's cancer was getting worse, so it didn't look like she would make it to Omaha either. The night of June 10, the Beavers had dogpiled, celebrating a Super Regional win and, as a result, a trip to the College World Series. It was also the one-year anniversary of J-Rod losing his dad. It also happened to be Petey's dad Walt's birthday. How sweet it would have been to celebrate the most monumental win of his career with his dad on his birthday. Instead, he celebrated with fresh pain lingering in his heart. It isn't so hard to see why the members of this team could rally around a guy like Max Gordon. At this point in his life, he was the living embodiment of loss and redemption.[1]

As it was, Petey's brother and mom had surprised him by driving up to Corvallis to see him play in the Super Regional. It was the first time his mom had seen him play for Oregon State. She was in the stands as he dogpiled with his teammates, cementing a trip to college baseball's premiere tournament.

There was also a freshman pitcher, Andrew Moore, whose grandfather had died the previous May, having never gotten to see his grandson put on a Beavers uniform. Between his own, Petey's, J-Rod's, and Max's backgrounds, the team was playing on a distinct plane of motivation; the whole team knew that people would be in Omaha who weren't counted in the stadium attendance.

Petey's mother, Debbie, had basically lived in a hospital for the past couple months while receiving treatment for her worsening lung cancer. With her own illness precluding her from earning enough to straighten up her late husband's medical costs, the family found themselves dealing with extremely tight finances. With her health declining, Debbie didn't see a way she could make the trip to Omaha with the rest of the Beavers' parents. That was, at least, until the endlessly philanthropic Marty Reser heard about the issue and stepped in.

Reser and other parents chipped in to pay for Debbie's round-trip plane ticket as well as her hotel for her entire stay in Omaha. Everybody hoped she would still have a reason to be there on the tournament's final day, watching her son and his teammates crowned national champions. It was the kind of thing the Oregon State family did for one of its own, especially at such a crucial stage of the season.

"The importance of family on that team, not just with players, but with parents was very apparent," Max remembers. "All of us on the team got along, and the parents were just extensions of their kids, so the parents all got along really well too. It was one massive, happy family, so everybody was pulling for the other parents' kid to do well when they would pinch hit for their kid. It was quite a unique thing."

Having drummed up the funds and having paid for a huge chunk out of his own pocket, Marty Reser gave Andy Peterson the good news.

Andy, in turn, shared the good news with his mom and she was set toward Omaha. With very little time between the Super Regional win and the College World Series opening ceremonies, it was tight, but everyone managed to make their arrangements as the biggest games of their sons' lives loomed ahead. Having made it safely into the heart of Nebraska, the team made its way out to TD Ameritrade Park, one of college baseball's great cathedrals—made famous as Rosenblatt Stadium—and the permanent host of the College World Series. That afternoon, it literally rained on the Beavers' parade as the skies opened up while teams were being announced onto the field for opening ceremonies. It was one of the more exciting parts of the tournament's festivities, but Oregon State's introduction was dampened by the gloomy, ugly weather above.

"You all are going to walk out there, then we're going to leave and everybody is going to go home," the coordinating staff instructed the team in between claps of thunder.

The team did exactly that, and with less-than-anticipated fanfare, the PA announcer summoned onto the field the eight remaining college baseball teams in 2013: Oregon State, Mississippi State, Louisville, Indiana, UCLA, North Carolina, North Carolina State, and LSU. As quickly as they entered, they all sprinted to shelter and the stadium was cleared out. Just like that, it was on: in less than 24 hours, the games would begin.

Max was more than happy to be in Omaha, even in the downpour, because he had taken one major risk that even his parents never knew about: when he saw a month earlier that his graduation ceremony fell on the same weekend as the College World Series, he knew there was no point in even registering. He hadn't signed up, and he hadn't sent out any invites. Had the squad not made it this far, he would have found himself in serious trouble with his parents and relatives who would have been enraged at his stupidity. But he wasn't looking so stupid, now.

"I was calling my shot," he beams.

After practicing at a nearby high school field in preparation for their first game, the Beavers finally practiced at TD Ameritrade Park the next day, ahead of their first game against Mississippi State. Moths were flying everywhere, partly due to the moisture that had permeated the air the day before. Being the loving teammates they were, Max and others convinced Nate Esposito that if he didn't eat one of the moths, the team would lose to Mississippi State that day.

"No, I'm not doing that. I don't care," Max remembers Espo saying.

"Okay, you want to lose? You want it to be your fault?" his teammates shot back.

"No, that's bullshit," Espo said.

Long story short, Espo ended up eating a moth before the game. He wasn't going to be the one to cost the team its first College World Series game after all. With the superstitious bit out of the way, the team got locked in for the first pitch against the Bulldogs. When the team took the field, there was no rain. As the national anthem wrapped up, Max went through his pre-game ritual; he bent down on one knee, keeping his hat in one hand and Nick's toe tag in the other. There, as time stood still for a few seconds, he shared a moment with his brother, knowing the pride he would take in knowing that his little bro was about to take the field in Omaha. He allowed himself only a moment to savor it all before refocusing on the momentous task at hand. He quickly got up, ran back to the dugout, and dialed in for Game 1 of the College World Series.

On a 79-degree, partly cloudy Omaha afternoon in front of nearly 25,000 fans, freshman Andrew Moore delivered the first pitch against Adam Frazier, and the game was underway. Frazier doubled to start the game for the Bulldogs, but Moore escaped the inning unscathed, stranding the runner at second and putting up his first clean inning in a College World Series game. The Beavers' leadoff man, Tyler Smith, grounded to third base, but the throw to first was airmailed, allowing OSU to put a runner in scoring position with nobody out. Petey followed by bunting him over to third base successfully, setting the stage for Conforto and Davis to do some serious damage. Conforto did just that, clubbing a double to left-center, which easily scored Smith and gave the Beavers a 1–0 lead. Looking for more, Davis popped out to shortstop to put the Bulldogs within one out of stopping the bleeding. Before they could get it, Danny Hayes came through with a

Max is announced as the Beavers take the field for their first game of the 2013 College World Series on June 15.

two-out single that scored Conforto and doubled the Beavers' lead. By the time Mississippi State finally got out of the jam, Oregon State led, 2–0.

Looking to quickly climb back into it, the Bulldogs were aggressive against Moore, who had put together a stellar freshman campaign. In 119 innings, Moore struck out 70 batters while going 14–1 with an unbelievable 1.36 ERA in his first collegiate season. Second baseman Brett Pirtle was hit by a 2–2 pitch and first baseman Wes Rea followed with a double down the left-field line, which gave Mississippi State runners on second and third with nobody out. A base hit would easily tie the game. Feeling the pressure, Moore walked C.T. Bradford, which brought up Sam Frost, the third baseman whose throwing error had enabled the Beavers to score two runs the previous inning.

Frost more than made up for his gaffe in the field with a bases-loaded single, which kept the carousel moving and the bases loaded. The Beavers' lead was cut in half. Demarcus Henderson followed with a single to right field, which was mishandled by Dylan Davis, allowing two runs to score. Just like that, the Beavers had coughed up a two-run lead and fallen behind, 3–2. Still having runners on second and third with just one out, Moore and the Beavers were in serious trouble. As the lineup rolled back over, Frazier flied out to left field as Frost tag up. Conforto caught it and fired it home with a strong crow hop. J-Rod was waiting at home plate to catch the frozen rope, and he tagged Frost as he tried to cross the plate. Once again, Conforto's rocket arm had gotten them out of a pickle. Mercifully for the Beavers, the inning was over with that electric double play, which ended the threat. Mississippi State had taken the lead, but at least they hadn't broken it open.

After ground outs by each of his teammates hitting before him, Max strode up for the first College World Series at-bat of his career. "Here we go boys," he said to himself, his eyes gazing up his bat as he looked to the sky, which seemed just about as far away as where he came from. Max Gordon stepped into the left-handed batter's box competing for his teammates, his parents in the stands, and for those who could only be felt in Omaha within himself.

Kendall Graveman fired a first-pitch strike to get ahead in the count. Followed by two straight balls, Max got back in the driver's seat. Graveman battled back with another strike to even things up at 2–2, then got Max to strike out swinging to end the inning. After a huge first frame, the bottom of the order had gone down in 1–2–3 in the second.

Still trailing 3–2 in the fourth inning, the Beavers managed to string a few hits together. Hayes led off the inning with a walk. Following a Barnes strikeout, Kavin Keyes tripled down the left field line, which scored Hayes and brought the crowd to their feet. The go-ahead run was just 90 feet away with one out in the inning. J-Rod was fixing to give the Beavers the lead when he tattooed a pitch to right field, but it was hit too hard, and right at future major league star Hunter Renfroe, to score the run. Renfroe made the grab, and Max came up with two outs and the chance to be a hero in his second plate appearance. On a 1–0 pitch, he grounded to shortstop. Though he ran his heart out until he cleared first base, the Bulldogs completed the routine play and retired Max to avert the fourth-inning crisis.

In the fifth inning, Conforto continued his hot day at the plate by smacking a one-out double which hopped over the fence. This kept Petey, who had started the at-bat on first base and would've scored easily, on third base. Davis followed with a productive out, a groundout to second base, which scored Petey and advanced Conforto to third. Slowly, but surely, the Beavers had retaken the lead, 4–3 midway through the game. Into the eighth inning, the score held with the Bulldogs desperate to at least knot things up with only a few outs left to work with.

After settling down following a rough first inning, Moore pitched admirably. After allowing a one-out single in the eighth, he was pulled in favor of Matt Boyd, who had come up big for the Beavers in clutch situations all year. Renfroe quickly welcomed him to the College World Series with a base hit, giving the Bulldogs two runners with just one out. Boyd followed that up by striking Pirtle out, putting the Beavers four outs away from a Game 1 win. Jumping on Boyd's next pitch, Rea flipped the script. He turned on the Boyd offering and sent it deep into the right-center gap, scoring both Alex Detz and Renfroe. Now, the Beavers suddenly found themselves six outs from defeat.

With two on and one out in the bottom of the eighth, the bottom of the Beavers' order once again had a chance to save the day: J-Rod flew out to right field, though, and it looked like a big situation would once again come down to Max at the plate. However, he was lifted for pinch-hitter Joey Jansen, who Coach Casey felt gave the Beavers a better chance in that spot. Jansen watched the first two pitches go by, both balls, and was in firm control of the count. He watched another pitch go by for strike one, followed by a foul ball on a big 2–1 hack, which brought him back to even. After another ball, and another foul ball, Jansen waited for the seventh pitch of the at-bat, having run the count full. Closer Jonathan Holder came right at him and Jansen swung right through it, ending the Beavers' threat and leaving them staring a Game 1 loss right in the face. Of course, Max felt a deep sense of disappointment at not having the opportunity at the plate in such a huge moment, but he understood, based on how he had performed in those moments earlier in the game.

Boyd and Scotty Schultz combined to keep the Bulldogs off the board in the ninth inning. It was now-or-never time. All they needed was a couple of base hits, and they could force extra innings. They had been in this situation before and had gotten the job done all season long.

The rally began in earnest with a Tyler Smith leadoff single on an 0–2 offering. In a rare occurrence, Petey couldn't bunt him over to second base and struck out trying, for the first out of the inning. Conforto followed that by drawing a tough walk. Once again, the Beavers had two runners on with just one out. A base hit would tie the game; an extra-base hit could win it. Davis, one of the Beavers' best hitters, struck out swinging to put OSU within one out of heartbreak. Danny Hayes, who had become a postseason hero for the Beavers that summer, strolled to the plate, the weight of the game squarely on his shoulders. On a 2–2 pitch, Hayes turned and clobbered a ball deep to right field, sending Oregon State fans to their feet. Max hopped the railing to get a better view of the ball flying over the fence for a walk-off, three-run homer.

"Get out of here!" he screamed as his teammates watched beside him.

The ball carried and then it died, falling into a backpedaling Renfroe's glove for the final out of the game.[2] Renfroe caught the ball at the base of the wall, just feet from home run territory, and quickly the Beavers had the wind knocked out of them. Just four home runs would be hit in that year's entire College World Series, prompting changes to the seams of the baseball in years to come. TD Ameritrade Park was a very difficult place to hit home runs, and as close as Hayes had come, the Beavers had nothing to show for it. They found themselves one loss from elimination.

While shocked, the team showed resolve in the locker room after the heartbreaking defeat, just as they had throughout this arduous postseason run. The Omaha buzz was gone, and they were no longer happy just being there. "It became a moment of 'I don't want to go home. I don't want to play just two games here. I want to play as long as I can,'" Max remembers.

Inspired by the 2006 Oregon State team, which lost its first game in Omaha only to string together one of the greatest runs in College World Series history and win the title, the Beavers saw some cause for hope. The Beavers were off the following day but learned they would face Louisville in their first elimination game. After going out to dinner as a group, everybody wound down in their hotel rooms. Shortly before he nodded off, Max felt the need to throw together a group text with every player on the team.

"This is going to be the last run for a lot of us," Max started. "Me and Ryan Barnes, a handful of other guys, this is it. We're not going to play after this. I'll be damned if tomorrow is the day that I have to take off the jersey forever. I'm not going to let anybody dictate the moment I have to retire from the game of baseball. Tomorrow, that's the end. If we lose tomorrow, it's over and I'm not ready to end it."

His message resonated, especially with guys like Conforto and Boyd, who knew they had promising professional careers in front of them. It put things into perspective and allowed them to remember that unlike them, not all their teammates were destined for such bright futures in the game which they had all played together for the past year or longer. Max vowed that he was showing up to play the following afternoon and he hoped everyone else would, too. Having finished up a project for class in the team hotel computer lab hours before he sent that text, though, Max had forgotten to reserve tickets for the following day's game for his parents and other family in town. That process inexplicably was not streamlined through NCAA and school administrators by 2013. Drifting off to sleep, he didn't even realize it. All that was on his mind was winning the following day and extending his baseball career.

Stan and Michelle arrived early for the Oregon State-Louisville elimination game. They were excited but had pits in their stomachs knowing this could be the last baseball game ever in which Max played. As they got to the front of the will-call line, Stan walked up to the counter to ask for the family's tickets.

"I'm Stan Gordon," he told the ticket agent.

"You're not on the list," he was told.

"My son is starting in center field today, I need a ticket," Stan replied, putting his driver's license up against the ticket window. Finally, they got the situation sorted out and the Gordons got their tickets, but not before a major scare. Not yet knowing that it was all sorted out, Max's sudden revelation sent him into a tailspin; while warming up on the field, Max realized his mistake and was freaking out. Conforto had to calm him down and tell him to worry about the game.

My parents are going to kill me, Max thought. Had they and his other family who made the trip out for the game missed his performance against Louisville, his prediction may not have been far off.

Max was a pest against the Cardinals, just the way he was against most opponents. Stan and Michelle recall once running into Dallas Buck, a star pitcher for the 2007 Oregon State national championship team, and he told them exactly what he would do if he were facing Max. "I would just hit him with the first pitch every time," he joked, but he wasn't laughing.

As a pitcher, the way Buck saw it, there was no use wasting bullets only for Max to work a walk, squib out a seeing-eye single, or reach base some other way after working an eight- or nine-pitch at-bat. He was truly a frustrating guy to face, especially at the bottom of the order. Louisville learned that lesson the hard way.

Dylan Davis, Max, and Michael Conforto (left to right) chat in the outfield during a pitching change at the 2013 College World Series.

The bottom of the Beavers order had failed to come through multiple times in the team's opening game loss to Mississippi State, and with his career on the line, Max was intent on making sure that wasn't the case in Game 2. Cardinals starter Jeff Thompson must have gotten Buck's advice, because with Max leading off the third inning of a scoreless game, he beaned him with his second pitch. For the first time, Max was on base at the College World Series. It was surreal. One pitch later, it became even more so when he scored on a double off the bat of Tyler Smith. Max was the first person to draw blood in this pivotal game, and he felt incredible. Helped by two Cardinals errors, OSU scratched across two more runs in the inning and led 3–0 a third of the way through the contest.

Max came up again in the fourth inning with the bases empty and one out. He fought off a 1–2 pitch and sent it the other way to left field for a single, marking his first hit in Omaha. Smith couldn't channel the magic in his third at-bat of the day and struck out looking, putting Max in danger of being stranded at first. With the heart of the Beavers order coming up, though, the rally wasn't quite finished. Petey and Conforto followed with back-to-back singles, loading the bases for Davis. When he sent the ball rolling into no man's land in the infield, Petey and Max both scored on a bizarre play, which extended their lead to five runs. Another crucial error kept the inning alive, pushing the score to 8–0 by the time Max came up for the second time in the frame, this time with the bases loaded.

Max is pumped after scoring a run against Louisville at the 2013 College World Series, which turned out to be perhaps the best game of his baseball career.

Having already reached base twice in the game, Max was trying to reach for the third time in two innings. Once again, he shot the ball the other way, and it scooted through the left side of the infield, scoring two more runs. By the time the Cardinals escaped, they found themselves down, 10–0. Max was following up his late-night, text chain speech with possibly his finest offensive performance in a Beavers uniform. In two innings with his team facing elimination, he had reached base three times, scored twice, and driven in two more runs.

The Beavers navigated through the rest of the game, holding onto a big lead. Final score: Oregon State 11, Louisville 4.[3] Blowing out a team in Omaha is no small feat, and the Beavers had done just that, knocking the Cardinals out of the tournament while getting one step closer to the best-of-three championship series. With the seven-run win, the team adopted the idea that they would be the ones blazing the trail home from Omaha.

Max, Tyler Smith, Ben Wetzler , and Pat Casey (left to right) at a post-game 2013 College World Series press conference.

"If you get us," the Beavers would warn, "We're the team that's going to send you home."

Having suffered the same fate against Mississippi State that the Beavers had, Indiana was next on OSU's list. The winner of that game would face the Bulldogs and would have to beat them twice in order to reach the championship series. The loser, of course, would be sent packing.

Following the big win over Louisville, Max returned to the hotel with the rest of the team and realized that the contact solution in his right eye-dropper was gone. He scrambled to find more eye solution, but all he had was allergy eye drops. Seeing no other choice, Max filled his right contact with allergy eye drops and kept both contact lenses soaking the entire next day, since the Beavers had the day off. Popping his contacts in before early BP at a local high school field, he was ready to go as his Beavers once again faced elimination.

During BP, Max kept waiting for his right contact lens to settle. His vision in that eye was still blurry, a sign that he hadn't placed the contact correctly. Multiple times, he took it out and tried to reset it on top of his eye, but nothing worked. Finally, still feeling it hadn't settled, he walked up to Joey Matthews and asked him if he could tell where he was going wrong.

"Joe Bags, is there something in my eye?" he asked.

"Bro, your eye is so dilated right now," Matthews responded. "Your pupil is huge."

He felt a pit of concern growing within him. The team piled into the bus and went from the high school field over to TD Ameritrade Park, and his contact still wasn't setting correctly. As soon as they got off the bus, Max went to the training room to talk with Josh, the Beavers' trainer.

"Josh, what's wrong with my eye?" Max asked.

"What did you do?" Josh responded upon seeing his dilated pupil.

"I don't know," Max responded.

"Well, can you see out of it?" Josh reasonably asked.

"Yeah," Max replied. He had a great round of BP even with his impaired vision, but he didn't have the same depth perception in the outfield. He didn't drop a fly ball during practice, but he didn't feel particularly comfortable out there.

"How'd you hit?" Josh came back.

"Great," Max divulged.

"Well, how about fly balls?" he continued.

"Eh, it was okay," Max said, clearly with less confidence.

"I don't know, man," Josh said. These conversations went on behind Coach Casey's back. The only way he would hear about this was if Max had to be scratched from the lineup. With only 20 minutes left before first pitch, Max had to make a decision.

"Are you going to be able to play?" Josh asked.

"I mean, I want to play," Max replied. In that moment, he realized with great chagrin that he couldn't. He had so much pride on college baseball's biggest stage that he would not play at less than 100 percent, drop a fly ball, and lose the game. If that became the final moment of his baseball career, he wouldn't be able to live with himself.

> It was the first time I couldn't muscle my way through something. I couldn't just bite my lip and say, "I'll be fine." It wasn't that type of situation, which sucked. I'd never had to deal with that. Whether it was a bum ankle or wrist or I got hit in the forearm, I was still able to get in there and play somehow. But it would've

been extremely immature and extremely irresponsible for me to put myself in that game.

Coming to one of the toughest realizations of his lifetime, Max had to chat with Coach Casey. Sitting in an office area in the locker room, Casey saw Max enter, and his starting center fielder quickly asked him to take a look at his eyes. Casey knew his center fielder was crazy, so he wasn't sure what he was looking for exactly.

"I can't see," Max cut right to the point.

"You can't see?" Casey asked, making sure he had heard his starting center fielder correctly 15 minutes before first pitch.

"I can't see out of my right eye," Max said.

"Can you play?" Casey asked, knowing Max had played through pain before.

"I can play, but I'm not going to be the reason we lose this game," Max replied. "I can only see out of one eye. I'm not going to be the guy to drop the ball."

"Do you want me to take your name out of the lineup?" Casey asked, words Max never wanted to hear. He had given everything to be in that lineup and now, on the biggest stage, he had to take himself out of it.

"Yeah," Max answered dejectedly.

"Okay," Casey said, "Go tell Hendrix to get ready."

Max nodded and walked back to the dugout to give the news to Jeff Hendrix, the freshman he'd been grooming for this moment since he saw his raw talent on display in fall camp.

"Hey man," Max said to Hendrix, feeling the burn of the words as they left his mouth. "You're starting."

"What?" Hendrix replied in disbelief.

"Yeah dude, you're the guy today. I can't see," Max responded. Hendrix knew about Max's eye as he had heard him talking about it in the outfield, but he didn't think it would keep him from playing. Nothing kept Max from playing.

"You're the guy," Max continued. "Just do what you've been doing. You're good enough. It's the same thing you've been doing all year long. Go in there and compete. Make sure you're talking with Mike, because he's going to help you in the outfield. If you have any problems, I'll be in the dugout to help you out. But just have fun and enjoy it. We don't get to do this a lot. It's a big moment."

With that, Hendrix was given a chance at creating his own moment with his team facing elimination.

Stan and Michelle sat in confusion as the announcement came over the public address system that Max had been scratched from the Beavers lineup. Quickly, they ran down the steps to the dugout and asked Max's teammates what was going on. At first, they thought he had scratched his eye and wondered if they needed to take him to the hospital. Once they got clarification, they went back to their seats disappointed, but not nearly as worried. It seemed to them that their son would not play at all that day, so they resigned themselves simply to being Beavers fans, cheering on the rest of their boys and hoping that Max would get another chance to take the field in Omaha.

Boyd toed the rubber for Oregon State, knowing he would be shouldering a lot of the Beavers' burden that afternoon. With runners on second and third and nobody out in the fourth inning of a scoreless game, the Beavers found a scoring chance. J-Rod strode to the plate with a shot to do some real damage. On the first pitch of his at bat, he drove the ball to right field, easily playable, but also deep enough to score Keyes from third. Rodriguez came through with a sac fly and, in a pitchers' duel, the Beavers had struck first.

Watching his team take a one-run lead into the fifth inning, Max noticed that his eye was starting to feel better. The team trainers had said it would take a couple of hours for his eye to return to normal, so it became a waiting game.

"It was terrible knowing I didn't have a say in what could be the end of the road for me," Max recalls. "I hated it, absolutely hated it."

He walked up to Casey, having decided that he was ready to come back in, and told him he'd be prepared to enter the game when needed.

"Coach, I'm good now," he told him. Casey told him to be ready to go, but he was probably going to let Hendrix bat one more time, because he didn't want Max hitting before taking the field, thus coming in cold in a one-run game. Still up 1–0 in the seventh inning, Hendrix got his final at-bat, an infield single he legged out. He was stranded there, though, and the teams moved to the bottom half of the inning.

"Coach, I'm really having a hard time seeing again," Max told his head coach. Then and there, the decision was made that he wasn't going to play that afternoon. Though the two went back and forth a few times throughout the contest, they decided that it wasn't worth the risk. "He almost went into the game," Casey remembers. "He got a little premature telling me he was ready to go, but I still remember his will to win as clear as day."

While Max was practically hyperventilating in the dugout, watching his team cling to a one-run lead, Boyd continued to spin a gem. Into the eighth he went, still nursing a 1–0 lead, and he allowed Casey Smith to reach base with a one-out single. Boyd proceeded to coax a fly ball out to center and struck out Justin Cureton looking to end the inning. OSU led by just one but was three outs from getting a revenge date with Mississippi State. Behind Coach Casey's full confidence, Boyd went back out for the ninth in an attempt at a complete-game shutout in Omaha.

As he watched his starting pitcher jog out to the mound, looking to close the deal, Max got closer to the edge of the dugout, still nervous as the three outs needed by the Beavers seemed to be a million miles away. After working the count full, leadoff man Chris Sujka started the ninth by watching strike three shoot past him. Power-hitting lefty Kyle Schwarber, who three years later would help the Chicago Cubs win their first World Series title in 108 years, popped out to right-center to put the Beavers within one out of advancing. Sam Travis delayed the Beavers' celebration with a base hit to right field. He was lifted for a pinch-runner, and the game's tying run was on first base. Boyd, now 120 pitches into his outing, stayed on the mound.

Nick Ramos, Indiana's cleanup hitter, strode to the plate with a chance to be a hero in the bottom of the ninth. After watching ball one go by, Ramos bounced it toward Keyes at third base. Max rose out of his seat, ready to explode. Keyes threw on the money to Hayes at first, and the Beavers were moving on. Boyd had thrown the game of his life: a complete-game, four-hit shutout, and Oregon State had survived, 1–0.[4] Instantly, Max ran over to Boyd and gave him a huge hug. "He just pitched the best game of his college career, and he'd also given me the opportunity to play at least one more game," Max remembers.

The stage was set: Mississippi State vs. Oregon State, Part II. With two days between the Indiana game and the Mississippi State game, Max was still nervous that his eye wouldn't get better in time. With a day to rest, though, and after taking the necessary precautions, his eye was back to normal with plenty of time to spare. The Beavers were itching for another chance to play the Bulldogs after the way their first game ended. This wasn't however, about revenge or redemption; this was business. They had only one goal now, and that was to win the national championship. By now, they had been in Omaha for a week, and it was time to put up or shut up.

Max started in center field and batted ninth. With one out in the top of the third inning in a scoreless game, Jake Rodriguez sliced a ball down the left field line for a double. That brought Max up with a chance to give the Beavers the lead. With nobody to hold on first and with a lefty up, first baseman Wes Rea played close to the line and deep, nearly on the outfield grass. On the fifth pitch he saw in his at-bat, Max got one he liked and roped it toward the right field line. Rea, playing deep already and using every inch of his 6' 5" frame, leapt and snagged the ball which a moment ago seemed ticketed for the right field wall. J-Rod would have scored easily, and Max may have had a double or a triple if the ball had sneaked past Rea's glove, but it did not. Thinking it was a sure base hit, Rodriguez had taken off and was caught leaning toward third when Rea caught the ball. The Bulldogs' first baseman whipped it over to second, and J-Rod was doubled off to end the inning. With the game still scoreless, the Beavers were delivered a gut punch.

Mississippi State struck first with a Bradford single in the fourth inning. Moore, getting a chance to vanquish the team that had gotten the best of him in the opener, held the Bulldogs to just that one run through four innings. In the fifth inning, the floodgates opened. All with two outs, Detz singled, Frazier singled, and Renfroe delivered the death blow with a soul-crushing three-run homer, giving Mississippi State a 4–0 lead. Max's career and Oregon State's season were just a handful of outs away from coming to a close.

Chasing those four runs, Max came up with the bases empty and one out in the sixth inning. He worked a walk and advanced to second on a Tyler Smith groundout. Petey came through with a single up the middle, which scored Max from second and helped the Beavers cut into the lead, which was now 4–1. Max had scored a run in the College World Series semifinal. That score held going into the eighth inning, when J-Rod gave OSU some life with a leadoff walk. Hitting behind him, Max was due to bat, but Casey had already informed him that he'd be lifted for a pinch-hitter, Joey Matthews. Matthews walked to the plate for just his second at-bat in the last two months following his violent collision with Conforto in the outfield against Utah.

"It felt like everything had come full circle between Joey and I," Max said, looking back on the moment he was replaced in the lineup.

> We had always been battling for the center field job, which I had somewhat won my senior year when Joey had a bad run of injury luck. When Case told me Joey was going to come in for me, I wasn't all that upset I didn't get to finish out the game. We busted our asses together, we worked hard to push each other to get to the point we both were at, so when he got the call to hit, it was pretty cool. I wanted him to have that at bat, I wanted him to have that moment, because he earned it.

After two months out of action, Joe Bags grounded out to third base, a productive at-bat which moved J-Rod to second. In a three-run game and with outs at a premium, though, the Beavers needed some quick offense to have any chance of salvaging the game. Smith followed with a groundout right back to the box, and Petey grounded out to short to end the inning. The Bulldogs were three outs from advancing to the College World Series championship series, and the Beavers were three outs from going home. Finally, in the ninth, OSU started hitting reliever Ross Mitchell hard. Conforto lined out to Rea to open the inning, the same fate Max had suffered earlier in the game. Now he watched, helplessly, from the dugout. Having already been pulled from the game, he would need his teammates to ensure that this wasn't the last time he'd wear the black-and-orange uniform.

Davis followed with a solid single to right-center, the second straight hitter to make good contact off Mitchell. Hayes slapped a single right up the middle. Oregon State had something brewing, as Keyes strode to the plate representing the tying run. Having seen him get hit hard three at-bats in a row, the Mississippi State coaching staff had seen enough of Mitchell. They called for closer Jonathan Holder to shut the door on the Beavers again. After falling behind 0–2, Keyes popped out to left field, pushing OSU within one out of elimination. Holding out hope as they watched Barnes stroll calmly up to the plate, the Beavers dugout held their collective breath. It seemed to happen very quickly. Barnes rolled over a pitch, sending the ball toward second base. With an easier force out at second, Pirtle tossed it to Frazier at second base and forced out Keyes. The dream died. As they had in each of the previous two seasons, the Beavers watched a team dance their way into the next round of the playoffs, but this time it happened just one step from the ultimate goal.[5]

Max sat still in the dugout, shocked. As he processed what he had just watched, he started to get emotional. As he did, Petey spotted him. Petey walked over to his dear friend who had just played his final baseball game. He wrapped his arms around him and began apologizing.

"I'm so sorry, man," he said, making the moment even more emotional for both young men. Max's parents got to watch him put his demons to bed and complete an outrageous physical and emotional journey before their very eyes; Petey's mom got to see him play in Omaha, and it was in this Nebraska city where she took her final steps. When she landed back home after the trip, the feeling in her legs was gone completely. The College World Series was the last time she saw her son play baseball, and it was the last time Petey got to see his mother stand up and cheer. Debbie Peterson died just six months later.

Petey and Max didn't exchange many words on the field that day. They just cried in each other's arms. It was the first time Petey had seen his roommate cry, and it was contagious. "I'll absolutely never forget that hug," Petey said. "That was the one that really, really got me."

"I remember grabbing onto Petey and that moment with him was when I realized, 'I'm not allowed to play baseball anymore,'" Max remembers with the sting still palpable in his voice.

Coach Casey came over and gave Max a hug too, knowing how much they had been through, how much they had grown together over the last three shared years of baseball. It was surreal for both of them: the old coach looked at the slight, wiry young man he had grown to love and respect as much as any other individual baseball had sent his way over the years. Max looked into the eyes of one of baseball's most legendary figures, and he felt a deep kinship with him. He had given him a new life, and short as they may have fallen of the ultimate goal, he had made him into a champion. Over the three seasons they were together, the two competitors had changed each other in ways which they could never have anticipated. They went and shook the hands of a few Mississippi State players, Rea and Renfroe among them, who congratulated them on a great season.

Coach Casey tried to do the same in the locker room after the game, stumbling over his words for the first time Max could remember. He told his team how proud he was of the adversity which they had overcome as individuals and as a family. Through all of that, they had won a Pac-12 championship and reached the College World Series. While they ultimately fell short of their No. 1 priority, Casey was incredibly proud of his team and he made sure they knew that.

Max kept his sunglasses on, not wanting his teammates to see him crying. He went and sat in the corner of the locker room near the showers and kept his head down, away from everybody else. "I was really emotional," Max details. "It was a big moment for me. Baseball was something I did for my entire life. It was in my personality to the point I was like, 'Now, what do I do?'"

Time came for the team to load back into the bus for a depressing trip back to the hotel. This forced Max to begrudgingly leave the locker room for the final time, jersey still on, sunglasses still masking his eyes. As he approached the bus, he saw his parents waiting for him. His dad stood there with a quaint smile on his face, right next to Michelle, who also smiled at her son, knowing how disappointed he must be after coming so far. Once he reached his parents, he grabbed his dad and the two men started crying in each other's embrace.

"We had this thing to keep the burden of Nick away from us and it was just gone all of a sudden," Max says of the end of his baseball career. "My dad was the guy who would come home from work and throw me balls, do all the things he probably didn't really want to do. He would be coming home from a long day at work, but he would always be there trying to help me out."

From the Scott Valley, to Ashland, to Corvallis, to Omaha, he and his dad had seen it all together. He had been Max's Little League coach, so when he embraced him on the sidewalk as the bus waited for players to file in, it was a culminating moment for both of them. They had been down to the depths of sorrow together, more than they even knew. Now they had seen the mountaintop together and were languishing in its fresh air. Max may not have any hardware to show for it, but he had left it all on the field, and both men knew that.

"We don't really ever say somebody doesn't have a shot," Coach Casey says. "But did I think Max would have the impact he did on our club by the time he left? No, I did not."

"Every day you get up, you have two choices and the first thing you choose is your attitude," Coach Bailey believes. "You choose your attitude no matter what circumstances you're in. Going through a situation, especially as young as he was and as devastating as that was, Max chose to live life despite the tragedy he went through. A lot of people would take that situation and say 'Whoa is me,' and end up living a miserable life because of it. His hard work and the way he supported his teammates make him a consummate Beaver."

The bus ride back to the hotel was quiet. Most of the guys didn't say a word. Max, the "consummate Beaver," wasn't among the few who did. When he got back to his hotel room, which he shared with Petey, he plopped onto the bed still in uniform and just lay there. Petey went to take a shower and didn't talk to Max. He could tell his pal wanted to be alone. The one thing Max knew he didn't want to do was take off his uniform. Casey's words echoed in his head: "Don't let anyone take the jersey off your back."

"It was like Superman taking off his cape and he doesn't get to wear it again," Max says. "So, I just sat there for the longest time."

Finally, Petey having showered, Max realized the jersey would have to come off at some point. Reluctantly, he took his Beavers uniform off for the final time, folded it perfectly, and placed his No. 4 jersey on the hotel bed. It was a jersey most talent evaluators thought he had no business even buying at the university bookstore. Today, he wore it while he played for a national championship.

Casey knew Max's size put him in an uphill battle; Bailey *knew* that his speed wouldn't translate him into a starting center fielder for the Beavers. As they saw him continue to improve over his three seasons, though, the uniform seemed to fit him better and better. He was no longer just a scrappy role player but had instead been a key piece in the best Oregon State squad that Pat Casey had assembled in many seasons.

As soon as he showered off the grass stains and dirt one last time, Max's identity crisis began.

"I didn't know what I was going to do," he remembers.

The healing from the loss would have to begin at some point, but that wouldn't come for several weeks. The moment he was able to move on from the memories of Mississippi State, who ultimately fell to UCLA in the College World Series national title series, his urge to play crept back again. It wasn't like he had any collegiate eligibility left, and he was not a professional prospect of any kind. Knowing first-hand that he had made crazier things happen before in his life, though, he began keeping a bag full of baseball gear ready in preparation for any opportunity that might come his way.

He figured that if, in the years to come, he ever got a call from someone in a faraway place about the chance to chase another baseball dream, wherever it was, he would be ready to grab his bag, hop in his car, and drive toward the next improbable step in his journey.

The day that call came, he had his bag ready to go.

CHAPTER 18

Life After Omaha

It was just like old times, doing work around their beautiful, cozy Ashland home. On this summer afternoon, Stan and Max were beginning a lofty project: tearing out the old deck and putting in a new one. It was not unlike the outdoor projects on which Max and Nick had helped years before. Stan had his chainsaw, which buzzed loudly as its thin teeth tore through pieces of old deck. He would get the piece cut most of the way off before Max finished the job by snapping it and throwing it in the back of his dad's pickup truck. It was the same truck he'd driven back from Sierra College in search of his life's direction.

Now here he was again: not quite sure what life without baseball might look like. Slowly coming to grips with the College World Series loss from earlier in the summer, he knew it was time to start writing the next chapter in what was becoming a very difficult, interesting life.

All morning long, the two would fill the trunk with boards from the deck and take them to the dump, then come back home to repeat the whole process. After dumping a fresh load of wooden boards, Max climbed back into the truck and felt his phone start to vibrate. He looked at it and realized he was getting a call from a number which he didn't recognize. Of course, not knowing what opportunity might be waiting on the other end of the line, he picked up.

"Hey man, I got your number from Aaron Nielsen," a man named Ernie Munoz told him.

Aaron Nielsen was a Medford Rogues assistant coach as well as a friend of Max's. The Rogues are a college summer league team which competes at a fairly high level, but nothing like summer leagues such as Cape Cod, Northwoods, or the Alaskan League. While talking about baseball and life at one point that summer, Nielsen casually mentioned a connection he had to professional ball.

"Dude, I've got a friend that coaches in the Pecos League. I can ask him if he needs an outfielder," he told Max.

"Absolutely, man. Anything," Max told his friend. He had told himself

213

that he would take any opportunity he could to keep playing baseball. About two weeks after that conversation, figuring nothing had come of it, here was this man, Ernie Munoz, on the other line giving him a call on Aaron Nielsen's behalf.

"One of our outfielders just went down last night," Munoz told Max. "He blew up his knee and we need another outfielder."

"Just tell me when I have to be there, man," Max replied without hesitation.

"Can you be here at 10 o'clock tomorrow night?" he asked.

"Yep, where am I going?" Max replied, as he looked down at his watch and saw that it was already noon.

"Alamogordo, New Mexico," Munoz told him.

"Okay, I'll see you there," Max answered, not knowing or caring how far he had to drive or what he'd be asked to do when he got there. He might as well have just hung up the phone once he heard the word "baseball." He found out it was longer than a 24-hour drive to Alamogordo, and he had to be there in less than 34. His dad had only heard Max's end of the conversation, so he eagerly awaited an explanation once his son hung up the phone.

"Hey, we have to get all this out of the truck and get home," Max told him with the last load of boards still sitting in the trunk at the dump site.

"Why?" Stan asked. He saw the look in Max's eye and thought, *Oh no.*

"I have to drive to New Mexico like right now," Max told his dad, earning him a blank stare in return. "Let's just go, I'll tell you more on the ride home."

After dropping the rest of the wood at the dump, the Gordon men drove back toward the house as Max explained his new plan. "Are you sure?" his dad asked. "Do you know who this guy is, do you know what you're doing?"

"Dad, I'm playing Indy Ball, I'm just going," Max said, his dad able to see the conviction in his face. Since he was little, he had worked out all the details of a plan and then presented it to his parents only once he had already reached the point of no return. It was clear this was another case of him following a dream, so nothing would stand in his way.

"Okay," his dad said, letting him know he supported his decision to keep chasing the baseball dream.

Knowing the clock was ticking, Max frantically started packing whatever he could back at the house when they returned. Since he already had his go-bag ready with all his baseball stuff, he just had to grab a few other items of clothing and personal belongings, and he was back out the door in record time. His mom watched in awe, not getting a word of explanation throughout the process. In his normal nonchalant manner when executing a plan like this, Max explained very little. "I'm headed to New Mexico, mom, see ya later!" he shouted flippantly as he slid by the door.

He gave her a quick hug on the way out the door and ran to his car with all the belongings he needed.

"What in the hell is he doing?" Michelle asked her husband.

Right as he began his drive, Max gave his mom a call to fill her in and get to New Mexico as quickly as possible. He dialed up the GPS and drove straight for Palm Springs, where he planned on getting a couple hours of shut-eye before getting back on the road and making a beeline for Alamogordo. He made relatively good time to Palm Springs, and at two in the morning, he stopped off at a gas station to rest his mind for a few hours. It was over 100 degrees, and even in the dead of night it quickly became apparent that resting would be impossible. After about 15 minutes of trying to fall asleep in the brutal heat, Max gave up.

Screw it, he thought as he climbed out of the car to fill it up with gas before continuing his journey. More than a day after he left Ashland, he pulled up in Alamogordo with a few hours to spare. Grampy Norman had taught him always to be on time, and with this potentially one-time-only opportunity, there was no way he would give the team an excuse not to give him a look.

"Do you have gray and white baseball pants?" he was asked upon arrival.

"I have some grays, but they have black and orange stripes on them," Max said, referring to the pants he'd worn at Oregon State.

"Well, they need to be white, no stripes," the staff replied.

In true Independent Ball fashion, Max stayed on someone's couch in a pool house. While the Independent League is a professional baseball league where players are mostly paid in opportunities to keep playing baseball, they also get a little bit of cash. At the pool house, Max pulled out his pocket knife and started cutting the black and orange stripes off his gray pants. Part of it felt like a grievous sin; he was shedding the pinstripes which he had given everything to earn. Then, however, he began to look at it differently. Really, he was keeping with the same spirit which had gotten him on the field at Goss Stadium in the first place: nothing is more sacred than getting onto the field.

Later, he would run to the store and buy some cheap white baseball pants. Like that, he was ready to give Independent Baseball a shot for the White Sands Pupfish of the Pecos League.

As he had partially anticipated, Max quickly learned that Independent Ball was not nearly as glorious as college had been. The crowds were small, and he described the level of play as a glorified men's league. Many of his teammates had been born a decade before him and already had families. In

the Indy League, one could find a healthy blend of both guys like Max looking to extend their baseball careers and guys in their mid-30s looking to
relive their former glory. For almost all participants, the Independent League
was a farewell tour following a lifetime love affair with the game of baseball.

Ernie Munoz, the man who had called Max to offer him a shot, was
the team's No. 3 hitter and starting catcher. It was a bizarre way for a baseball career to end, but Max had a lot of fun, and like every other stop along
his baseball career, he ended up making good friends. They had to find
their own ways to have fun because they were the worst team in the league.
The team had no bullpen, so Pupfish games tended to devolve into more
carnival-like atmospheres after a few innings.

In the 10 games in which he played, Max played well, hitting .294 and
getting on base at a .400 clip.[1] While his stay was relatively short, he had fulfilled another goal: getting paid to play baseball.

"It was the final tour where I got to fulfill my childhood dream of saying that I played professional baseball," Max says.

When he made the trip back to Oregon, Max could rest knowing that
he had maximized his playing career. A man who few thought had the talent to play in Division 1 had started in center field in the College World
Series and then played baseball professionally. A boy who few believed
would ever run to first base again had won an Oregon High School State
Championship on his way to a six-year baseball career.

His next step seemed to be the natural one; he was ready to get into
coaching. Some of the men who most influenced him throughout his life
were his coaches: Pat Casey, Coach K, Charlie Hall, Pat Bailey, Joe Carnahan, etc.

He wanted to inspire more kids to play like him—fearless, as if there
was nothing to lose. That road began with coaching the Ashland High
School JV team in the spring of 2014. He followed that up by accepting an
assistant coaching job with the Medford Rogues—the team bore the same
name as its town's hospital, Rogue Valley, the very one which had saved his
life—later that summer. One day, when heading down to batting practice
with the Rogues, his dad gave him a call.

"I am officially no longer working," Stan told his son. "I'm going to
retire."

"Congratulations, dad," Max told him. "That is so cool. You did it the
right way, working your butt off and Nick and me never wanted for anything. You did it right, man. Kudos to you, that's awesome. Congrats."

There was silence on the other end of the line for several seconds
before Max realized his dad was getting choked up. "What do I do now?" he
asked Max. "I can't go see the guys anymore, I can't go to work with them."

Instantly, Max could see the parallels between his dad's situation and his own; the relationships which Stan built in his job were built on the principles of fairness, selflessness, and caring for his fellow man. Those were the values Max tried to embody as he took on the next chapter of his life. He wanted to teach the next generation of players to love and care for each other. But that started right now, with showing his father that he loved and cared about him.

"Dad, now you can go fishing," he told him. "You can do all these things, you can go fishing, you can go hunting, you can play golf. You can live your life. You don't have to worry about waking up at six in the morning and having it snow on you all day. You can do whatever the hell you want, you can do anything in the world."

Max knew that he was also sort of talking to himself about his own situation. He was about to experience a newfound freedom; it didn't seem like it, but there was life beyond baseball.

Luckily for him, coaching helped replace a lot of the competitive juices Max had lost when his career came to an end, but it didn't replace all of them. Following that summer, he knew he would be heading south. He had been in touch with Terry Baumgartner, the man who had gone out of his way to find him a place to play while he prepared to try out for Oregon State. Coach Baumgartner was interested in a player on Ashland's varsity team and had called to ask Max about him. Toward the end of the phone call, Baumgartner made a comment that made Max's ears perk up.

"You know, if you ever want a job, just let me know," he told him.

"Okay, yeah I do," Max said back.

"What?" Baumgartner asked.

"Yeah, this is me letting you know," Max replied. He knew Baumgartner hadn't expected him to take him up on the offer immediately, but he needed to know if he was serious about having him or not. He had been through too much at this point to get his hopes up about a future in baseball.

Terry Baumgartner knew he needed an outfielders coach on his staff and had seen enough of Max when he was in Northern California and Oregon State that he knew he would work as hard for his staff as he had for his college teams.

"Oh, okay," Baumgartner said, surprised. "Let me get some stuff together and I'll give you a call back tomorrow."

Max waited eagerly for a call the next day as he anticipated what he hoped would be a formal job offer from Coach Baumgartner.

"This is what we can do," Baumgartner told him when he called back. "I can get you free rent at the dorms and you can work a couple other jobs and also coach."

"Hell yeah," Max accepted without negotiation.

Just as Pat Casey had done when he was coaching at George Fox, Max had to wear multiple hats. He painted the dugout, manicured the field, and of course, coached the team's outfielders. For two years, he held that post, quickly earning credibility with players who knew he had played in the College World Series. Terry Baumgartner was a calming presence for Max from a coaching perspective. Having assumed he would take on the boisterous persona of Coach Casey or Coach K, Max adopted a hybrid style of coaching thanks to Baumgartner's mostly laid-back approach. In big moments, though, he channeled his more eccentric coaches in order to get the guys riled up.

"I'll always revert back to Pat Casey or Coach K in terms of getting guys to be at their best when we need them to be," Max says.

Meanwhile, over at Oregon State, Coach Casey and Coach Bailey started to use Max's story to motivate new classes of Beavers baseball players. Before every season, Bailey plays a video showing what he wants his outfielders to do in terms of positioning, jump, route, etc. Years after he had played his final game in a Beavers uniform, Max's diving plays, many of which had ended up on SportsCenter, still take up a third of the film.

Pat Casey tells the story of his walk-on center fielder because his story is not only improbable, it can also be used to show current players that while the road to Omaha is a long one, it can be reached with the right amount of hard work and motivation. It also takes the right group of guys. Max's presence went a long way toward making any group of guys "the right group." Casey says of Max:

> He inspires me. Remembering what he did is an inspiration to me. That's why I bring it up, because he inspires me when I think about what he did to play, when I think about who he was. Guys hitting .400 and stuff like that, those things are vitally important. But nothing is more important than the character of a man, and nothing is more important than the impact he has as a teammate and what he's going to do in the future. I bring it up, because it's something that was vitally important to our success.

Max makes frequent trips back to Corvallis, a place where he accumulated plenty of notoriety thanks to Coach Casey's constant stories relayed to players over the years. "I love seeing the guy come back," Case says. "I love seeing him walk onto the field and he feels it. He walks onto the field or in the locker room at Oregon State like he's an All-American, and he was, because he was part of a team that went to the World Series."

Often, when Max comes back, players know who he is before he knows who they are. "Oh, you're Max Gordon?" he was asked at an alumni event. "Case still talks about you at least once a week. He's always talking about you, man. He won't give it up."

When Max called him to talk about walking on with the Beavers, Pat

Casey had already cemented himself as one of college baseball's most legendary coaches; he never would have imagined during that phone call that the young man on the other line would end up standing out from among the hundreds of players he coached over a decades-long career.

About 250 miles north in Seattle, on a May night in 2017, another former Pat Casey pupil had a big night planned; Max welcomed several friends to town. They stayed over at his place, for the next day promised to be a party. Max was settling in nicely to a new place he'd gotten since moving up to the Emerald City. His friends were excited; Max was nervous. The next day, they drove to their destination, got out and started walking among the thousands of others who were there to see the same thing. They were at Safeco Field, home of the Seattle Mariners.

Max and his buddies had pretty good seats, a few rows up and behind home plate. Everyone was excited and horsing around as first pitch approached. All of Max's friends in attendance grabbed him to shout how great their seats were and what a nice park it was.

It was nice, and the group was having a lot of fun. Max was still intensely nervous, but the nerves were not for him. He scanned the field intently until he saw a familiar face. He was nervous for his best friend. There, in the bullpen warming up, he saw Sam Gaviglio, who was preparing for his first start in the major leagues. He had been traded from the Cardinals to the Mariners in 2014, and after several years in the minors, he was getting his shot. Not only had Max been with Sam through thick and thin when they were teammates, but recently, he had provided much-needed support to Sam in a multitude of forms.

Back in Ashland that off-season, Max would catch Sam's bullpens for him. He didn't wear a catcher's mitt at first, receiving 90-mile-an-hour fastballs. "It was great, I couldn't have asked for a better off-season catcher," Sam remembers. "He just wore his outfielder's mitt to catch me and would wear a batting glove underneath. He made things easier on me that off-season."

Sam was battling some personal demons, too: His dad, with whom he was very close, had recently died. Just as Max had taken Nick's death, Sam took his dad's death hard. He didn't want to talk about it, but after attending a Sturgill Simpson concert, the buddies' favorite musician, with Max, he started to open up.

It had been hard for him to open up to his then-girlfriend, now-wife, Alaina, about what he was feeling, but Sam just knew that Max would understand what he was going through. In a troubled time, Sam had someone to help him initiate the healing process. When Sam was called up to the big leagues that May, it marked a major moment for a healing family.

Max knew the nerves wouldn't go away until the game began. He didn't have any doubt in Sam's abilities; he had seen him pitch in Triple-A for the Tacoma Rainiers and knew his buddy had the stuff to make it in the big leagues. Now, with a chance to prove it, there was nothing for Max to do but watch. "I knew everything that happened that day was important," Max explains. "I didn't say a ton, but I would get super amped up when he would strike somebody out."

Facing the White Sox, Sam made a good first impression. It was his first MLB start, so the team—not wanting to overwork a fresh prospect—held him to a pitch count of 80 and allowed him only five innings. He gave up just three hits, walked one, struck out two, and didn't allow a run. A clean five innings of work was how he opened his major league career. At Sam's hotel, where he had given Max and other buddies a key, his friends awaited him with champagne to toast his success when he arrived back. First in Ashland, then in Corvallis, now in Seattle, baseball once again brought Max and Sam together for a major milestone moment.

Max had recently taken a job at Driveline in Seattle, making it an easy trip to see his childhood friend make reality out of a lifelong dream. Driveline is a data-driven performance training center for baseball players ranging from teenagers to professionals doing their off-season and, in many cases, in-season work. It was founded in 2008, shortly after Max's and Nick's car accident. After eschewing a sales job there in hopes of a job as a hitting instructor, Max got the break he needed and was offered the job he wanted. There he now works on the swings of high school players looking to matriculate to big-time programs.

Using state-of-the-art technology, Max helps kids recognize their swing patterns and make subtle adjustments after reviewing video. Of course, he also makes sure they aren't getting soft on him and constantly pushes them to have the work ethic he had always shown in the batter's box years ago. It wasn't long after starting work at Driveline that he got to watch a new group seal the deal in Omaha. They had heard plenty about Max.

The 2018 Oregon State baseball team suffered the same fate as the 2013 team, losing its first game of the College World Series. They battled back, though, and knocked off Washington and North Carolina to get within two wins of a College World Series championship series berth. They had to win two games against none other than Mississippi State, who had knocked out Max's Beavers five years earlier.

OSU outslugged the Bulldogs in Game 1, 12–2, setting up a winner-take-all second game with the victor advancing to play Arkansas in the final. In a game that was close most of the day, the Beavers pulled away late and bounced the Bulldogs from the tournament with a 5–2 win.

In the championship, they ran into a buzzsaw in the form of the Arkansas Razorbacks as they fell in Game 1, 4–1. With one out left in Game

2, the Beavers caught a break: a foul pop fly by Cadyn Grenier went past the first-base line. Three fielders gave chase, but nobody called it and the ball bounced foul off the turf and into the stands. Instead of winning the College World Series, the Razorbacks had to go back to the drawing board, with the tying run standing at third base. Grenier had new life. One strike from elimination, he came through with a base hit through the right side to tie the game 3–3.

The next batter, Trevor Larnach, launched his 19th home run of the season down the right-field line and gave Oregon State a 5–3 lead, one they wouldn't relinquish for the rest of the game.

Somehow, the Beavers had forced a decisive Game 3, where the winner would claim the national title. Behind freshman phenom Kevin Abel, who pitched a complete-game shutout, the Beavers blanked the Razorbacks, 5–0, to claim the school's third national title ever. Five years after Max's crew got so close, a new crop of Beavers rushed the field and swarmed each other in an epic championship dogpile. These Beavers had been the culmination of a new tradition of teams at Oregon State which had been rebooted with Max and his group: Another undersized center fielder, Steven Kwan, one of the Beavers' many stars, wore the same No. 4 jersey which Max had worn as he leapt onto the dogpile.

After Oregon State was done celebrating, Pat Casey decided to go out on top. Shortly after the team won it all for the third time under his command, he announced his retirement. He was named an assistant to the athletic director and handed the reins over to Pat Bailey, who took over as interim head coach for the 2019 season. The team hired two-time national champion Beavers catcher Mitch Canham for the permanent role one year later.

While Max now makes a living critiquing other players' swings, he's still working on perfecting his own—on the golf course. His goal is to compete on the Senior Tour when he turns 50, something that seems possible given his 75-to-80-stroke average. When he turns 40, he hopes to compete in an Iron Man, something which he and Josh Scarminach always talked about doing, but for which they never found the time (yet).

Another major milestone was crossed off the list: coaching at a Division-1 program. Max was hired by the University of Michigan as a volunteer assistant coach in February 2020. Within weeks, the Wolverines became the first team in the history of Big Ten baseball to be ranked No. 1 in the country.

Max came from a small town where no one knew who he was to being that town's golden child. He went from being a small-town boy in a big-town program to being the big man on campus. Every time someone cast doubt Max Gordon's way, he made them eat their words.

Most still don't know his name, because he never got to the major leagues. To someone of Max's stature and talent level, though, the College World Series *was* his World Series. It was the pinnacle. As unknown as he may be to the mainstream, national baseball audience, his impact on the people and programs through which he worked over the years would never forget his will power, work ethic or how much he cared about the people around him. He had played like a champion, every chance he got.

Baseball became a platform for Max to show how he would live life after losing Nick. Down in the depths of the darkest moments of his life, Max had found the courage to play not only for himself, but for everyone who loved him and helped him get to the heights he would reach. When he lost Coach K, he thought he was playing for two. When he lost his grandpa, it became three. By the time he finally came around to the idea that he had lost Nick, however, he had made another realization altogether: all this time, he was playing for love. For the love of the game, for the love of those for whom he played, and for the love of his parents, the only two people on earth who would ever fully understand his journey.

It taught him that as he had done in baseball, he would live the rest of his life in pursuit of the things that made him feel genuinely alive. Up to this point, those things have been baseball, family, and surrounding himself with friends worth fighting to keep. Still a young man, looking back on all of his accomplishments and the trove of hardships he left in his wake, Max doesn't worry about the future so much anymore. The same blind determination and reckless abandon which became hallmarks of his outfield performances at Goss Stadium will be the same thing propelling him through the next big leap, and the next, and the next. He knows now that if he brings the right people with him in his mind and in his heart, then the next leap will always be a leap in the right direction. And each time that direction changes, all he has to do is close his eyes and think of something new.

Here we go, boys.

Afterword
by Pat Casey

Max Gordon certainly didn't wow me or the coaching staff early on. As it was time to make some tough decisions, he wasn't in our roster plans for the upcoming season. We appreciated his hard-nosed hustle-all-the-time attitude, but his talent fell short of the level we expect from the players we recruit. Many student athletes, of course, were much more physically gifted and talented than Max.

At that time, it was hard to imagine him making the team, let alone becoming such an important part of Oregon State Baseball. We did not anticipate keeping him on the roster at the end of his first fall with us, and we were ready to recommend he attend a Junior College where he could more realistically play every day.

However, a meeting near Christmas break changed my perception of this young man completely. I discovered he was living in a camper at the fairgrounds. I also found out that he would have to leave Oregon State if he did not make the team. The impact those discoveries had on me was immediate and profound, and I suddenly had a deeper understanding for who Max was and what he represented.

It was no longer about pure talent. I left that meeting knowing Max had the makeup and attitude to influence our team without ever stepping into the batter's box. We needed Max and over time, I realized just how much he needed us as well in order to overcome the challenges and struggles he was facing head on in his own life.

Max was undersized and didn't display many of the tools our coaches normally look for in the recruiting process. His physical abilities simply didn't fit the mold of the type of player we bring to Oregon State. To put it simply: he wasn't on our radar. However, as our fateful meeting foreshadowed and Max's three years in Corvallis proved, you may be able to measure a player's physical tools, but you can't measure a man's heart, desire, passion or will to win.

Max is the embodiment of these intangible attributes that are so often overlooked. Never in my wildest dreams did I imagine Max would *make* our team at Oregon State, let alone have a lasting impact on our program. My own doubts were trumped by his dream. When nobody else could fathom it, Max envisioned not only making the roster, but eventually becoming an everyday player. To anyone, that would be a tall order, but especially to Max who was on a team full of supremely talented and highly recruited players. When most would have, Max didn't let those challenges get in the way of his dream: becoming an integral part of Beaver Baseball.

After that Christmas break meeting, we embarked on a journey that nobody could have seen coming. From his first practice until he took off the black and orange for good, Max was an inspiration to our coaches, players, staff, community and Beaver Nation as a whole. To this day, I'm motivated by Max's courage and undeniable will to overcome all the roadblocks put in his way in order to succeed at the highest level.

He went from a walk-on to a starting center fielder in the College World Series. Still today, I constantly talk about the influence he had on all of us during his career at Oregon State and beyond. That influence, I believe, will be etched forever in the storied history of the Oregon State Baseball program.

Pat Casey coached collegiate baseball for 31 seasons, winning 1,071 games, 900 of which came at Oregon State, where he coached from 1995 to 2018. Casey's 21 College World Series wins rank ninth all-time, and he is one of just a handful of coaches to win three or more national titles. He has coached more than 20 players who have gone on to play in the major leagues.

Chapter Notes

Chapter 1

1. City of Etna. Accessed March 21, 2019. https://www.cityofetna.org/.
2. "Etna, California Population," *World Population Review*, January 1, 2020, accessed February 5, 2020. https://worldpopulationreview.com/us-cities/etna-ca-population/.
3. Weaverville Joss House State Historic Park. *California Department of Parks and Recreation*, January 30, 2020, accessed February 6, 2020. https://www.parks.ca.gov/?page_id=457.

Chapter 2

1. "David C. Kitchell Obituary," *Mail Tribune* (Medford, OR), November 23, 2007.
2. "Pacific Rim Bowl," *Ashland Football Club*, January 2018, accessed March 30, 2019. http://www.ashlandfootballclub.com/SectionIndex.asp?SectionID=13.
3. "2006 Baseball Schedule," *Oregon State Athletics*, 2019, accessed April 5, 2019. https://osubeavers.com/sports/baseball/schedule/2006.

Chapter 5

1. Specht, Sanne, "Ashland Teen in Critical Condition," *Mail Tribune*, January 4, 2008.

Chapter 8

1. "Ashland 2008 Baseball Schedule," *MaxPreps*, Updated January 1, 2019, accessed March 3, 2019. http://www.maxpreps.com/high-schools/ashland-grizzlies-(ashland,or)/baseball-spring-08/schedule.htm.

Chapter 9

1. "2009 Sierra College," *The Baseball Cube*, updated March 12, 2019, accessed March 20, 2019. http://www.thebaseballcube.com/college/schools/stats.asp?Y=2009&T=21213.

Chapter 10

1. Youmans, Matt, "UNLV Fires Baseball Coach Gouldsmith," *Las Vegas Review-Journal*, May 18, 2010.
2. "Brainspotting (BSP)," *GoodTherapy*, Updated March 8, 2018, accessed March 27, 2019. https://www.goodtherapy.org/learn-about-therapy/types/brainspotting-therapy.

Chapter 12

1. "Pat Casey," *Baseball-Reference.com*, accessed April 5, 2019. https://www.baseball-reference.com/register/player.fcgi?id=casey-002pat.
2. "Goss Stadium at Coleman Field," *Oregon State Athletics*, updated January 1, 2019, accessed April 7, 2019. https://osubeavers.com/facilities/goss-stadium-at-coleman-field/5.
3. "1998 Oregon State University," *The Baseball Cube*, accessed April 7, 2019. http://www.thebaseballcube.com/college/schools/stats.asp?Y=1998&T=20272.

4. "2005 Baseball Schedule," *Oregon State Athletics*, updated January 1, 2019, accessed April 7, 2019. https://osubeavers.com/sports/baseball/schedule/2005.

Chapter 13

1. Schnell, Lindsay, "His Curveball Is Back, But Josh Osich Says He's Still Not at 100 Percent Yet," *The Oregonian*, May 5, 2011.

Chapter 14

1. Oregon State Athletics Staff, "Tyler Smith Gives Beavers Opening-Day Win with Single in 11th," *Oregon State Baseball*, February 19, 2011, accessed April 11, 2019. https://osubeavers.com/news/2011/2/19/207845313.aspx.

2. Oregon State Athletics Staff, "Baseball Loses Pitcher's Duel in Sunday Nightcap," February 20, 2011, accessed April 12, 2019. https://osubeavers.com/news/2011/2/20/207823411.aspx.

3. Oregon State Athletics Staff, "Beavers' Late-Inning Comeback Denied in Fresno," February 21, 2011, accessed April 12, 2019. https://osubeavers.com/news/2011/2/21/207836707.aspx.

4. Oregon State Athletics Staff, "Stamps' Ninth-Inning Walk Caps OSU Baseball's Five-Run Comeback," April 9, 2011, accessed April 13, 2019. https://osubeavers.com/news/2011/4/9/207830010.aspx.

5. Oregon State Athletics Staff, "Oregon State Loses in Season Finale, Will Host NCAA Regional," May 29, 2011, accessed April 14, 2019. https://osubeavers.com/news/2011/5/29/207864781.aspx.

6. Oregon State Athletics Staff, "It's a Win: Oregon State Headed Back to a Super Regional," June 5, 2011, accessed April 15, 2019. https://osubeavers.com/news/2011/6/5/207833473.aspx.

7. Oregon State Athletics Staff, "Baseball's Season Ends with Loss at Vanderbilt," June 11, 2011, accessed April 15, 2019. https://osubeavers.com/news/2011/6/11/207864631.aspx.

Chapter 15

1. Beseda, Jim, "Oregon State's Pat Casey Considering Stepping Down as Baseball Coach," *The Oregonian*, July 21, 2011.

2. Winthrop Athletics Staff, "Former Baseball Player Conrad Funk Concludes 16-Year Playing Career in Canada," August 9, 2011, accessed April 17, 2019. https://winthropeagles.com/news/2011/8/9/BB_0809110946.aspx.

3. "Sam Gaviglio," *Baseball-Reference.com*, accessed April 17, 2019. https://www.baseball-reference.com/players/g/gavigsa01.shtml.

4. Oregon State Athletics Staff, "Baseball Loses at San Diego State," February 24, 2012, accessed April 18, 2019. https://osubeavers.com/news/2012/2/24/207868036.aspx.

5. Oregon State Athletics Staff, "Beavers Tally Comeback in Nike College Showcase Finale," March 11, 2012, accessed April 18, 2019. https://osubeavers.com/news/2012/3/11/207831142.aspx.

6. Oregon State Athletics Staff, "It's a Sweep: Starr, Beavers Shut Down Oregon in Season Finale," May 27, 2012, accessed April 18, 2019. https://osubeavers.com/news/2012/5/27/207818779.aspx.

7. Oregon State Athletics Staff, "Baseball's Season Ends in 10-Inning Affair," June 3, 2012, accessed April 19, 2019. https://osubeavers.com/news/2012/6/3/207858954.aspx.

Chapter 16

1. Oregon State Athletics Staff, "2013 Oregon State Baseball Individual Game-by-Game for Oregon State," *Oregon State Baseball*, July 9, 2013.

2. Oregon State Athletics Staff, "No. 6 Beavers Take Civil War Series With 12–2 Win," May 19, 2013, accessed April 20, 2019. https://osubeavers.com/news/2013/5/19/207850592.aspx.

3. Oregon State Athletics Staff, "Beavers Defeat K-State, Advance to Fifth College World Series," June 10, 2013, accessed April 21, 2019. https://osubeavers.com/news/2013/6/10/208466430.aspx.

Chapter 17

1. Quick, Jason, "College World Series: At Oregon State, 'There's Something Special' About This Team's Motivation," *The Oregonian*, June 14, 2013, accessed April 23, 2019.

2. Oregon State Athletics Staff, "Beavers

Drop College World Series Opener to Mississippi State," June 15, 2013, accessed April 23, 2019. https://osubeavers.com/news/2013/6/15/208466437.aspx.

3. Oregon State Athletics Staff, "Beavers Down Louisville at College World Series," June 17, 2013, accessed April 24, 2019. https://osubeavers.com/news/2013/6/17/208610964.aspx.

4. Oregon State Athletics Staff, "Boyd's Complete Game Keeps Beavers Alive at CWS," June 19, 2013, accessed April 25, 2019. https://osubeavers.com/news/2013/6/19/208611161.aspx.

5. Oregon State Athletics Staff, "Beavers' Season Ends at College World Series," June 21, 2013, accessed April 26, 2019. https://osubeavers.com/news/2013/6/21/208611260.aspx.

Chapter 18

1. "Max Gordon," *Baseball-Reference.com*, accessed April 28, 2019. https://www.baseball-reference.com/register/player.fcgi?id=gordon000max.

Bibliography

Interviews

Bailey, Pat. Interview with Jacob Kornhauser. February 19, 2019.
Baumgartner, Terry. Interview with Jacob Kornhauser. February 14, 2019.
Carnahan, Joe. Interview with Jacob Kornhauser. March 15, 2019.
Casey, Pat. Interviews with Jacob Kornhauser. February 27 and 28, 2019.
Gaviglio, Sam. Interview with Jacob Kornhauser. February 13, 2019.
Gordon, Max. Interviews with Jacob Kornhauser. January 8 through April 5, 2019.
Gordon, Stan, and Michelle Gordon. Interview with Jacob Kornhauser. February 20, 2019.
Gorton, Ryan. Interview with Jacob Kornhauser. March 14, 2019.
Hall, Charlie. Interview with Jacob Kornhauser. February 17, 2019.
Kozinski, Leslie, and Chad Kozinski. Interview with Jacob Kornhauser. April 2, 2019.
Peterson, Andy. Interview with Jacob Kornhauser. March 28, 2019.
Matthews, Joey. Interview with Jacob Kornhauser. March 17, 2019.
Scarminach, Josh. Interview with Jacob Kornhauser. March 31, 2019.
Weeks, Sean. Interview with Jacob Kornhauser. February 5, 2019.
Willson, Rob. Interview with Jacob Kornhauser. March 27, 2019.

Articles

"1998 Oregon State University." *The Baseball Cube*. Updated January 1, 2019. Accessed April 7, 2019. http://www.thebaseballcube.com/college/schools/stats.asp?Y=1998&T=20272.
"2005 Baseball Schedule." Oregon State Athletics. Updated January 1, 2019. Accessed April 7, 2019. https://osubeavers.com/sports/baseball/schedule/2005.
"2006 Baseball Schedule." Oregon State Athletics. 2019. Accessed April 5, 2019. https://osubeavers.com/sports/baseball/schedule/2006.
"2009 Sierra College." *The Baseball Cube*. Updated March 12, 2019. Accessed March 20, 2019. http://www.thebaseballcube.com/college/schools/stats.asp?Y=2009&T=21213
"Ashland 2008 Baseball Schedule." *MaxPreps*. Updated January 1, 2019. Accessed March 3, 2019. http://www.maxpreps.com/high-schools/ashland-grizzlies-(ashland,or)/baseball-spring-08/schedule.htm.
Beseda, Jim. "Oregon State's Pat Casey Considering Stepping Down as Baseball Coach." *The Oregonian* (Portland), July 21, 2011.
"Brainspotting (BSP)." *GoodTherapy*. Updated March 8, 2018. Accessed March 27, 2019. https://www.goodtherapy.org/learn-about-therapy/types/brainspotting-therapy.
City of Etna. Accessed March 21, 2019. https://www.cityofetna.org/.
"David C. Kitchell Obituary." *Mail Tribune* (Medford, OR), November 23, 2007.
"Etna, California Population." *World Population Review*, January 1, 2020. Accessed February 5, 2020. https://worldpopulationreview.com/us-cities/etna-ca-population/.
"Goss Stadium at Coleman Field." *Oregon State Athletics*. Updated January 1, 2019. Accessed April 7, 2019. https://osubeavers.com/facilities/goss-stadium-at-coleman-field/5.

"Max Gordon." Baseball-Reference.com. Accessed April 28, 2019. https://www.baseball-reference.com/register/player.fcgi?id=gordon000max.

Oregon State Athletics. "2013 Oregon State Baseball Individual Game-by-Game for Oregon State." Oregon State Baseball, July 9, 2013.

Oregon State Athletics Staff "Baseball Loses at San Diego State." February 24, 2012. Accessed April 18, 2019. https://osubeavers.com/news/2012/2/24/207868036.aspx.

Oregon State Athletics Staff. "Baseball Loses Pitcher's Duel in Sunday Nightcap." February 20, 2011. Accessed April 12, 2019. https://osubeavers.com/news/2011/2/20/207823411.aspx.

Oregon State Athletics Staff. "Baseball's Season Ends in 10-Inning Affair." June 3, 2012. Accessed April 19, 2019. https://osubeavers.com/news/2012/6/3/207858954.aspx.

Oregon State Athletics Staff. "Baseball's Season Ends with Loss at Vanderbilt." June 11, 2011. Accessed April 15, 2019. https://osubeavers.com/news/2011/6/11/207864631.aspx.

Oregon State Athletics Staff. "Beavers Defeat K-State, Advance to Fifth College World Series." June 10, 2013. Accessed April 21, 2019. https://osubeavers.com/news/2013/6/10/208466430.aspx.

Oregon State Athletics Staff. "Beavers Down Louisville at College World Series." June 17, 2013. Accessed April 24, 2019. https://osubeavers.com/news/2013/6/17/208610964.aspx.

Oregon State Athletics Staff. "Beavers Drop College World Series Opener to Mississippi State." June 15, 2013. Accessed April 23, 2019. https://osubeavers.com/news/2013/6/15/208466437.aspx.

Oregon State Athletics Staff. "Beavers' Late-Inning Comeback Denied in Fresno." February 21, 2011. Accessed April 12, 2019. https://osubeavers.com/news/2011/2/21/207836707.aspx.

Oregon State Athletics Staff. "Beavers' Season Ends at College World Series." June 21, 2013. Accessed April 26, 2019. https://osubeavers.com/news/2013/6/21/208611260.aspx.

Oregon State Athletics Staff. "Beavers Tally Comeback in Nike College Showcase Finale." March 11, 2012. Accessed April 18, 2019. https://osubeavers.com/news/2012/3/11/207831142.aspx.

Oregon State Athletics Staff. "Boyd's Complete Game Keeps Beavers Alive At CWS." June 19, 2013. Accessed April 25, 2019. https://osubeavers.com/news/2013/6/19/208611161.aspx.

Oregon State Athletics Staff. "It's a Sweep: Starr, Beavers Shut Down Oregon In Season Finale." May 27, 2012. Accessed April 18, 2019. https://osubeavers.com/news/2012/5/27/207818779.aspx.

Oregon State Athletics Staff. "It's a Win: Oregon State Headed Back to a Super Regional." June 5, 2011. Accessed April 15, 2019. https://osubeavers.com/news/2011/6/5/207833473.aspx.

Oregon State Athletics Staff. "Josh Osich Throws Fourth No-Hitter in Oregon State Baseball History." April 30, 2011. Accessed April 14, 2019. https://osubeavers.com/news/2011/4/30/207859512.aspx.

Oregon State Athletics Staff. "No. 6 Beavers Take Civil War Series with 12–2 Win." May 19, 2013. Accessed April 20, 2019. https://osubeavers.com/news/2013/5/19/207850592.aspx.

Oregon State Athletics Staff. "Oregon State Loses in Season Finale, Will Host NCAA Regional." May 29, 2011. Accessed April 14, 2019. https://osubeavers.com/news/2011/5/29/207864781.aspx.

Oregon State Athletics Staff. "Stamps' Ninth-Inning Walk Caps OSU Baseball's Five-Run Comeback." April 9, 2011. Accessed April 13, 2019. https://osubeavers.com/news/2011/4/9/207830010.aspx.

Oregon State Athletics Staff. "Tyler Smith Gives Beavers Opening-Day Win with Single in 11th." Oregon State Baseball. February 19, 2011. Accessed April 11, 2019. https://osubeavers.com/news/2011/2/19/207845313.aspx.

"Pacific Rim Bowl." Ashland Football Club. January 2018. Accessed March 30, 2019. http://www.ashlandfootballclub.com/SectionIndex.asp?SectionID=13.

"Pat Casey." Baseball-Reference.com. Accessed April 5, 2019. https://www.baseball-reference.com/register/player.fcgi?id=casey-002pat.

Quick, Jason. "College World Series: At Oregon State, 'There's Something Special' About this Team's Motivation." The Oregonian, June 14, 2013. Accessed April 23, 2019.

"Sam Gaviglio." Baseball-Reference.com. Accessed April 17, 2019. https://www.baseball-reference.com/players/g/gavigsa01.shtml.

Schnell, Lindsay. "His Curveball Is Back, but Josh Osich Says He's Still Not at 100 Percent Yet." *The Oregonian,* May 5, 2011.

Specht, Sanne. "Ashland Teen in Critical Condition." *Mail Tribune,* January 4, 2008.

Weaverville Joss House State Historic Park. California Department of Parks and Recreation. January 30, 2020. Accessed February 6, 2020. https://www.parks.ca.gov/?page_id=457.

Winthrop Athletics Staff. "Former Baseball Player Conrad Funk Concludes 16-Year Playing Career in Canada." August 9, 2011. Accessed April 17, 2019. https://winthropeagles.com/news/2011/8/9/BB_0809110946.aspx.

Youmans, Matt. "UNLV Fires Baseball Coach Gouldsmith." *Las Vegas Review-Journal,* May 18, 2010.

Index

233